I particularly enjoyed the information on affirmations and how you have a process that allows you to go into your main affirmation in 'bite size pieces'. This truly helps with overwhelm. I've already started using your idea and it will help me along my path to better finances, health and overall well being."

.... Serb Kandola Spiritually Advanced Intuitive

"This is a must-have book to read and reread! You are bound to find new ways to enrich your life each time you pick this book up. Throughout this book, you'll find new and innovative ways to pursue your passions in life !"

June Russell, Discriminating Spiritual Reader and Reviewer

Powerful meditations Dianne … you're amazing! I will use the [tips for] letting go… Every session had useful tips and meditations to manifest our intentions. Very practical. I'll use the vision board, writing intentions and raising my vibration in my everyday life

…. Anon, Coquitlam

[The work] "allowed me to get in touch with levels of awareness & inner knowledge that I had never known existed. Dianne's thoughtful & enlightened teaching style is a pleasure & she is a remarkable resource to have along on any inner journey."

… Joy Borthwick, Gastric Band Hypnotherapist. Burnaby BC

From Fear to Eternity

212 Ways to
Let Go of Limiting Beliefs
and
Shift Your Energy
into
Higher Consciousness Living

GINA-DIANNE HARDING

B.Sc. Nursing, Master Public Health., M.Div.

BALBOA.
PRESS
A DIVISION OF HAY HOUSE

Balboa Press books may be ordered through booksellers or by contacting:

Balboa Press
A Division of Hay House
1663 Liberty Drive
Bloomington, IN 47403
www.balboapress.com
1-(877) 407-4847

Because of the dynamic nature of the Internet, any web addresses or links contained in this book may have changed since publication and may no longer be valid. The views expressed in this work are solely those of the author and do not necessarily reflect the views of the publisher, and the publisher hereby disclaims any responsibility for them.

ISBN: 978-1-4525-4184-6 (sc)
ISBN: 978-1-4525-4186-0 (hc)
ISBN: 978-1-4525-4185-3 (e)

Library of Congress Control Number: 2011919627

The author of this book does not dispense medical advice or prescribe the use of any technique as a form of treatment for physical, emotional, or medical problems without the advice of a physician, either directly or indirectly. The intent of the author is only to offer information of a general nature to help you in your quest for emotional and spiritual well-being. In the event you use any of the information in this book for yourself, which is your constitutional right, the author and the publisher assume no responsibility for your actions.

Printed in the United States of America

Balboa Press rev. date: 11/15/2011

To my Parents, whose love and support I treasure,

To my beloved son Jonathan: You have
always been a bright light in my heart,

and

To the People who are destined to read this book.

Contents

Preface

Rapid changes, ecological disasters, system collapses and their resulting impact have left many people feeling overwhelmed, even frightened at the prospect of unwanted change in their personal lives. The media fuel that fear, and the unconscious collective spews forth this negative or low vibration energy. Personal or societal change can be confusing, especially during times when social systems are no longer Serving our needs. However we can experience a different life of personal peace and enjoyment when we choose to engage in alternative patterns of beliefs and activities consistent with higher vibrational living.

Thought leaders representing many segments of society agree we are at a tipping point. We can make choices that result in a sustainable world, where we respect and connect to each other and everything around us, or we can continue on the road to systemic collapse and environmental exhaustion. This tipping point coincides with predictions that we are moving into another age, made by various wisdom traditions.

The earth and humanity have had long evolutionary cycles that have led to the information age we are currently living in. As a society, we are familiar with shorter cycles, such as the 290 days from conception to birth, the 365 days of the year; the natural cycles of the four seasons, the manmade seasons defined by marketing campaigns, the 28 day moon cycle and the 30 day monthly calendar cycle.

We are coming up to the end of at least three cycles in the next couple of years:

- **2,160 years** (1/12 of the precession) - the length of time it takes for the precession of the equinoxes to move the spring equinox through one constellation into another. (Astrologically and astronomically we are moving into the Age of Aquarius from the Piscean age).[1]

- **5125 years** – the length of one age.
- **25,625 years** - the length of one precession of equinox cycle (5 ages).[2]

A precession of the equinoxes occurs when the sun and earth are aligned astronomically with the exact centre of the Milky Way. In 1964, expert John Major Jenkins identified the date of the upcoming precession as December 21, 2012. Is it coincidence that this was the day the ancient Mayan culture ended many of their calendars? Many Maya scholars believe the Maya knew this precession marked the end of one age and the beginning of the next, because the end of their calendar coincides with a precession. It is one of the factors that support the generally accepted belief that the ancient Maya were an advanced civilization.

The destabilization of our society and ecology, combined with the fact that the Mayan calendar ends in 2012 is being sensationalized and labelled by some of the media as the catastrophic end of the world. In actuality, systems are shifting to make room for a new sustainable way of living. There is a great need for clarity and understanding about 2012. Information is available that is based on scientific fact, prophecy and metaphysical teachings. In this book I will share the knowledge and wisdom I've learned from some of the respected thought leaders and wisdom teachers who are guiding our transformation from business as usual towards living a purposeful, meaning filled life. I have had the great honour to meet and learn from several indigenous wisdom keepers, healers, scientists, futurists and spiritual and metaphysical leaders. They all believe that if we choose, we can create a sustainable world where everyone can have the necessities for a healthy life, and we can fulfill our potential, repair the environment and live happily, cooperating and collaborating as a global community.

Here we stand at the beginning of another age. Will we tap into our limitless potential to shift ourselves and humanity into higher-conscious living? Or will we succumb to fear-based limited beliefs, thoughts and emotions, which suck our vibrational energy and keep us mired in quiet desperation?

We have the capacity to save humanity from extinction by transforming our limiting beliefs, thoughts and emotions into higher vibration conscious living. We, ourselves, must change. Others will change when and how they are meant to.

I believe that to sustain higher consciousness most effectively, it is essential that we understand vibrational energy. Quantum physics has determined that everything in the universe has energy. Our electromagnetic vibrations resonate at varying frequencies depending on our thoughts, feelings, beliefs, health, sensitivity to other humans, what is around us and more.

This book will help you make choices so you can move past overwhelming fear into limitless possibilities and live in higher-conscious vibration in your day-to-day life. You can ensure a brighter future for yourself and your children and grandchildren, not just for seven generations into the future, but for eternity.

You hold in your hands a resource you can return to time and again to glean information and tools to enable you to move more easily into harmony. As you read you will realize that everything that is happening in our world serves to show us what we do and do not want in the upcoming age. It will provide an alternative explanation from the fear based media hype, and show you how to reframe what is happening on a global scale, and especially in your everyday life.

You will learn to alchemically transform information, habits and behaviours that are lower vibration lead energy, into higher vibration gold energy, through practical, useful tools and tips that I have personally used and taught. These will allow you to manage your energy, overcome overwhelm and let go of beliefs that no longer serve you, so that you can choose to ascend into a world of higher vibration and higher-conscious living.

Acknowledgements

My thanks go to Serb Kandola, June Russell and Sandi Vitoria for providing feedback regarding the content of the manuscript. Serb has unearthed a gift for promotion, providing several meaningful comments about the value of this book for the reader.

I am really grateful to my editor, Angela Royea, for her support, encouragement and calming, accepting presence. Getting editorial correction was painless and her eagle eye and accurate editing made my revisions much faster.

My thanks go to Donna Kozik whose Book in a Weekend course got me started on the process and amazingly my first draft was done in a week! (The next 14 months were spent in editing and rewriting).

I am glad I was guided to Christine Kloser, whose transformational author series provided information and smoothed the process of finding a publisher and readied me for marketing my book. She brought a sense of the sacred to the last couple of months of editing and proposal writing.

I am thankful that my soul sister Joy Borthwick provided her faith, support and grounding energy. She always encouraged and reminded me of my expertise. She could also relate and provide advice from her perspective as a published author.

Thanks to Trudy Woodcock, The Mayan Cosmic Institute for letting me know when I had less than accurate information in my manuscript and for her gift for planning and implementing the Mayan Sacred Tours and Shamanism workshops which have been such an important part of my spiritual path.

I am ever appreciative of my dear friend, Lois Alionis. Her interest and upbeat enthusiasm helped me stay in higher vibration and she always put things in perspective when daily life intervened with my book creation time.

What can I say about my Earth Angels, Carla Kraft, Dianne Thiessen and Sharon Watts who cared enough to devote their time and effort so I am alive to share my message.

Of course I am grateful to the beings of the highest vibration, the superconscious energy and all the teachers and lessons that have brought me to this point on my spiritual path.

I am also grateful that you have been called to read this book. The Maya have a saying In Lak'ech Ala K'in, It means 'I am you, and you are me'. I recognize the spirit in you and I am grateful you are here.

Introduction

When I first read this line in Walden over 10 years ago, I could totally relate. I was living that life. Fast forward to a later date, when I was asked a simple question: "Are you everything you want to be?"... "I'm not just talking about having the stuff you want to have," the facilitator continued, "I mean the person that you're being each and every day... is that person the most fulfilled version of you imaginable?"

Well, at this moment, I can answer, Yes! So, how did I make the shift from living in desperation to living a fulfilled life?

I've experienced ALCHEMY. **What is alchemy?** Traditionally, alchemy was a process of changing a base metal, such as lead, into a valuable metal, such as gold. It has been practiced throughout the ages. The greatest challenge in the process was to find the philosophers stone, which was the key to transforming the base common material into the desired precious one. This process also led to the transformation of the Alchemists themselves, – they came to understand their personal connection with the Divine Energy of Creation, aspired to love all people, nature, and All That IS as God or however they understood this energy). During the Renaissance, when people were still being persecuted for beliefs outside of those dictated by the Church, the practice of alchemy was often used as a covert way to develop a more spiritually based practice. The allegorical symbolism enabled people who were familiar with the symbols to share their beliefs. The scope of alchemy is wide, ranging from a practical scientific perspective to hermetic philosophy, to metaphysical, mystical, and spiritual approaches.

Alchemy has been a symbol for transformation in mystery schools where the educated elite and priests and priestesses learned secret metaphysical teachings, including the manipulation of energy. The basics were shared in clandestine metaphysical communities for centuries. Alchemists were, however, expected to find the secret to the philosophers' stone through their own devices. Today many people, if they know what alchemy is, still think of it as turning base metals into gold. However the concept of alchemy is becoming somewhat more mainstream. If you do a Google search you will find over 55 million references to alchemy, 5 million for spiritual alchemy and almost 1 million for metaphysical alchemy. Amazon. com has a selection of over 5,500 books on the subject.

If I tried to explain alchemy in general terms I'd say it is the process of transforming one possibility into another. If we relate alchemy and energy, we see that "Alchemy is accomplished by changing the frequency of thought, altering the harmonics of matter and applying the elements of Love to create the desired result".[3]

Today more and more people are hoping or realizing there is more to life than eating, sleeping, working and (if you have the desire and the energy) making love. They don't want to believe that the world is 'going to hell in a hand basket', that economic, societal and systemic collapse and environmental disasters are inevitable. They want to believe somebody can do something about it, and a little voice may be saying in their ear, "Maybe it's you". It doesn't have to mean a huge change like moving to another country, leaving your family and becoming a missionary, although a few of you may find that that's exactly what the 'more' in your life entails. What I mean by 'more to life' involves a transformation in how you think, feel and perceive the world, and how you relate to others. It means moving from living in the collective unconscious into the higher vibration energy of higher consciousness.

Perhaps off in the distance, you are hearing the music of "To Dream the Impossible Dream". *You* sure don't know of anyone who is doing more than trying to get by. Or perhaps, just perhaps, you have seen something on PBS or in documentaries, read or heard something on Oprah, or dared to dream. There are people who are doing what they love and attracting what they desire in their lives. You may have even tried some of the techniques you've seen in DVDs or books with some success, although perhaps not in anything big. Perhaps inside, you feel as if something big is going to happen. Maybe it wouldn't hurt to be optimistic.

I'm very fortunate. The people I have in my life are for the most part positive and enthusiastic about their lives. They are doing what they love or they love what they do. When asked how the recession is affecting them, they say "What recession"? It is more than just positive thinking; they are living in higher vibration energy. They are grateful for, and focus on, the good things they have in their life. They have learned the alchemical secret and have chosen to transform a heavy lead perspective to a light golden one, hence their genuine lack of experience of a recession.

This book will give you information and examples that you can apply in your everyday life. You will learn more about energy and how it can work to improve your life. I will explain what I mean by low and high vibration energy and why it is one of the simplest and best ways I know to live a life fulfilling your desires for good health, abundance, happiness, relationships, life's work and spiritual goals. You will come to understand why this knowledge is so important at this time when we must choose whether humanity will continue to thrive or merely survive. This book is unique because you will not only gain knowledge, you will also gain new skills to transform your life.

There are a number of tools you can use to learn how to experience higher vibrations. I share these in Section Three of the book, but I'll give you a sneak preview of 'upcoming attractions'.

1. Be aware of what is around you and use your five senses to perceive the miracle of everything in the environment you are in.
2. Give your mind and feelings a quick break by finding something ironic, bizarre, funny-ha ha or funny-odd in any situation. Humor lightens and raises your vibration by changing the focus of your

attention, thereby detaching you from the seriousness or drama of a situation.

3. Focus on being grateful for what you already have. This feeling of gratitude will take you into the highest vibration many of us can achieve at this time.

4. Think about something (not someone) you love. Feel that sensation inside your body and allow it to uplift you.

Voilá, you have alchemically transformed your energy from the dense lower vibration of a person living in quiet desperation, to higher vibration awareness. Now that you know what it *consciously* feels like to experience a higher energy frequency, experiment with what will move you into that energy. You may even wish to write your findings down so when you are feeling low and can't think clearly, you can re-energize yourself. This book gives you many more ideas, techniques, tools, and tips to increase and then sustain your vibrations.

I believe there is a reason for almost everything that happens to you and me. There is a reason you have picked up this book. It is written at a critical time in our history as a human race. Experts are saying if we want to survive it is essential that we make choices to live differently. I believe those choices will come from higher-conscious awareness, from the higher vibration of a critical mass of people. Because you've been attracted to this book, I believe you are one of this critical mass.

The apparent disintegration of our world is happening at a time when knowledge about geological cycles, wisdom from ancient and indigenous cultures, and current scientific knowledge about earth changes and cosmic events, all indicate there is a great shift taking place. Many people are capitalizing on the uncertainty of the times and creating fear that (once again) we are nearing the end of the world. I don't believe it would be overstating it to say that life as we know it now *will change*. Some may call this a crisis. In the spirit of moving out of fear, I prefer to consider that we have an opportunity to make our existence better.

In the literature, the change we are experiencing is referred to by many terms. Some are interchangeable and others have subtle differences in their meaning. They include, 'The Shift', 'The Great Shift', 'The Shift of the Ages', '2012', 'The End of the Mayan Calendar', 'The Precession of the Equinoxes', 'The End of an Age', 'The Next Age', 'The New Age', 'The Golden Age', 'The End of the World', 'The End of a Cycle', 'The Next Stage in Human Evolution', The Age of Homo Universalis or the Universal Human', 'The New Reality', 'The Tipping Point', and 'The Cycle of the Ages'. I will use many of these terms depending on the context.

Visionaries in the field of human evolution say that in order for humanity to survive with our knowledge and wisdom intact, we need to move into higher consciousness. Almost all experts in every field say that we first need to change ourselves, our expectations, our perceptions, and our habits and beliefs. They also agree that positive energy shifts are occurring already. These increased flows of energy are creating significant changes. Some experts believe that these shifts are resulting in some interesting symptoms that more and more people are experiencing. Many people are noticing odd physical sensations such as dizziness, sore muscles, poor balance, and poor memory. These come and go. Can they be related to energy? I will explore this with you in the second chapter, *Are You Awake?*

The Mayan calendar is ending on December 21, 2012, not because it's the end of the world, but because it is the start of what the Maya timekeepers anticipated as the Golden Age. We have been preparing for it for many years. Being aware that there may be something more to life and consciously choosing higher vibration is part of our preparation. *Right now, The Shift in Consciousness is accelerating!* There are now scientifically measurable flows of higher energy moving within, around and through the Earth and each of us. As you will discover further in the book, I have studied the literature, learned from master teachers of ancient oral wisdom, and studied how energy affects our life and evolution. I know in Reality, without a doubt, we are currently in the process of coming to the end of an age. I think many of us are sick and tired of how life is unfolding in the world today. I know I am eagerly anticipating the next age. Ancient wisdom keepers and credible experts of many branches of science have verified this is happening. However, we need to be aware that we probably will not wake up Dec. 22, 2012 in a perfect world. The dawn of this next age is an astronomical event and is the peak of a human energetic transition that has been building for decades if not longer.

There is a theory that when a critical mass of people makes the shift into higher-conscious living, then the majority of society will follow (much like the 100th monkey concept,[4] or the way buyers respond to a new type of technology; when enough early adopters use a new product then the majority will step forward and try it out). [5, 6]

In my day to day life, as well as in the actions of humanity, I see growing evidence of an exponential increase in our desire and actions to reach out, to collaborate and cooperate with each other and live with compassion, in harmony, connectedness and respect for all life forms. I also realize that we will likely continue to evolve and refine our new ideals and values well into the decades and centuries of the next age.

As I write this I have a whimsical vision. Perhaps we may shift more quickly. Only the Universe knows how many people it takes for the '100th monkey' to tip us into the 'golden age of humanity'. Wouldn't it be fun if the Creator Energy set off fireworks, horns and bells and a great cacophony, followed by an angelic chorus and the incredibly moving songs of nature as that person, whose shift into high vibration consciousness tips all of humanity into living fulfilled joyful existences was awarded the keys to the omniverse?

This book will explore more about The Shift and provide a more balanced perspective regarding 2012. I will also look at how to manage our increasing energetic sensitivity as we alchemically transform and move into our preferred future. *I welcome you as we embark on this energetic journey together.*

SECTION ONE

Everything Is Energy

I know what I am meant to do during this shift:
That is to contribute to the understanding of
the mind-body-spirit-energy relationship in a new way.

...Gina-Dianne Harding

Chapter 1

Everything is Energy

What is all life?

What is every flower, every rock, every tree, every human being?
Energy!

ALL LIFE IS ENERGY, and we are transmitting it every moment.
We are beaming it...little tiny signals, like radio frequencies, and the
world is responding in kind.

Oprah

What do you think when you read the words *everything is energy*?

Depending on your perspective, it may include any of the following:

You may think of electricity, so necessary in our lives. If you are mindful of
ecology you might include alternative forms of energy, including wind and
solar energy, which are converted into usable forms to replace electricity,
to generate light, heat, irrigation and other useful outcomes.

You might also think of people in terms of having lots of physical energy
or conversely, of being exhausted. You might wish you had as much energy
as your dog, especially when it's going for a walk. Or perhaps you'd prefer
to be like your cat, able to lie in a relaxed state and be content to do
nothing but doze for hours. Your mental energy can be evidenced by the
relative chaos or order of your thoughts. Energy created from emotions
can vary from despair to bliss, and it very much affects your physical

energy. Spiritual or metaphysical energy can shift you out of yearning and emptiness into wholeness and fulfillment.

If you are a Highly Sensitive Person (I prefer the term "Highly Energetically Aware Person"), you have a much different perspective about energy. It's likely you can sense the energy that was happening in a room you just entered, despite how the people are acting now. You may also be easily overwhelmed by crowds, noise, energy and light, and you could be a psychic sponge, soaking up energy from everyone around you.

Yet another type of energy is electromagnetic energy. It affects the earth as well as individuals by its vibrational frequency. People who do energy work complementary to mainstream medicine use electromagnetic energy as one of their tools.

If you are a biologist you might be aware of another aspect of energy, which involves studying the response of items you would not expect to have a response. For example, did you know that plants hooked up to energy sensors register a chaotic response when someone who has previously uprooted or torn them comes into the lab. Marcel Vogel found that his instruments "measured even greater reactions from plants when he *thought* about burning, tearing, or uprooting them than when he actually did so".[7] The other plants in the room also responded.[8] Since these experiments were conducted, the responsiveness of plants has been demonstrated in a variety of circumstances.

The above examples are just a smattering of ways one can consider the statement "Everything is Energy". As you can see, energy is a word we use in a variety of ways, to express many different multidimensional concepts.

Are you consciously aware that *all* living things have energy? Trees, insects, pests, fish, birds, animals, and water have all been shown to have energy. This is a key concept in this book. Before I share with you the importance of this conscious awareness, I want to make another point that leads to an amazing finding.

Everything Has Energy?

Albert Einstein established the traditional definition of energy in his famous equation: $E=mc^2$. The idea that all matter is energy is well accepted today. "Matter is a universal substance, primary energy or vibration, from which we are all composed. Vibrational medicine involves the manipulation of basic vibrational or energetic levels of substance. We can connect with Universal Energy and manipulate substances to achieve many miraculous events, including healing". [9]

Another way of considering energy is by exploring the field of quantum physics, which is the study of individual particles of energy smaller than an atom. "It's the science of things so small that the quantum nature of reality has an effect".[10]

Quantum Theory explains how much of the *'woo-woo'* stuff happens. In the past, scientists believed that because quantum phenomena occurred at such a small level, it had no relevance to traditional physics and could be ignored. However, more recent findings demonstrate that quantum happenings affect both sub-atomic and conventional physics levels.[11] Research in quantum physics demonstrates strange behavior which has been used to explain a variety of paradoxical phenomena including the nature of the interaction between mind and matter, consciousness and particles. [12, 13]

A quantum energy field is created by the exchange of energy between quantum particles. Even at the coldest place in the universe where the movement of these particles is extremely slow, this energy exchange occurs. This slow movement also happens within dense objects such as rocks and metal. *This is a very important fact and key to the principles belief necessary to understand and accept the information in this book.*

The conclusion we can reach is **not only do living things have energy, but objects we consider inanimate do as well.**

Do You Mean Things Like Rocks, Gems, Wood Furniture, and Cars?

Yes, that and more. They have measurable energy too. Rocks, crystals and gems for example, have energy that resonates with human energy and therefore can be used for healing because they encourage a shift in your vibrational fields. The crystalline energy in the stones resonates with the crystalline structure of the body.

Why Is This Important?

Everything has Energy. What use is this information? It provides a foundation on which you can base your beliefs and actions, implement the techniques, tips and tools presented here and ultimately change your life and, should you wish, create a better world.

It allows you to connect with what I refer to as All That IS. I believe when we connect and realize the energy that's in you and me is the same as the energy around us, it is easier to focus on what we are doing and its effects. We feel and act with more respect for our environment. For me, it changes my relationship with my car knowing the metal frame has quantum particles that are vibrating at a certain frequency, or that a soda pop can may exchange particles with the environment as it breaks down. Do you feel a shift in your perception? This perceptual change when I perceive energy in everything I encounter, affects my ability to manipulate energy more easily so I can create what I want in my life.

I first learned that other people besides me could sense the energy present in inanimate objects about seven years ago. At that time if I dared to speak to anyone I knew about what I was learning, they rolled their eyes and kindly called me eccentric. I was attending a seminar at a spiritual retreat, where I was shown how to see auras. The first thing the wise old soul leading the exercise did was to ask us to look for the aura of a wooden stool. He had been a carpenter and connected with the energy in this piece of furniture. Once I opened up to the possibility that furniture could have an aura, I was able to see a white light around the stool and feel a connection to it.

Are You Willing to Take a Short Walk in the World of "Woo- Woo?

What is woo - woo? You may have heard of a 1960's TV show called The Twilight Zone which featured paranormal, futuristic, or somewhat disturbing situations. In 2002, it was actually named in TV Guide's 50 Greatest TV Shows of All Time. The show's introductory music was characterized by a riff that people would describe as Woo-ooo-ooo-ooo and that eventually became a slang phrase used to indicate scepticism about unusual or out of the ordinary events.[14] If you want to hear a short sound clip, go to http://www.youtube.com/watch?v=NzlG28B-R8Y

When you walk in the world of woo-woo, keep an open mind, believe anything is possible and go with your inner guidance, you may discover information and ideas in this book that are - just perhaps - life changing! In fact, you'll find out that modern science can now explain and demonstrate many phenomena in repeatable experiments. Hence, ancient teaching and practices have been validated by current scientific research.

Much of the metaphysical and spiritual information and practices of the ancient wisdom teachers are based on concepts of energy. Manipulation of energy was known and practiced in Sumeria, Mesopotamia, Egypt, Greece and Rome. The practice of alchemy was one of the energy crafts undertaken in many cultures. In addition to converting base metals into gold, alchemy was also an energetically transformational spiritual practice. The wisdom keepers and shamans of indigenous tribes all over the world, including Maya, Inca, North American and Australian Aboriginal peoples, trained each generation in their arts. Pre-Christian religions that worshipped Goddess and God energy, the Celtic Druids, members of mystery schools through the ages, and groups like the Masons, who have metaphysical knowledge they share at the highest level of initiation, apparently all had knowledge of how to use energy (also known to some as magic) to aid in their physical, mental, emotional and spiritual transformation.

Some of these groups had another key belief crucial to alchemy, energy and the current energy shifts occurring in the world. This belief, which I will refer to throughout the book, is that *We Are All One*. This means we are all connected to each other and All That IS, which includes the energy of the Four Directions (North, south, east, west), and the energy of Above (sun, moon, sky and cosmos), Below (mother earth) and Within (our inner wisdom and guidance). We are all connected through Source Energy (this may be known as God, Goddess, The Creator, All That IS, Universal

Energy, Divine Energy, or whatever Name you are most comfortable with). In other words, the energy we are connected to includes everything, seen and unseen, in every dimension.

Is This Stuff True?

The wonderfully exciting thing is that leading edge scientists are now confirming what the ancient practitioners, teachers through the ages and their students knew, both intuitively and through oral tradition. The unfortunate challenge is that old traditional science and medicine are resistant to incorporating this knowledge into their practices. The critics have pointed out some valid concerns, citing poor research methods and finding the researchers may have a bias because of their own beliefs. From my experience in research in my undergraduate and master's programs, I have noted that there is often disagreement between scientists. The result of much medical research has been called biased since they are funded by the pharmaceutical companies. Fortunately this new information is bypassing the professions that are reluctant to change beliefs that have existed for many years. Publicly owned broadcasting and special interest television channels are airing programs that deal with information that was never before shared with the general public. Of course, the internet has had a huge impact on the availability of esoteric information that was previously only accessible to a chosen few. However, I encourage you to be discerning about the information you find, including what is in this book. I have referenced much of my writing, so you can follow up any areas that interest you. I personally resonate with much of this new information, and at the same time I bear in mind that it may not all be scientifically provable. For the sake of those who have chosen science as their primary path to higher consciousness, I hold out hope that their findings prove true.

Have you ever watched or read any PBS documentaries that talk about string theory, quantum physics, or biogenetic research? Have you seen the movie, What The Bleep Do We Know!? The science of quantum physics is explaining things that until recently were seen as science fiction phenomena, as unbelievable to us as travel in space shuttles was to my 90 year old parents when they were young.

This esoteric information is becoming more mainstream, thanks to shows like Oprah, too. She did an online dialogue series with Eckhart Tolle based on his book 'The New Earth'. Other spiritual and metaphysical authors, including Wayne Dyer, Deepak Chopra, and Esther Hicks and Abraham are being studied by an increasing number of people. Even the mainstream movie 'The Matrix' has a lot of metaphysical concepts that have created awareness in the collective conscious. Movies such as 'The Secret,' despite having what many long term practitioners of the Law of Attraction feel are serious flaws, have brought the concept that there are Universal Laws to the public's attention. If you wish to know more about these laws, refer to the resources in the back of this book.

The 6ᵗʰ Sense

At this point in the book, I'd like to remind you to keep an open mind as I continue to build a framework to help you understand the concept that *Everything Is Energy.*

In addition to our five senses of seeing, hearing, smelling, tasting and touching, you may accept that some very intuitive or highly energetically aware people have a sixth sense. One of the ways this can reveal itself is in the ability to see auras or energy in a person's etheric energy body. (We have physical, mental, emotional, spiritual and etheric bodies). These auras can indicate our health as well. Some people are able to intuit the state of a person's health and offer a remedy for any illness. People have other intuitive gifts as well. These include clairvoyance (seeing invisible things), clairaudience (hearing guidance) and clairsentience (knowing something intuitively).

One advantage of these intuitive gifts is being able to sense things a lot of people have not learned to perceive. This includes the ability to channel higher vibration beings such as ascended masters, saints and archangels, or intelligent energies. It could be said that these intuitive people are able to use their energetic gifts to move into higher dimensions and connect with the higher vibration energies of what are believed to be Angels, Spiritual Guides and Ascended Masters. Ascended Masters refers to great teachers who have once lived on earth, like Jesus Christ, or Confucius.[15] Although some are associated with religions, many are considered to be great masters and teachers who provide *all* of humanity with great wisdom and higher truths. As such, they are respected by all spiritual seekers.

"So yes," you the reader might say, "I believe some people are truly psychic. My great aunt Alice used to know if an accident or death was going to happen. My friend can tell who is calling her on the phone without call display. I've noticed lately, I sometimes know what someone is going to say before they say it. But that's all coincidence, right?"

Well, it is widely recognized in the metaphysical community that many more people are becoming more sensitive to energy because of The Shift. In fact, there is a widely growing belief that everyone is experiencing more extrasensory phenomena and that we are all becoming more intuitive. There are even books in the business section of bookstores that relate to using your intuition as an edge in business. You may want to play with the idea of opening to higher vibration energy – you already do it if you meditate or pray, or even if you commune with Mother Earth and nature when you go for a walk.

What is Vibration?

I began this chapter listing some of the ways we use the word energy and established the fact that everything is energy. I will now narrow the focus to the human energy system and how it is affected by vibration.

Everything has a rate at which it vibrates, also known as its resonant frequency.

The human energy system includes many forms and frequencies of vibration. All molecules in the physical body can be measured as vibrating energy. Alternative energy practitioners work not only with physical energy, but also with the energy of mental, emotional, spiritual and etheric bodies. Their intuitive knowing is being validated now that there is scientific equipment that can even measure the light fields (auras) of objects. The energy from these light fields is technically known as bio-photon emissions.

It's important to keep the difference between physical and nonphysical vibration in mind. Your physical energy is maintained by a balance of food, rest and activity. It is stored like fuel and represents your capacity to do something. Non-physical vibration, as I use the term in this book, has more to do with describing your thoughts, emotions and beliefs.

Imagine if you will an opera singer who hits a note and creates a sound wave that's moving at the exact frequency or vibration as a crystal goblet. Because the two are resonating at the same frequency, the crystal goblet breaks. This is an example of physical vibration. The same principle is used in some healing practices. There are specific frequencies that mediate healing. Treatment with different forms and frequencies of energies balance the body, mind and spirit. [16]

Tuning forks are an example of a fairly common low tech vibrational diagnostic tool. They are used by health practitioners as a screening tool to determine if the reason for hearing loss is due to structural or nerve damage. A friend's chiropractor used a tuning fork to determine if she had broken her finger. She reports that broken bones are very painful if a tuning fork is applied. An example of a physical vibration treatment tool is a crystal bowl. These are used in alternative healing and the bowls work by vibrating at a certain frequency when struck. We hear these as a note. Different areas of the healthy body resonate with one of these tones. If an area is unhealthy it vibrates at a different frequency. The resonance of the bowls at that particular vibratory tone will cause the unhealthy part to align with its frequency and return to that healthy vibration.

Equipment that generates sound waves, light and ultrasonic waves are other forms of vibrational energy tools which have been used in healing. Each oscillates at a different frequency and can be used to return the part of the body with a matching frequency to a healthy state. In addition to use for specific individuals, musical artists compose frequency and wave based music and sounds to balance a listener's energy. You can purchase CDs with crystal bowls, and synthesized sounds which use a variety of tones and vibrations, and relax while your body aligns with healthy frequencies.

What Do You Mean by Lower and Higher Vibration?

People places and things have different rates of vibration which may change depending on what is occurring in and around them. For example, you may have heard it said, "Oh, he's such a downer" or "I'm so depressed -- I have no energy". If a person is very critical and pessimistic, we might say "they are so negative". These words describe the energies of low non-physical vibration. Often being in or around low vibration energy can decrease your own energy if you don't know how to manage it. It can be exhausting; your thoughts may become confused, you may have difficulty concentrating. Your outlook and perceptions about a situation may be skewed; you may lack a sense of direction regarding your next step. Your creative ability is also affected. One of the most common causes of low vibration is negative thought. Thoughts about ourselves, such as, "I'm such a loser, I'll never get a job" or "it always rains when I want to do something special" put you in a lower vibration. Remember the children's song *"nobody likes me; everybody hates me, going to the garden to eat some worms"?* That song is an excellent example of lower vibration thoughts. Messages are often programmed in the subconscious mind from birth up until seven years of age.[17, 18] As an adult, when you unconsciously go through your day, you are living the life and beliefs of the people whose programs were downloaded to you as a child.[19]

The core reason for negative or low vibration thought is the presence of limiting beliefs and values which create your thoughts. These beliefs are limiting because of the universal Law of Attraction, which basically states, 'you achieve what you believe'. This law also incorporates the principle that you attract what you focus on. If you think and feel worried about what you *don't* want, that is often what will occur. Instead, be aware of incidents in your day that result in feeling happiness, peace or connection with others. These create higher vibrational frequencies. Focus on really feeling those feelings, with gratitude that they occurred. You will attract more and more situations that result in these higher vibration feelings and thoughts.

Emotional, non-physical energy is intertwined with thoughts and is the power behind creating anything. People with high vibration energy are optimistic, enthusiastic, passionate and happy; their magnetic energy draws other people to them like ants to a picnic. Usually they have such joy and love of life; they attract people, money and success easily and effortlessly.

Lower vibration energy emotions such as fear, anger, depression, lack, doubt or frustration sooner or later shut people down, cause mental and physical exhaustion and attract nothing but lack: of love, money and happiness.

You may have noticed that I choose to use the terms higher and lower vibration when describing thoughts beliefs and emotions. It is easier to understand there is no judgment attached to vibration or the thoughts, feelings and beliefs that cause them. I prefer to use the less judgmental terms low and high vibration instead of good or bad, positive or negative. These terms are also more accurate and it's easier to be detached from disapproval when we look at ourselves, others and life in general, as forms of energy.

Past cultures, mystery schools and exclusive esoteric organizations understood the power of thoughts words and emotions and deliberately used this energy. They practiced the art of being in high vibrations and thus in high consciousness. They had more awareness of the potential power of thought than the general population and understood the principles behind it.

Today we are rediscovering this knowledge and skill. Ancient wisdom teachers of indigenous tribes have been guided to share their knowledge to help us make much needed changes in our chaotic unsustainable world, and make the transition to new ways of living. We have realized energy generated by the non-physical (thoughts and emotions) doesn't behave in the same way as physical energy. We can effect changes in our immediate environment or on the other side of the world, with non-physical energy. Distance is irrelevant.

Fascinating examples of vibratory energy levels are presented in David Hawkins book 'Transcending the Levels of Consciousness'. Dr. Hawkins has used his knowledge of many fields of science, including kinesiology, non-linear dynamics and complex computer analysis, in his research on the range of non-physical vibratory energies. He has mapped the energy fields of human consciousness and provided measurements of the energy of single cell life forms, insects, reptiles and animals. [20] I remember reading one of his books for the first time many years ago and being amazed he had calibrated even the purr of a cat or wagging tail of a dog.

In humans, the lowest category of vibrations are ego driven actions, thoughts and emotions, including hate and shame which measure even lower than fear. Indifference is a slightly higher frequency in this category. In 2006, according to Hawkins' measurements, 78 percent of the world's population was ego driven. [21]

In the next category, the range of frequencies measures the higher levels of consciousness associated with the linear mind, such as courage, willingness and acceptance. According to Hawkins, this range also includes inspiration, hope, optimism and intention at a slightly higher vibration. Forgiveness and harmony measure in an even higher range and the highest level of vibration in this category includes wisdom, reason and abstraction. [22]

The spiritual reality of love, joy and ecstasy are in the next energy range. Hawkins identified extremely rare high vibration states ascending from transcendence to peace, bliss, and illumination. Higher still is self realization, followed by the highest vibrational level of full enlightenment and pure consciousness. [23]

Experimental Findings

There are several thought provoking experiments that have validated intuitive knowledge about energy. I include a few to stimulate your curiosity and whet your appetite for more.

One hard to believe quantum experiment has demonstrated that there are particles whose behaviour depends upon the presence of an observer. This is sometimes misinterpreted to mean that reality changes as the observer changes.

"What the heck does this mean? Basically, it means that if there is an observer watching a certain point in the experiment, the outcome of the experiment is different than it is when no one is watching that same point."[24] Just as you will find when we look at the tool of reframing your perspective in Section Three, "it could behave differently or not exist at all." [25]

Other research has theorized that the effects of high vibrational thought occur in a similar way to quantum principles of non-location. A simplified description of this principle is that once subatomic particles are in contact, they remain cognizant of and influenced by each other instantaneously over any distance forever. [26]

I am certainly not a physicist, but the reason this seems to be important is that it corroborates the idea that high vibration originating in one person can increase the vibration of someone or something anywhere in the universe, whether it's the energy of a person standing next to them, or the energy of a town half way around the world that is in shambles from a natural disasters. In other words, the energy of a thought can intentionally be directed to someone or something in any part of the world. This principle partially explains remote healing by an energy worker to a person who has consciously made a free will choice to be open to that healing energy.

This phenomenon could also explain why group meditation can measurably change events occurring in society during the time period when meditation is occurring. "The increased coherence and orderliness in individual consciousness appears to spill over into society and can be measured indirectly via changes in social indices".[27]

A well known study demonstrating this occurred in 1993 in Washington DC. The study was overseen and analyzed by a review panel which had representation from independent scientists and key community leaders. A group of almost 4,000 people trained in transcendental meditation gathered for eight weeks. During this time violent crimes including rape, assaults and murders were reduced by over 20 percent. "The odds that this would happen by chance are less than 2 in 1 billion. Rigorous statistical analyses ruled out an extensive list of alternative explanations. Drawing on terminology from quantum field theories, [the principal researcher] John Hagelin, an eminent physicist, referred to the findings as a field effect of consciousness". [28, 29]

The Global Coherence Organization and The Heart Math Institute have research based techniques, which I share later in the book, that support people who want to send their energy to help others.

Further evidence that validates the power and importance of energy as an instrument of change is found in other experiments, when for example, during a period of focused attention such as in meditation, energy surges in the meditators have been demonstrated to increase their energetic vibration. When studies of healing practitioners are done, their energy surges are 100,000 times higher than their electromagnetic energy in a normal state. Intention Experiment research has shown that electrical frequencies and molecular structure of matter are changed by intention. [30, 31]

The ability to enter and maintain a state of high vibration is very significant and research has also demonstrated how prayer and transcendental meditation have had varied outcomes from healed acutely ill and terminally ill people [32] to increasing periods of peace in war torn areas. Millions of people from around the globe joined together on November 13, 1998, for a worldwide peace vigil called, "There's Nothing to Fear." because peace talks had broken down between then President Clinton and Saddam Hussein "That same day planes were in the air waiting for the order to go ahead and begin the bombing. Within hours of the vigil, Clinton gave an unprecedented stand down order, calling the planes back, not once, but twice". [33]

It is not possible to scientifically measure the connection between people praying for world peace and the 'outbreak of peace' there certainly a growing body of evidence that appears to indicate a strong correlation.

Understanding of what has previously been seen as mystical intervention is changing rapidly. In the last ten years, published findings in the fields of theoretical and functional magnetic resonance imaging have pinpointed the specific brain locations of mystical and spiritual experiences. This information, in combination with continued study in metaphysics and quantum physics research will no doubt clarify why inconceivable outcomes are being achieved in the field of vibrational energetics.[34]

Connecting with Higher-Conscious Energy

Activities such as meditation, healing and prayer are ways of connecting with spiritual energy.

What do I mean by that? As a writer and educator, there are times I have felt uncomfortable using the term *spiritual* because many people don't differentiate spirituality and religion. I was contemplating this when, synchronously, I came across a blog by Scott H. Young.[35] He cited Tony Schwartz and Jim Loehr, authors of 'The Power of Full Engagement', who describe spirituality as being the energy of purpose for our lives, and suggest that this energy is the most powerful and important form of energy needed to live successfully. They believe, as I do, that a strong sense of purpose creates energy even when physical, mental or emotional energy is drained.

That same day I also stumbled upon a description of 'spirit' by Dr. Darren Weissman. He describes spirit as the electromagnetic field of the body. The electromagnetic field has what's called a *super-conscious.* "The super-conscious is where the mind resides and where all emotions begin. Every experience in your life is because of energetic attraction or repulsion by the electromagnetic force of the super-conscious mind."[36]

To me spiritual includes knowing there is an energy that created All That IS, seen and unseen, in a multiverse that is infinite and eternal. Everyone experiences this energy differently. I *choose* to experience it as an intensely unconditionally loving, peace filled energy with many higher vibration qualities, including unity, joy, order, balance, abundance, wisdom, generosity, compassion, courage and wholeness.

Preview of Upcoming Events

By now you are probably wondering, "How can I raise my vibration?" Although I will reveal more in the 'how to' chapters, I want to offer a simple technique now. You are now intellectually familiar with some higher vibration emotions. People can regulate the flow of energy and turn their vibrations up or down, much like the volume on a TV. Try to change your vibration right now by tuning into a "feel good" emotion. Think of a high vibration (positive) feeling you have experienced, or choose one from the paragraph above. Now imagine turning up the intensity of the energy like you would turn up the volume of the TV.

Some people have a challenge feeling anything. Section Three describes why and shows you how to feel again.

Is it True we Leak Energy?
Are there Energy Vampires who Suck Our Energy?

Yes! And our energy doesn't have to be depleted! We are sending out and receiving energy all the time. If you are holding on to limiting beliefs or values which are not your own, if you carry a lot of memories (good or bad) from the past or are worried about the future, if your actions are based on what others will think, you are losing energy. It's like an invisible hose that runs between you and other people, situations, memories or beliefs. The hose has little holes in it and streams of energy drain from it, much like the soaker hose in your garden. No wonder you have no energy for what you are doing!

Energy can also be drained by what are sensationally known as energy vampires. Can you think of anyone you know - perhaps even a good friend, who when you are with them you end up feeling exhausted? If they say things like, "I always feel so much better when I talk to you" and, "I feel like I can carry on with my day when before I was so dragged out", they likely are taking your energy unconsciously. I explain how you can resolve it in several ways in Section Three.

The hose can run the other way too, with people sending you their energy or you taking theirs on. If you know someone who says, "I wish I was sick instead of you" or, "It's my duty and responsibility to take care of you", there is a good possibility they are using their energy to try to 'make' you better. On the other hand, if someone is jealous, resentful, or angry with you, they may unknowingly send that energy your way. You receive it and whoa! "Why am I feeling so crappy when a moment ago I was so happy?" You do not have to deplete your own energy or allow others to deplete it. You too, may occasionally be an energy vampire when you are in need. Mutual energy exchange, give and take, is what life's about, so it's ok as long as you aren't always using others to maintain or enhance your energy.

When I do energy work with people I often sense an area of low vibration energy that I experience as a black tarry mess or an inflamed wound. I may even get a mental picture of a knife in someone's back or arrows piercing an area of their body. When I ask what's going on, whether they're experiencing any challenges in their personal or professional life, I often hear that indeed they have an uneasy feeling or actually know someone is out to get them, betray them, and take credit for the work they've done. In addition, they often report feeling generally unwell, almost as if they are living under a cloud. They also state that life isn't as sharp and in focus as it used to be. Once I remove the unhealthy energy, I etherically cut and cauterize the hose and clean the area, and my clients report having more energy and being more like their old selves. I show them ways to prevent attachment of unhealthy hoses and how to avoid other kinds of energy leaks. I'll share some of these in Section Three.

What Can I Expect When I Live in Higher Energy?

When you learn techniques and tools to live in higher vibration energy you feel lighter, less dense, optimistic, happy for no reason, more loving, unconditionally accepting and loving. You attract people of like mind and energy so there is more harmony. You are vibrating at such a high level, that the lower vibration energy of psychic attacks or vampires does not resonate with your frequency and cannot affect you. When you lose your limiting beliefs and fears and learn to manage your energy and feelings of fear, anxiety and overwhelm, you find yourself making choices that are based on *your* needs and desires; and you also find it much easier to attract positive experiences into your life.

Key Concepts About Vibration

Vibrational energy is a vast subject. A small part of this is knowing how to manifest your desires. Understanding and using manifesting techniques in our daily lives is crucial to being able to shift into the next age. Therefore, a basic understanding of vibration as it relates to nonphysical energy is essential. More specifically, it is essential to know that in order to attract anything - you have to be at the same resonant frequency, or be a resonant match. I will say it again. *Vibrational energy must match the energy of the person, situation or object you desire.* This is a key principle in the Law of Attraction. It is what makes it possible to bring what you desire into our 3rd dimensional world. When information about the Law of Attraction first appeared in the mainstream I believe it alluded to this principle. However it didn't stress the other important principle of needing to feel emotions when attracting your desired life. Emotions are key indicators of whether you are aligned with Source Energy and your point of attraction. If you do not get what you want, it is almost always only because you are holding yourself in a vibrational pattern that does not match the vibration of your desire – it's not because you do not want it enough or because you are not intelligent enough, not worthy enough, not because fate is against you or because someone else has gotten it instead (i.e. lack of enough to go around). These are the limiting beliefs that are vibrating at a lower energy. I discuss the concept and techniques for manifestation further in Section Three.

Duality is another fundamental principle related to vibration in our 3D world. Duality allows us to see the difference between negative and positive and higher and lower vibration. Right and wrong, good and bad, love and hate are examples of dualistic concepts. Although ideally we would like to live with only the higher vibrational aspects of duality, the good thing about this contrast is that identifying what we don't want helps us know what we do want to experience in our lives. We can focus on creating a steady, strong energy flow that attracts what we want. This is what is called manifesting and can be used for material tangible items. You can also manifest less tangible qualities such as a more peaceful, joy filled, healthy, happy life and healthy relationships, a job you love, wisdom, love, courage, compassion, and many other positive or higher vibration traits.

Vibrational match and duality are two key concepts which are part of an online eight week course I offer. It is specifically geared to helping you release beliefs that no longer serve you, so you can more easily materialize your desires. It goes way beyond the scope of the *Law of Attraction,* as presented in the book and movie, 'The Secret', and helps address the frustration some people experience, when using the methods described in 'The Secret's' does not get them the expected results. Participants in my course achieve many things including better health, more fulfilled lives, changes in their beliefs and successful risk taking, based on these new beliefs.

Summary

The key points presented in this chapter are:

- Everything, live and inanimate, is energy.
- Modern science, including quantum physics, is showing that ancient beliefs and the effects of practices previously considered "woo woo" can be demonstrated using the newest scientific technology.
- Quantum physics explains scientifically how "We Are All Connected".
- Everything physical, mental, emotional and spiritual, in all planes and dimensions, has a rate or frequency at which it vibrates.
- You give and receive energy all the time, whether or not you are conscious or awakened.
- In order to experience the life you wish to lead, your vibration must match the vibration of what you desire.

In the next chapter, I will begin to explore the differences being between unconsciously existing in lower vibration energy, and thriving in higher-conscious living, including a discussion of changes you may experiences in your physical, mental, emotional and spiritual awareness as you awaken during the 'Shift of the Ages'. The planet itself is shifting into higher vibration energy, so you will experience personal transitional changes regardless of whether or not you choose to move into higher vibration consciousness. The personal transitional changes are more intense if you choose to stay in lower vibration energy because you are not matching planetary vibratory energy.

CHAPTER 2

Are You Awake?

> Why must we answer the call to awaken? Because the most magical things become absorbed into the daily mind's steady geographies of endurance, anxiety, and contentment. Once you awaken, you know how precious your time here in this body is. You 're no longer willing to squander your essence on undertakings that do not nourish your true self. Now you are impatient for growth. You want your work to become an expression of your innate gifts. You want your relationships to voyage beyond the pallid frontiers to where the danger of transformation dwells. You want your God to be wild and call you to where your destiny awaits. When your soul awakens anew, you begin to inherit your true life, the one you were meant for. You leave the kingdom of repetitive talk, and weary roles [to discover] who you are and who you are being called to become. .....
>
> John O'Donohue

Are You awake? If you're thinking, "Well this isn't a dream, so I must be awake," read on to discover that when you live in the 3D world, you are almost certainly living in a dream world even if you aren't physically sleeping.

What Does Being Awake Mean?

When you are asleep, you believe the life you are leading is all there is. You have your own, idiosyncratic truths. Your truth is probably different from those of the person next to you because it's based on your personal beliefs and limited life experiences. The government, bureaucracy and media all have their versions of truth. This makes up the collective conscious belief, which is fear based and tends to expect the worst. Most people make choices based on this negative outlook. This is why metaphysics says you are living in an illusion. In the context of this book and in most spiritual and metaphysical circles, being awakened means realizing there is an energy greater than yours that directs matter in the universe. This force is often called God. It is also referred to as The Divine Source, Father-Mother God, the Universe, The Creator of All That IS, The Goddess, Your Higher Power, or Your Higher Self. I will use these terms interchangeably and suggest you substitute the word that feels best as you read.

When you are awake you want to make a *conscious* connection with this Creator and all of creation; other people, animals, nature, the earth, the sun, moon and stars. Everything you can see, feel, hear, smell and taste. You are aware that there are many things we humans cannot experience with our five senses. You have a desire to live a life that is focused on more than your own limited self. An awakened person deliberately focuses on being aware of what is happening in every moment, and does not dwell on the dramas of the past or worry about the future. You want to make thoughtful decisions, be discerning about what information you choose to read and which TV shows to watch. You make choices clearly based on their ramifications for yourself and others. I really resonate with the ideas lived by some North American Native Indian Tribes who consider the implications of their decisions for the next seven generations.

An awakened person knows there is a greater Truth that applies to everything in the universe. It is not based on religious dogma, man-made laws or mass consciousness. It is the higher Truth taught by all the great masters and conveyed by many great poets and artists. This Truth is "We Are All One" and we are made from energy of the highest vibration. Highest vibration energy includes attributes such as love, peace, harmony, cooperation, compassion, order, balance, abundance, wisdom, wholeness, unity, depth, generosity, courage, trust, acceptance and clarity, anything that increases your sense of aliveness and connection to everything.

When you are awakened you are consciously aware and choose what you say and what you do. Of course, being human, sometimes we are thinking about ten things we have to do and unconsciously miss something or someone important. These missed precious moments are often what keep us from being in higher vibration and consciousness.

So, if you want to live in higher consciousness, intend to be aware in every now moment so you don't miss the gifts that each moment brings.

> ALERT: One thing to realize is once you are awakened, you cannot go back to sleep.
> You may choose to ignore this state, but deep inside, it is always there.

Common Triggers That Wake You Up

Do You Feel There Must Be More to Your Life?

At some point in your life, providing that you have your basic needs of food, clothing, shelter and safety met, you ask yourself "Is this all there is to life?" You may feel aimless, empty, bored; tired of doing the same old thing, or living for the moment. You may regret being a martyr and taking care of everyone else. You might feel angry because everyone is taking you for granted, or feel you were meant for greater things. I have even heard many young people say there is no point in trying --because the world is going to end and no one will be around in a few years anyway.

You May Be at a Transition Point in Your Life.

Your children may have left the nest and you suddenly don't feel needed. You may have achieved your goals and be considered a success. You may have to retire when your whole identity is tied up in what you do. You may be looking back on your life and realizing it isn't what you wanted it to be.

Is Your World Falling Apart?

You may have lost your job, your partner may have left you, or you may have been thrown out of your apartment because you no longer have money. A loved one might die. You could be in a life changing accident, experience a severe, deep depression, find out you have a terminal illness, or have a near death experience. In my experience, a major trauma is one of the most common events to wake people up. The trauma may not necessarily be a recent one. It may be a suppressed event from the past that emerges and exposes your limiting beliefs.

Have You Had a Mystical Experience?
Have you seen an angel? Received a message? Seen a white light and been told to take some action? This happened to me and really woke me up. It resulted in my making a re-commitment to my spiritual growth.

I am sometimes quite slow in picking up the message that I need to change something I'm doing because my life's work is taking me into something else. If I don't pick up the more subtle messages, the universe provides increasingly obvious cues. I hope you learn from my experiences and become alert to the whispering guidance you receive. I used to say, "I want to experience everything" without qualification. I did. Now I say, "I want to experience everything beautiful, holy and good" or, "I want to experience everything that is for my, and others', greatest and highest good, easily and effortlessly!" That easily and effortlessly qualifier is important for you to remember. Life doesn't have to be a struggle.

> **Try this:**
>
> *Given the above:*
>
> - Are you Awakened?
> - Did you experience any of the aforementioned triggers?
> - What has been your experience?
> - You may want to journal about them.

My experience of awakening actually was a little bit of all of the above triggers. I was raised in a Christian household. I enjoyed going to church every Sunday when I was growing up. A couple of significant experiences made an impact on how I was living my life up until a decade ago. When I was about ten years old, my dad was rushed to hospital for emergency surgery. Immediately following he had a cardiac arrest; his heart stopped. The doctors were not able to say whether he would live. As is common in a crisis, I bargained with God, promising if he let my dad live, I would be really good and not do anything to upset him or my mom. That Sunday was Easter, and a neighbour took me to church. The minister asked the congregation to pray for my dad and our family. A bit later that day, my mom came home. She told me the doctor had come out to see her about the same time we were in church, and told her, "He's going to make it, he's decided to live."

I grew up knowing I had experienced an Easter miracle. Even as an adult I was very careful to do the *right* thing, always wanting to know and follow the rules. I also wanted to help make everyone's life better. Whenever my dad or even my mom got critically ill, I subconsciously thought it was my fault, and I was breaking my promise to God. I wasn't aware of this limiting belief until I was in my early 40s!

Another key belief I absorbed as a child was from the powerful words of the communion service. "I am not worthy... to gather up the crumbs from under thy table," I repeated week after week. This thought was planted deeply in my psyche. It was only in the last decade that I healed this belief and I realized I *am* worthy!

Of course, these were not the only incidents that affected the way I believed and behaved. I was generally happy, although I had the usual angst about other things in my life. When children misunderstand a significant event, they often subconsciously carry that belief through their life. I had a normal, happy childhood and the way I perceived these events in particular, shaped how I responded to the events that unfolded later in my life.

I was very successful in my career, but one thing niggled away in the back of my mind. I blamed myself for not being able to make a difference in the health care system I worked in. I felt it was my responsibility to ensure that the people in my nursing units could practice in an environment that had enough staff and equipment to allow them to provide excellent care. I also believed that if I provided this, they would love their jobs and enjoy coming to work. Even though there was not enough money in a tight healthcare budget, I had an expectation that if I was a good enough manager and just tried hard enough, I would be able to get the equipment and budget when other much more experienced people couldn't.

In addition to the unrealistic stresses I placed on myself, I also experienced a lot of "good and bad" personal and professional stress over a period of seven years. During that time, I worked full time while studying for a Master of Public Health degree, changed job locations, was promoted, got a divorce, ruptured my spleen and had a car accident that resulted in chronic dizziness. I really enjoyed the work I did and got an adrenaline high from it, so I often chose to work 60 or more hours a week during a reorganization.

Near the end of this period, a caring friend and colleague told me she was worried that I might be depressed. Without going into detail about the changes in my behaviour, I realized she could be right. I sought medical help and counselling, which weren't successful. I was off on a stress leave from work and at one point I came to believe I had tried everything I could. I felt as if I would never get out of the tarry black pit of waste I had sunk into.

I believed my son would be better off with no mother rather than with me. I felt empty, as if I had no soul. I still knew God was there, but I felt I wasn't able to make the connection. I thought God would be merciful to me for taking my own life because I was mentally ill.

I planned my suicide on a date when my son would be at Cubs camp, and told my parents I was going to stay with a friend who had been trying to encourage me during my illness. I'd planned it so no one I knew would find me and no one would be at risk of being hurt. I was a robot, with no feelings of uncertainty or regret.

A couple of days before THE DAY, I managed to be alone and out walking beside a river, reviewing my plan, making sure I hadn't forgotten

27

anything. *This is where the mystical experience occurred.* Out of nowhere, I saw a very big, bright white light. In my mind, I heard the instructions. "Go see Sharon." She is a healer friend who had been working with me and providing short term relief for my depressive symptoms. She managed to help me get clear enough to see I had one more thing I needed to try: to go to the hospital emergency. I went believing the medical staff wouldn't think I was seriously ill and would discharge me and then I could kill myself with a clear conscience, knowing I had done all I could. You can see the irrational thinking going on with this mental illness.

Fortunately, I was referred to the mental health team and admitted to hospital. I received the help I needed with medicine and nurturing care. I could then look at what had become of my life and I realized I had unhealthy beliefs that hadn't been serving me. I realized I had severely neglected myself and had become so run down physically, mentally, emotionally and spiritually that I had absolutely no reserves of serotonin, a chemical produced by the brain, which regulates moods.

I'm telling this story in detail in case the reader thinks they know someone who might be considering suicide, or is experiencing something similar. It is important to seek help and tell health professionals clearly what is going on. The myth that someone who says they want to commit suicide won't really do it is FALSE. I learned this in my nursing education from mental health experts in the field of suicide.

Following discharge I attended outpatient classes and learned to make a life almost as if I'd had no past experiences of living in our culture. I learned how to change my thinking, change some values and beliefs, and some very basic skills for living a healthy life. I also found a New Thought church, which supported the healthier habits I was developing. I learned about the power of thought, and how to manifest what I wanted in life. When I accepted the belief that we always do the best we can with the information we have, I began to feel less guilty and to be less self-judgmental. I started to love, accept and be kind to myself for who I was-- not for what I did or what others thought about me. I still see a professional who helps me set realistic expectations and challenges any beliefs that come up that are not healthy or reality based.

In this last decade, I've learned how to move from living on a roller coaster with deep highs and deep lows, and from being in low vibration, to living in high vibration. I've gathered a lot of tools, some of which I use frequently, and some of which I find useful to share with clients. I've also been inspired and guided to develop new tools.

I also manage my life more realistically. It has been a long road, but I have found following a spiritual path, exploring new ideas, and learning to discern which energies I resonate with has resulted in a life that is more peaceful and content. I have better relationships, am more productive in the work I do and see the abundance I attract in my life. I still fall back into unconsciousness and experience overwhelms and depressed thoughts from time to time, but it happens less frequently and I experience it less deeply. I am awakened and can choose to be in higher consciousness for longer periods of time. I am really grateful to have experienced everything I have and to learn to appreciate the small successes and take baby steps with more self-acceptance.

Where Does High Vibration Energy Come From?

High vibration energy has a variety of origins. Humans can create higher vibration energy by connecting with Source. This energy is limitless and available to people who are realizing they want more from their lives. I've heard that one of the events resulting from 9/11 was that a lot of people decided they did not want to engage in escalating wars and violence. They made the decision to awaken. Because there were so many people wanting this, it resulted in higher vibration and higher consciousness across the whole planet.

Are you familiar with the 100th monkey phenomenon? Apparently a monkey on an island started washing his food before he ate it. Another monkey copied, and then several started washing their food at the same time. More and more monkeys adopted this practice until 100 monkeys were washing their food. Once that 100th monkey began washing his food, all the monkeys on the island began washing their food. Not only that, but the monkeys on another island that had no access to the first group also began washing their food.[37] This is a good example to demonstrate that once a critical mass is reached, a new phenomenon will become widely used. So, it is expected that the critical mass of people are awakening at this time. There are many formulae for determining the number of persons needed on earth to trigger a collective higher consciousness. One I've heard quoted is the square root of 1% of a population.[38] That really seems like an easily reached goal. A more recent figure is 11% of the population can make a difference.[39]

I see more people reaching out to assist others, taking turns to merge in traffic, and looking each other in the eyes as they pass by on the streets. I've been listening to people discussing the cleanup efforts ordinary citizens from across the lower mainland undertook following the recent Stanley Cup riot in my city of Vancouver Canada. The general consensus was that this wouldn't have happened even a decade ago. The volunteers value the beauty of our city and, rather than looking the other way took responsibility and acted to demonstrate their disgust towards the attitudes of the rioters. These visible examples have reinforced my trust and created assurance in my mind that the world will survive. I am seeing more creative, sustainable and inclusive programs. I know the shift into the next age is happening because more and more people like you are moving into an awakened place of higher consciousness.

High vibration energy is generated by Lightworkers (people who are more awake, live in higher vibration energies and hold this energy for the planet.) There is also divine energy coming in as a result of people asking for more peace, sustainability and enough for all.

Indigenous wisdom teachers, evolutionaries, spiritual and metaphysical leaders, teach that the planet itself is a living being, shifting into higher vibration energy. Energy from sunspots, solar flares, solar storms and other changes in the cosmos, are also changing earth's vibration. While science knows the energy of free-flowing electrons is constantly replenished by solar radiation and lightning, (in 2010 and 2011 solar flare activity is very high), you generally don't hear them relate this to its effects on people in general.

How Do Energy Shifts Affect Us?

The higher vibration energy is resulting in physical, mental, emotional and spiritual transitional changes regardless of whether you are still asleep or consciously choosing higher vibration. Whereas in the past only more energetically aware people noticed these changes, my theory is that now, as even more energy comes in, the changes are going to be more intense if you choose to stay in lower vibration energy because you are not matching increasing planetary vibratory energy.

The increased energies have been so strong, many people who have made the decision to move into higher vibration and higher consciousness experience increased sensitivity. They are more attuned to the moods of others and to nonverbal communication and may notice more seeming coincidences occurring in their lives. They may even recognize new intuitive abilities. Because of this and some of the symptoms below, a lot of people approach me asking if I think they're going crazy.

Indicators That You Are Waking Up

Several metaphysical and spiritual energy experts have documented symptoms that people experience as a result of the shift to higher energy currently happening. There is a surprisingly large community of people who have experienced these signs and therefore, are able to articulate them to other sensitive people, not familiar with these signals. People who resist these energies may feel as if they're being dragged through a tunnel backwards or sucked into a vortex of chaos and confusion where nothing seems familiar. If you are awakened and open to unlimited possibilities, you have a much easier time, although you may still experience symptoms such as the following:

Physical

Unusual aches and pains;

Being very cold for a brief time no matter what you do to warm up;

Night sweats and hot flashes (in men and women of any age);

Experiencing pulses of unusual energy moving right through your body;

Whirling, Dizziness, feeling off balance;

Feeling as if part of your body on one side is asymmetrical compared with the same part on the other side.

The need to eat every couple of hours because of low blood sugar;

Ringing or buzzing in the ears or other odd sensations in the head including feeling as if energy is coming into the top of your crown.

Emotional

Emotional ups and downs-feeling as if you are on a roller coaster;

Panic attacks, anxiety, or depression;

Feeling comfortable only in your own personal haven at home;

Unable to cope with lower vibrating energy of such things as TV News or people who are angry, negative or complainers

Feeling you don't belong (now or in the past) and longing for people who "get" you.

Yearning for something, but you don't know what.

Mental

Absent mindedness

Forgetting what just happened;

Can't think of the words you want to use;

Forgetting what you were going to say.

Fuzzy mind or unclear thoughts

Spiritual

Knowing that you are here to accomplish something, but you may not be sure what it is;

Finding that spiritual and personal growth information no longer draws you.

Other

Losing friends, jobs and family;

Unexpected financial loss;

Seeing the same numbers repeatedly on license plates, digital displays etc.;

Seeing the exact same minute on the clock every night when you suddenly wake up;

Feeling uneasy when in crowds, noisy stores, places with bright lights and being exhausted when you get home;

Feeling compelled to move somewhere you've never been drawn to;

Difficulty being around people who are living in an ego based state or creating drama in their lives;[40]

If you do experience these indicators your best course of action is to let their energy flow, rest and drink lots of water. Now that you know that you are expanding and letting more light and higher-conscious vibration in, you can be excited that this cosmic gift is coming to you. Let it amaze you, be in wonderment and be grateful that you know why you are having these experiences

It is always important to see a doctor if you are experiencing any of these signs or symptoms. I recently had a retinal detachment, which I initially attributed to energy shifts because I was on a sacred study tour. If I hadn't decided to double check with a retinologist, I probably would have gone blind in the affected eye. As usual, there were many layers to this incident. I had been learning to use my intuitive "3rd eye" and was not paying attention to the guidance I was getting, so the messages were becoming more obvious. In addition, there was a lot of higher knowledge that I needed to download, so the universe ensured I had an enforced quiet downtime. This was not "punishment"- I always ask Spirit that my experiences occur for the greatest and highest good of myself and everyone involved, and I always recommend this to my clients.

So, be discerning and also aware that transitional symptoms and experiences may be related to our spiritual expansion process, as we begin to vibrate at a higher-conscious frequency and retain and express more light.

Moving on Up

As we evolve in our spiritual transmutation process, we release lower frequency energies, and transform our body-mind, emotions and spirit by aligning ourselves with new and higher vibrational energies. This ensures our shift into a new and higher way of living and being. Sooner or later, we realize that we are no longer subject to many of the signs and symptoms of waking up. This is an indicator that we are ready to shift to a higher frequency. After we move to the next level we often feel supercharged and do everything better. Eventually, we may experience some of the above symptoms again, feeling lethargic and having difficulty accomplishing anything. This is normal. Our bodies and minds are adapting to the higher vibrations, and the signs will again decrease. It can be discouraging if we are not aware that this process occurs. We may beat ourselves up and wonder why we can't stay in higher vibration. However, when you recognize that it is part of a cycle, it makes it easier to allow yourself some time to adjust.

There comes a time in our spiritual evolution when we have higher vibration light in our body so we can connect with others more easily. We have integrated our life lessons and have experienced some important insights that change our behaviour. We:

- Become aware no one needs to be "fixed" (including our self);
- Realize we no longer need to refer to anyone or anything outside our self; the answers from Source consciousness are within;
- Rarely experience lack - our needs are met easily and effortlessly;

- See the value and necessity of collaboration rather than feeling ego based ``shoulds`` to make something thing happen by ourselves;
- See the bigger picture, the ramifications of our actions, how others can contribute, and where we fit in.
- Connect instantly to Source wisdom - we don't need long periods of meditation listening for the small still voice;
- Stop offering our services - allowing others to ask for it;
- Despite outward chaos, feel protected and experience a deep down knowing that everything is OK, peaceful and serene;
- Make our first priority our personal happiness and health;
- Allow others to suffer, knowing this is important for their growth; it has a higher purpose, and comforting interferes with the process;
- Have stronger boundaries and have a strong sense of what is appropriate for our self at that time rather than going along with what others want us to do or believe;
- Become visibly impatient with people who do not take responsibility and only appear to be making an effort to move into higher consciousness;
- Stop wanting to accumulate material goods and are content to appreciate them where they are. No longer concern ourselves with getting what we want, and allowing things to unfold in a flexible way;
- Realize that the behaviour of others has nothing to do with us, all that happens it not about us, therefore we no longer take things personally;
- Become very aware of and connect to the beauty of what is around us;
- Give up the desire to *save* anyone or anything;
- Realize we are imperfectly perfect;
- Decide on something based on our gut feeling rather than a logical process;
- Spend more of our time and focus on just *one* of our passions, instead of pursuing many interests. [41]

We may still feel restless, as if something big is going to happen, but rather than calling it fear we know to be alert and call the feeling excitement or anticipation. Kryon, channelled by Lee Carroll, attributes this to Kundalini Energy and says it is a physically real, chemical reaction and feeling. We do get used to this surging energy and recognize it as positive.[42]

My Friends and Family Think I've Lost It

A commonly expressed question or concern among people who are awakening is related to friends and loved ones who do not seem interested in their new passion. It is really essential to remember everyone has his or her own path and often it does not appear to be similar to the one you are on. That's OK. Everyone has different lessons to learn so we can all become fully conscious beings. It may happen at a different time or rate. It is most important NOT to try to get people to change, Please focus on yourself and your own path. Sometimes when people see the differences in your life they'll ask you what you are doing differently and, because it is their own idea, may be open to change.

Since not everyone has the same vibration as yours, they may resonate with other teachers. We all choose unique ways to grow. It's as if our GPS's (Guided Path Sensors©) are programmed differently. Some people program theirs to go straight as the crow flies and struggle through whatever may be in the way. Others choose the fastest route and are not distracted from the task at hand. Many choose the road more traveled, and they might get caught and distracted by the traffic. Some people pick what appears to be a slow winding scenic route that flows around what's in the way, and use little effort. Several don't seem to have a GPS and have a fun time exploring the road and not getting anywhere their whole life. Many of us would choose to worry about them, especially if they were a partner or children. That will decrease our vibrational frequency and distract us from our spiritual path. Worry is a big lesson or a road block we need to release as we move along on our spiritual path. We need to remember some people start off at daybreak, others at noon and others may not leave until after dinner. But I believe we all end up at the same place in our soul's own time.

As I'm writing this I'm reminded of the story of the owner of a vineyard who hires labourers throughout the day. He speaks with each person and tells them how much he will pay them. The men hired in the morning overhear him talking with the ones hired at lunch, promising these new workers the same amount he had promised them. The morning workers think "Oh boy! I guess I will get more pay". The same thing occurs with the workers hired in the evening. At the end of the workday, the owner pays all the men the same amount of money. The workers hired earlier in the day complain that the men who only worked the evening got the same pay as the men who worked the entire day. But, the owner didn't cheat them -- he paid what he had said he would.

The moral of the story is that it doesn't matter when you start on your path. We will all have the same outcome.

So too, as we travel with our GPS on whatever path we choose, remember we all make a difference. Even the ones who seem to have hurt a person actually helped them learn important lessons. People who have selected the fast path may have helped a large group at one time by sharing their knowledge or writing a book. People on the slow path may have chosen to use a lot of time with a few individuals. People who have a "hard" life may have chosen lots of lessons to reach higher consciousness sooner. People who seem to have an easy life may have let go of limiting beliefs and learned how to manifest their desires. In the end, perhaps after several incarnations, we are all awakened in higher vibration and conscious awareness.

How Long Does It Take To Move Into Higher Consciousness?

Transformation is happening much more quickly now than in the past because there are so many more Lightworkers on the planet. I find the process of how and why this occurred extremely enlightening.

One of the factors that affects the time it takes to move into higher consciousness is the beliefs and values that have occurred at various times in history. From a bird's eye, big picture viewpoint, the length of time it takes to move into higher consciousness also changes depending on the energy of the age. Ages last about 2500 years, and we are now at the end of one age, moving into another. The one we are ending began around the time of Jesus. The energy of this age has been paternalistic, restrictive and a key belief is "We (those in power) know what's best for you". The age we are moving into has more balanced male and female energies; it values allowing, harmony and cooperation instead of power and competition. As I explain this in more detail, the different lengths of time it takes to move into higher consciousness will become evident.

In the past people had to work hard to provide for the basic needs of their families. There was no time or energy to think of higher things. Of course this is still true today. Yet there have always been those who have learned about universal laws and energetic principles, and have achieved higher consciousness. In some civilizations, these people were from the elite or part of the church, with a lifestyle that allowed them to ask more metaphysical and philosophical questions.

However, people took many decades to experience higher consciousness for many other reasons. A primary factor was that energy was very dense and heavy. The flow of energy was slow because information was by word of mouth or, if it was printed, it was inaccessible to most. Collective conscious beliefs were entrenched and the status quo was maintained. If you longed to understand why you were here, you had to put a lot of time and effort into studying and raising your vibration.

Even in the early 1900s, although we were only about a century away from the next age, the heavy patriarchal energy and the accepted mass conscious beliefs resulted in a very slow process of enlightenment for people who wanted to move into higher consciousness. Instead, people valued accumulation and acquisition of material goods, rather than spiritual growth. In fact by the mid 1950s, advertisers had convinced U.S. consumers that it was their responsibility and their duty as loyal citizens to buy the biggest and the best.

Changes in the collective conscious energy became evident as each generation birthed more and more people who were remembering how to live in higher consciousness. There have always been awakened people but by the 1960s, there was a large core group, the flower children, who valued peace and held a new vision of what could be. In fact the song "The Age of Aquarius" foretold the coming next age which has subtly been establishing itself. I wondered why this vision didn't take root and how disillusioned flower people had turned into the old guard. I was told by a wise woman that one reason was that the new energy remained in the thoughts and emotions of the flower children's higher energy centres, or chakras; it was not grounded into third dimensional reality.[43] This explanation demonstrates the importance of having balanced chakras and experiencing life using all chakra energy. In the first few years of growing in my spiritual and metaphysical life, I loved focusing on developing and being in my higher chakras, spiritually connecting with the higher energy. In the last few years I've begun to understand the importance of also using the lower chakras and the necessity of being grounded to accomplish my purpose.

If we look at how long it takes to move into higher vibration today it is important to recognize the large group of people who became adults in the late 70s. They grew up feeling they didn't belong in a society that had paternalistic characteristics, beliefs and values. These people, who are known as light workers and wayShowers (way-Show-er- one who is a guide along a spiritual development path), carry the beliefs and values of the energies of our next age. Their work has been to increase the vibration of the planet and hold the energy so more people will feel called to wake up. In the last decade we have reached a place in the evolution and awakening of humanity where many awakened souls moved into the places light workers had been holding the energy. It seems like there is a big enough group with a high enough frequency to evolve much faster.

Because of the Lightworkers, the collective energy on the planet today makes it possible for people to wake up, remember the Truth and move into higher consciousness in a very short time. It may only take a couple of years or even less, especially if they choose to work with a wayShower who can assist them to manage their overwhelm, release beliefs that no longer serve them and teach them about energy management. The wayShower can help them with tools and strategies that increase their vibration, and provide them with information about universal laws, the power of thought, and other metaphysical and spiritual wisdom formerly available only in mystery schools, or through indigenous peoples.

Thanks to the Lightworkers, the energy is now stable enough for large numbers of Indigo children to come in and live in awakened awareness. They do not even need to experience the process many of us have gone through. If the number of Indigos living on the planet today had been born in the 1940s, they couldn't have survived because there would have been so much dense, immovable energy based on old beliefs of the age.

Tell Me More About Indigo Children

A large group of children born after 1987 are highly intuitive, have a well-developed sense of right and wrong and have the knowledge and skills that are needed to live in the upcoming age. Although perhaps in the not so distant future we will stop using labels to differentiate and separate people, these children are called Indigos because of their deep blue aura. Some even have a blue tinge to their skin. Indigos have been born in gradually increasing numbers in past generations. They are often the Lightworkers, metaphysicians, perhaps people who were burned as witches, or tortured in the inquisition. They had different wisdom, often connect more with nature and used natural substances such as herbs, minerals. These were the people who may have gone to mystery schools where they learned esoteric insights. In the past generation the inception of new thought churches often had members who were indigos. One common characteristic of these early indigos was a feeling of not belonging, wondering how they were born into the family they were, being the odd person out and just feeling different and having unusual perspectives compared to their peers. A larger contingent was born in each generation, gradually raising the vibrational frequency of the planet, until it was possible for the group on the planet today who are here in enough numbers to increase the rapidity of The Shift

They are here to help us make the transition, and because of their higher vibration energy they are often misfits in the system. We initially saw some changes occurring in schools. Because of their different learning styles, old rigid education systems with energies based in the past ages are slowly and painfully breaking down. New, innovative, creative ways of learning are developing, but they are slow to be implemented and are not available in most traditional schools. (*I'm looking forward to seeing what happens in the job market, since the '87 birth cohort has graduated from school*).

I had an experience of learning with these delightful individuals when I was in the seminary. We had a few young adults in the program. They were bright and intuitive but were having difficulty learning because of the structure of the classes. Our enlightened intuitive leaders, led by James Twyman, worked with them and they were encouraged to learn in the best way that met their needs. So a couple of them didn't attend the live classes but listened to the lectures on their own. Everyone was encouraged to get up and go to the back of the room if we felt moved to do so. There we could move, sway and respond to the energetic vibration and waves. As one who had learned to survive in the educational system of my time, I found it was so freeing to be able to incorporate all my senses in the learning process. I believe I integrated the learning at a cellular, mind, body and spirit level more quickly than when I had experienced traditional, familiar methods.

When I was having coffee the other day, the conversation turned to how kids today learn to use a mouse at 2 years old, are constantly texting and tuning out with their electronic devices. The person I was chatting with believes this is going to result in negative outcomes for the kids, families and society. Because I believe in limitless high vibration possibilities and I know that there are more children who have come in with these advanced energies, I felt uncomfortable with that conclusion. Yet I was unable to clearly identify why. Upon reflection and connection I realized that these children see their poor fit in society just as the highly energetically aware Lightworkers who came before them and likewise felt like they don't belong. They may be using the technology to distract themselves until they get into a position where they can "be the change they want." I don't believe it's dumbing them down. There are people like my friend who are challenging some of the young people to live up to their potential, who believe they can make something of themselves and be successful. Many people are using their unique talent and helping children and adults learn to change the system and work within it. I was privileged to get a grant and work with high school students in the district to plan unique AIDs education projects when the HIV epidemic was beginning to spread to women and children. The children I worked with developed unique creative ways to clarify myths and provide accurate information about the spread and prevention of HIV, despite limitations imposed on the project by a parent advisory group and some principals.

I have faith that today's children and youth will change the world based on that, and many other experiences and examples from colleagues, and social media.

There is another group of children called Crystal children being born to Indigos adults. They are called Crystal children because apparently their DNA cell structure and make up is more crystalline in nature than ours. If you wish to find out more, there are many books available about indigo, crystal and other highly evolved children.

I also want to give you a heads up to tuck into your memory bank. Because of the overlap during the new and old age, we will still have people being born in the next few generations who have old energies. It is important for people to use their increasing sensitivity, so all people with will be unconditionally accepted; and their viewpoints, skills and strengths valued. I envision a community where everyone is nurtured and helped to find a place in life where their talents and skills are recognized and honoured, and they thrive.

> ### *End of Chapter Reflections*
>
> Are you enjoying your journey?
>
> How would you define being awakened?
>
> How did you wake up?
>
> How is your GPS set? Where are you on your path?
>
> How far along the path are you? Do you want to reset your Guided Path Sensors©?
>
> Are you just awakening and wondering "what now"?
>
> Have you been seeking your life purpose?
>
> Do you know your purpose and are well on your way to fulfilling it?
>
> Are you drawn to materials that will help increase your knowledge and fulfill your desire for spiritual growth?
>
> Do you believe you have read enough information and are seeking your wisdom from within?
>
> Are you living your life's purpose? Is there anything missing or any areas you are strengthening? Do you have all the resources you need in place or know how and where to access them?

Summary

This chapter explored the meaning of being awakened instead of living in the 3D dream, or illusion. The four most common triggers of awakening are discussed: feeling as if there must be more to one's life, being in a transition period, having one's life seemingly fall apart, and having a mystical experience.

I hope you were as reassured as my clients are when you learned that the weird physical, mental, emotional and spiritual symptoms you may have been experiencing are normal occurrences because of the earth's evolving higher vibration energy patterns. By saying YES and consciously choosing to live in higher consciousness, you will experience these symptoms with less intensity than people who are still unconscious. Life will also be easier when you are in higher frequency, although you may experiences fluctuations as you adjust, plateau and shift again.

It is important to remember everyone has their own path and our GPS`s (Guided Path Sensors©) are programmed for different routes. This difference also occurs according to cycles in our human evolution and the evolution of the earth, as described in a brief historical review of personal growth in the age we are transitioning from.

CHAPTER 3

Why Move Into Higher Consciousness

The *unconsciousness* with which we have been evolving as a civilization is taking us rapidly toward collective extinction -- following in the footsteps of the vast majority of "failed experiments" (extinct species) in Earth's history -- and taking many more with us.

This century's evolutionary challenge -- to become a civilization capable of conscious evolution -- is not only what can "save" us, but is also one of the most significant evolutionary leaps in human history. All the crises of our age are manifestations of our challenge to consciously evolve. *www.co-intelligence.org/**Evolution**.html*

Our Life is Currently Unsustainable

In many areas of the developed world economic structures are crumbling. Banks are closing their doors, loans are being called in for the full amount owing, credit card companies seem to assume everyone is going to default on their payments and make their policies inflexible not for long term responsible customers who may need a bit of a break. The health care, education and social systems are also breaking down. A lack of integrity is evident as government officials and other people in positions of trust, or those who act as role models by virtue of their popularity (notoriety), are being outed by scandals. Many people are experiencing stress, anxiety and suffering as their jobs, health and relationships collapse around them.

In addition we seem to be experiencing an unusual number of natural disasters. We are overusing natural resources and some areas are being restricted in their use of electricity in brown outs, in the use of water and other things we see as essential to our daily life. Even in Vancouver where our four seasons are cold and wet, wet with occasional showers of cherry blossom petals, summer, and wetter, we experience restrictions around watering our lawns in the summer.

We Live in a World of Fear.

Much of western society is experiencing the fear of "what if it happens to me" or if it has already happened, "what do I do now?" Fear governs their life and limits the choices they make.

The media escalates fear in the way it chooses to report local and world events. Not only are we fearful about our own situation, but people are responding with fear to the news of suicide bombings, shooting sprees, drug wars, local gangs of preteens and teens, and more societal breakdown.

We are numbing the feelings we experience as we hear about and see when the media captures personal, private anguish and terror on television. We are starting to view it as business as usual. So what level is the great majority of energy vibrating at?

The law of attraction says: like attracts like and what we focus on grows; it seems to many that life goes in a spiral cycle of increasing negative energy.

The news doesn't even have to sensationalize events to evoke low vibration responses. I heard a story on the news a couple of weeks ago about a woman who was killed in an accident when she was hit while standing beside her car on the shoulder of a very busy highway in Toronto, Canada. It wasn't a sensational accident. It wasn't presented in the context of a saftey reminder. It seemed to serve no useful purpose.

While I am deeply sorry for this woman's family, did I really need or want to hear about this tragedy halfway across the country? Since I was not involved in the situation or know anyone who was, and since I was listening consciously, it didn't result in lowering my vibration because of fear of the same happening to me. Just by being reported however, it contributed to keeping the general collective unconscious in lower vibration energy.

Even businesses are reacting from a fear base. I can actually sense the fear when I call a business for assistance with a concern. Even if the person I am connected with seems pleasant,, their manner is such that they have made a judgement that everyone is the same and wants to "rip their company of". It is almost as if the senior manager is standing over their shoulder telling them to watch out. Sometimes when I go into a business I can sense their desperation for a sale and I hear conversations focusing on the bottom line. Since you attract what you focus on, Guess what that business will find at the end of the month? Lower profits.

One last aspect of fear I want to mention is the western world's penchant for *seeking out fear for "fun"* This is demonstrated by the popularity of extreme sports, horror movies and books. I wonder if the thought behind seeking these activities out is related to a belief that, "if I get over my big fears, the little ones won't bother me."

What's your opinion?

> There is No Peace for Those who Live in Fear.
>
> –Gino Ojeb commenting on the Vancouver Canucks
> hockey team's chances in the playoffs.

Although one purpose of this book is to help you shift out of fear, I won't be focusing on it. There is a universal law that suggests that "What you focus on you create." Instead, I will offer information to help you get a handle on how to let go of what you don't want, in a detached manner, and shift into living in higher vibration consciousness.

We Are in a Perfect State for Change to Occur

First we need to acknowledge the disconnect between how the majority of people say they want to live and how they live now. This can be quite a positive state for change. The most likely time for people to change is when they are experiencing chaos. Alchemists know that a substance is most easily transformed when it is in an unstable state, so our world is ripe for transformation.

Because We Can

It is the end of current cycles and ages and the beginning of a new: Geologists, astronomers, scientists and ancient wisdom cultures validate the evidence that this is an excellent time for shifting.

We Can Personally Live an Enriched Life

We CAN live more consistently in love, peace, acceptance and joy and because of that, we will finally access limitless possibilities and do what we are meant to do!

A Practical Comparison of Higher and Lower Vibration Consciousness. There are many ways of explaining transformation of low energetic vibration into higher vibration, which can result in higher consciousness. One way to understand the practical difference between higher and lower vibration energies is by considering your chakra or energy centres in your body.

What are chakras? The most basic definition is that they are energy centres that have specific qualities associated with them. They are dormant in most of the population. [44] Awakening and developing each chakra has implications for physical, mental, emotional and spiritual health and growth. Balancing them will allow a person to increase their vibration and activate and develop their higher consciousness. The first three chakras are often seen as more related to the material world - living in 3D world of form, while the development of the upper three correlates more with the higher dimensions connecting with Source Energy or growing into higher consciousness and awareness of the self and others. You can have lower vibration (shadow aspects) in all chakras if they are not balanced and experiencing freely flowing energy.

For the sake of brevity I will select one or two of the main qualities or characteristics I associate with each chakra and use these as an example.

Each chakra vibrates at a different frequency. The chakras can be unbalanced by either excess or deficient energy. If this occurs, a person will experience lower vibration energy. Once the situation is remedied the chakras will have an ability to move into their higher vibration. However, a person needs to consciously make an effort to learn, practice and incorporate spiritual principles in their everyday life in order to maintain balance. Although a person has a dominant chakra that provides them with special skills, strengths and potential challenges throughout their lives, they can also experience imbalance in other chakras, depending on situations and current life lessons. For further information on this fascinating topic I refer you to the book 'The Eye of the Lotus', written by my teacher, Dr. Richard Jelusich.

As an example, the first or root chakra has to do with having basic needs such as safety, security, food, shelter, clothing, etc. met. Its lower vibration energy could be fear of lacking these. When this chakra is balanced and functioning well, people have the opportunity to move into and live in the higher octave of trust and confidence, and the ability to manifest these basic needs.

Similarly the second chakra deals with sexuality and creativity. Lower octaves of unbalanced energy could involve over-focusing or under-focusing on these areas, to the exclusion of other aspects of a healthy life. A higher octave might result in a shift away from imbalanced sexuality and an evolution from carnal to tantric sexuality. Ego driven creativity for recognition may become inspired (from the Latin in spiritus, meaning 'in spirit') by a higher Source or higher ideals and connection with All That IS.

One of the primary aspects of the third chakra is will and power. This can be evident in the lower vibration of a person who wants power over others and uses their will to achieve something that will result in loss to someone else. This is often the motivating factor behind competition in business, school, even in relationships. These qualities may seem to be essential in getting ahead, but can be associated in extremes with ruthlessness.

In a higher vibration this can become the power of the self. It manifests in cooperation, desires for win-win outcomes and the use of power to ensure everyone gets a fair outcome. This reminds me of how, in some indigenous tribes, the sign of being successful is how much you give away to ensure others have enough or more to enjoy. I keep reading and hearing that there is enough food, water and resources for everyone on the planet to have more than enough of what they need. When we expect and achieve this as a world belief and value, we will have alchemically transformed to the highest vibration of the third chakra.

The fourth or heart chakra is the bridge between the lower and upper three chakras. The heart is commonly associated with love. For people in the western world, this may be the most difficult chakra to shift. People with lower vibration heart energy experience lack of self-love. Thoughts and feelings range from self hatred: "no one will ever love me" or, "I'm afraid to love anyone" to inadequacy: "I'm not good enough." It exhibits behaviours such as poor self-care, nutritional choices, grooming, ignoring self and wanting to get love by helping others to the exclusion of one's own self. Other common behaviours include being unable to give or receive love, having walls around your heart, inability to commit and neediness.

The maxim, love others as you love yourself, applies to this chakra. In my opinion, as a society, we *do* this very well; because we don't love ourselves, we can't love others. This is so evident in every aspect of today's world, expressed as intolerance, judgment, unreasonable expectations and so much more.

Because of our inability to love, it may be confusing when we look to the higher octave or the higher vibration aspect of love. We assume the love we think we want is what is portrayed in the movie Jerry McGuire where the famous quote has become so familiar. "You complete me." But the motivation behind how we view our ideal love is very connected to our beliefs.

Our beliefs are a major factor in keeping us in lower vibration and I will go into detail on how to shift our beliefs, thoughts and emotions in the third section of the book.

I would define true higher vibration love as being unconditional love for all energy, and being able to connect to and receive healthy unconditional love. We would be completely whole and not need anything to complete us. In a relationship, high vibration love would be about having a resonant match in a partner not in the way that it would be boring sameness, but in fact would be stimulating and one person's passion for life would energize their partner's.

The fifth, throat chakra is about speaking your truth. In its lower aspect, we often say what we think others want to hear. Another way this manifests is when we don't speak up because we don't want to create conflict, we want to be nice. Marianne Williamson has written an inspirational message made famous by Nelson Mandela. She says we don't want people to know how valuable our contribution is; because our greatest fear is that others will feel inadequate because of our greatness. The higher vibration of the throat chakra expresses as clear inspired communication.

One important bit of information to be aware of is that lower vibrations often result in physical symptoms and can lead to significant illnesses. For example, a common fifth chakra malady is a sore throat. If you choose not to speak your truth, the blocked energy may result in an acute sore throat (if there is one particular current situation you are having a challenge communicating about), or a chronic one if you habitually swallow your words. Treatments have been developed that match a resonant frequency, which can destroy illnesses and even tumours. Just as when the voice of an opera singer reaches the resonant frequency of a crystal glass and shatters the glass, the administration of a resonant vibration can shake apart a virus, bacteria, tumour or organism responsible for many physical illnesses. These frequencies were identified by Royal Rife.[45] Another valuable resource in identifying the core emotional reasons for maladies is the book, 'Heal Your Body', by Louise L. Hay.

The sixth chakra, commonly referred to as the third eye, is the centre of your intuition. If this centre isn't balanced you may not connect with your intuition, or the messages you receive may be confused or incorrect, ego driven, or move through filters of your own beliefs and values. You may connect with lower vibration messages, may feel frustrated and give up listening for higher guidance. When you move into higher vibration sixth chakra energy, you will receive clear guidance from the highest vibration, your intuition will be accurate and you can confidently move forward and act with assurance.

Your seventh or crown chakra connects you with Divine Source Energy of the highest vibration. If you are in low vibration energy because this chakra is blocked or out of balance, you won't connect with high vibration energy. You'll be unable to connect with your higher power. You may feel empty, soulless, purposeless and aimless. You may live life superficially, connecting with others on a surface level. You'll never really feel pleasure - not feel touched by others who care about you, not appreciate beauty or any higher vibration such music, art, nature, or the innocence and wonder of children. You may just have a feeling that something is missing -- a longing or yearning for ... you're not sure what.

When you transform your energy into its highest vibration, you experience the bliss of being connected with *All That IS*. You may feel light and your heart may feel expanded. You know *All's Right with the World*. You can see beyond the 3D reality and look at life as Shakespeare does:

> All the world's a stage and all the men and women merely players.
>
> They have their exits and their entrances and one man in his time plays many parts;[46]

I love this metaphor, and frequently use it as an example of how we can choose higher vibration energy to live in higher consciousness. We can think of ourselves as both the playwright and the actor, and the world as the play. When we are the actor, we are in what I call, the illusion of our lives; or we are asleep – dreaming, because we believe our experiences and the world around us are real. However the Truth is, when the rehearsal is over, we take off our costumes, become our Real (or higher-conscious) Self and live in the True Reality of highest consciousness.

When your crown chakra is balanced, you have the potential to make a powerful alchemical transformation through the process of remembering life is an illusion. Living Life as your Real Self is truly being in higher consciousness. When we wake from the dream of our 3D life and realize who we truly are, we can accomplish anything and change our life and if we wish we can even change the world.

In my work with clients I use several tools and techniques to address unbalanced, deficient or excessive chakra energies. This allows them to begin to undertake alchemical transformation. I also show clients how to change their lifestyle into one of higher vibration, and provide hints on how to maintain the changes. You can find some of these hints in the "How To Move Into Higher Vibration" chapter in Section Three.

What Do You Want in Life?

What do you think you would hear if you were to ask a large group of people how they want to live and what they want to experience in life? You might hear, "I want to have enough money to do what I want and enough time to do it." Perhaps, "Have a job that I love, with great benefits and enough flexibility to take off when I want. I want to travel, have an environmentally sporty car or an SUV, a big house with a maid, cook and gardener."

In addition to the material things people would mention, you would likely hear less tangible desires mentioned such as a good relationship, happy, healthy children, good health, the ability to donate money to good causes and help others. Probably people would want to live in a safe community where they would know their neighbours and would watch out for each other. In this community they might exchange their skills with someone when they need help with their garden or with updating their bathroom or they need the extra bread someone has in their freezer because there is a snowstorm and they can't get through the drifts.

You might hear even less tangible, more metaphysical, spiritual or esoteric desires, such as feeling peaceful, being creative, being able to give and receive love in all its forms, living in order and balance, feeling comfortable and confident to speak up, share perspectives, speak our truth and be listened to, respected and unconditionally accepted. Some people may mention the need to feel connected to other people and to do their bit for the environment or other causes, the desire to be compassionate, to listen to their gut feelings, to be more sensitive to other peoples energy (moods or feelings) or be more intuitive.

Some may express higher conciousness desires such as having experiences that uplift the spirit and expand their heart, to know and live their greater purpose, to pay attention to higher vibration messages from their wise self, Higher Self or angels, ascended masters, and guides of the highest vibration; to connect spiritually to a being of the highest vibration, something that is greater than the self, internally or externally.

One aspect that may be mentioned and is currently occuring in some organizations and communities is being cooperative rather than competitive. I love the anecdote Gregg Braden tells of children who have Downs Syndrome and participated in a race. One of them fell near the start line. The boy who was going to win looked back and when he saw the child struggling to get back up, he walked back to help. All the other children walked back too and they all hooked their arms together and walked over the finish line together.[47]

Try this:

In order to feel yourself in higher vibration, I'd like to give you an opportunity before you read any farther;

Make your own list of what you would like to experience, both material and less tangible, in your life.

Then imagine yourself having one or more of them right now and experience all the great feelings you have. Really put yourself into the picture. Imagine seeing, touching, smelling, tasting and hearing -- emotionally and physically. Note where you feel it in your body and be aware of what it feels like; perhaps a tingle, a burn, numbness like pins and needles or goosebumps.

People usually feel very positve or high vibration energy when they imagine what they have in their life during this exercise. I feel my heart expand and feel lighter when I am in high vibration or higher conciousness. It reminds me of 'The Grinch Who Stole Christmas' when the Grinch's heart grew 3 sizes!

If you notice your vibration lowers or you feel angry sad or heavier as you imagine having one of the things on your list, just note it and go on to others. Then read ahead to the section on journalling in part three of the book.

By moving into and sustaining higher-conscious vibration, you will be lifting energy for humanity and the planet. Just doing this fairly simple thing will make a big difference in the world, helping to shift us from fear to an eternity (of at least 5,300 years) of the upcoming Golden Age. More people will awaken through the higher vibration energy you hold for them, and the critical mass we create will be aware of the need for and want to create a sustainable world, cooperatively and respectfully. We will know we are all the energy of Source of Life and recognize our similarities.

Those of us who are coming to understand and welcome this challenge to become conscious evolutionary agents are discovering new sources of inspiration and meaning in it, and find ourselves working in community with truly remarkable companions.[48] When you have a vision for how you can live and what you desire you will know it can manifest for every person on earth who desires it.

Summary

This chapter presented five factors that are driving our movement into higher consciousness. The first three, a currently unsustainable world and the fear being spread by the media, are among the global problems that result in being in a perfect state for collective change. The last two factors are more personal: we are shifting into higher consciousness because we can, and The Shift will result in a more enriched life.

If you completed the exercise where you listed what you'd like to experience in life, then you'll be ready for Section Three. If you haven't, you may wish to do it before you get to Section Three, since it will enhance your experiences of how to move into higher vibration.

In the next chapter we'll explore some hitches that people often don't recognize when they live in higher vibration, as well as the benefits of living in higher consciousness. You'll also see how your life might change.

CHAPTER 4

The Benefits of Living in Higher Vibrational Consciousness

> To change your mood or mental state, Change your vibration...
>
> The Kybalion (classic hermetic manual)

As humans living consciously in the third dimensional world, we find ourselves moving between higher and lower vibration. People who are well along their path often express how frustrating it is to recognize they have slipped back into patterns they thought they had worked through, and worked through and worked through, and left behind. "Why is this coming up again!!??," they wonder about the lack of consistency in their behaviour.

However, just knowing how it feels to be in higher vibration makes it easier to detach from the thoughts and feelings that "bring you down." When you realize Truth --- "this is coming up so I can release it;" the thought, feeling or behaviour evokes less reaction. Each time it comes up it is a relief to know that the universe is offering one more opportunity to make a healthy choice and reaffirm our commitment to living an awakened life in higher consciousness. You can even start to see the humour in it and be playful with your Higher Self. "Oh look, here comes issue 'X' again. Wow, I guess I still need to let go of some part of it." Or, it may be an opportunity to learn to forgive yourself for slipping into unconscious behaviour, and realize it is perfectly normal.

As an example, when I was brainstorming the benefits of living in higher vibration energy, I found myself reflecting that I don't very often come into contact with crabby dissatisfied people who live fear based lives. When I do, I sometimes challenge myself to try and make them smile. *Oops. Did you catch that? I am engaging with them and trying to change them. Changing others and believing I have the power to make people do something is not higher vibrational thinking. Unconditional acceptance and recognizing everyone chooses how they respond, is. The lower vibration ego, which operates when you slip into unconsciousness thinking and feeling, can still react in a habitual way even after you conciously let go of beliefs that no longer serve you.* So, as I write this I smile and recognize the "universe's playfulness" and "nudge nudge, wink wink" the reminder that I'm human.

I read another viewpoint regarding being human and slipping into old habits as opposed to knowing it all and living a perfect life with interest. Alchemists believed that as long as they were transforming and transmuting themselves they would be successful in manifesting; if they finished they would lose their ability to transform anything. "... For it is only in their unfinished state that phenomenon are transmutable".[49]

EGO as an Ally in Higher Consciousness

When you choose to live in higher consciousness, you recruit your ego and connect with it as an ally.

My EGO isn't my ENEMY?
Your ego is not your enemy. Many self help books tell you that you must be the master of your ego. This power over someone or something view is not in alignment with my perspective of higher-conscious living. Your ego doesn't have to be subdued. In fact, it's important to acknowledge all it does for you, know what it does well and be grateful for that. The ego is great at doing things that are automatic in your life; habits like brushing your teeth -- imagine if you had to think about what to do every time you brushed. When you drive to work and you realize you don't know what went on between the time you passed the first traffic light until you got to your parking spot, you can thank your ego. (and your lucky stars!!)

Living in the Moment

Having said that, being on autopilot isn't a practice of higher-conscious living. Quite the opposite: one practice many people choose to have when they are living in awareness is mindfulness, or awareness of what they are doing. When brushing their teeth they would consciously feel the sensations and be in the moment, focusing on what they are doing.

Living in the moment is a practice that eliminates fear and anxiety. When you are completely focused on what is happening, past and future worries can't intrude. Canon Geoffery Dibbs, a wise man, influential in my spiritual development, once suggested that I save my worries for a scheduled time every week. When that time arrived, I found I couldn't remember most of what I worried about.

Think of all the wasted energy you leak worrying about 'no things'. How much better we'd feel if we could use that energy for accomplishing something positive we wanted to do. Like a savings account in a bank; this energy would be available when we had a deadline or unexpected stress, and we could withdraw it without compromising our health and happiness.

I'll show you more exercises to manage worry when you get to Section Three.

Beneficial Life Changes When You Live in the Moment.
When you live in higher vibration your life may change in the following ways: You may,

- Have positive thoughts; move from negative thinking and feelings and behaviour to connecting with inner wisdom and making wiser decisions,
- Be able to manage overwhelm,
- Be aware of limiting thoughts, negative thoughts and feelings when they arise and choose to reframe them into ones that move you into higher vibration,

- Live knowing you have unlimited possibilities instead of limiting beliefs which hold you back in relationships, career and daily life,
- Make clear, good decisions instead of feeling unable to think,
- Discover that more information, opportunities and choices come to you,
- Attract experiences that move you into higher dimensions,
- Be drawn to following your passion,
- Be restored to your natural high vibration frequency and feel comfortable being your authentic self instead of worrying "what's wrong with me" or what will people think?"
- Know how to take care of yourself; what to do if you do move out of higher vibration or you start getting frustrated,
- Increase your focus, concentration, and conscious awareness, control of your attention, instead of being distracted by mind chatter and living in your head,
- Have more fun,
- Know the importance of experiencing feelings instead of being afraid of being out of control, or stuffing them and having stunted emotions.
- Recognize feelings are not are good or bad. Allow lower vibration energies to flow through you and be released,
- Feel more balanced and your energy will flow,
- Connect with other people, nature, the cosmos and the "All That IS" instead of feeling separate, alone and unloved,
- Act responsibly and respectfully with a sense of ease with all humanity and the planet.
- Move forward on your path instead of being stuck and feeling paralyzed,
- Have a better income because of increased productivity, committment and be more effective and efficient practices,
- Know that there is no right or wrong – everyone has their own truth,
- Instead of experiencing burnout, being ineffective and doing more while achieving fewer results,
- Be more creative, connected to your intuition and Higher Source,

- Feel 'all's right with the world' and have a sense of direction instead of feeling aimless and not knowing which way to turn or where to start,
- Communicate your truth more clearly,
- Accept your responsibility that you create what happens in your life,
- Easily focus on other people, show up and listen, be supportive and responsive to others instead of using all your energy being focused on your own problems and worries,
- Have better relationships, sense your heart expand and be more loving to yourself and others: be open and able to receive love,
- Move from a fear based lack perspective to a trust that Source, (Universal Energy , God) will provide(cocreate) with some effort from you,
- Feel lighter as the knot in your stomach diappears,
- Feel content, relaxed and balanced rather than wanting to crawl into bed and stay there,
- Experience improved health,with your body operating as best it can rather than having a poor immune system and more frequent illness because of stress,
- Choose to not let other people's (customers, families, friends) criticism, moods, or behaviour affect you,
- Overcome your need to blame, judge, control, and prove yourself,
- Live in the "I AM" rather than the " I am not",
- Get excited by the synchronicities that occur, and what you attract when you are in the flow,
- Unconditionally accept others and their behaviour, while taking action to respect your own needs,
- Accept and nurture your desires and dreams whether they might be judged too big or small by others,
- Be more patient with yourself and the manifesting process,
- Be aware of cycles in life and live in harmony with them. (Resisting and fighting against cycles burns valuable energy and it's easier to slip into lower vibration),
- Expect natural cycles of give and receive to occur [i.e. peaks and valleys of energy (sleep or rest, eat, act; high creativity, lying fallow; productivity, inaction; work, play)] and take them in stride,

- Accept uncertainty gracefully,
- Understand and accept that you may not know the outcome of what you are guided to do, but be willing to take the next steps in the process,
- Feel more certain that you are moving in right direction (even if you don't know what that is),
- Act from higher consciousness, love and integrity and be detached from the outcome of situations,
- Know even 'bad guys' are providing contrast so we know what we don't want and what we do want,
- Experience less drama,
- Live with inner peace and a profound sense of self worth,
- Recognize that it is not in the best interest of others or yourself to take care of everyone or solve the world's problems (we need to learn our own lessons).
- Feel certain everything is unfolding as it should in your life and in the world and is happening for the greatest and highest good of all involved,
- AND
- Make a difference.

When a critical mass of high vibrational beings is reached, humanity will achieve its highest potential: freedom, liberation and the unification of science, spirituality and philosophy.

www.creativeconsciousevolution.com

At this point I want to include a quote from Jim Self, of Mastering Alchemy. com, which provides a wonderful perspective relating to the experience of living in higher consciousness.

Because you have increased the speed of your energy field, changed your energetic alignment to fourth dimensional frequency and merged with the Soul, you now have expanded your access to the Soul's memory banks and the capacity to know your purpose and your agreements with the Soul.

By having access to your list of spiritual tasks and consciously setting out to complete them, another very interesting experience occurs. The noise, drama and discomfort you have experienced interacting with various people while moving around in this life… shifts. Those people who have been the most difficult to deal with now become the actors of your play. The noise becomes the costumes, props and staging designed to assist you in identifying and fulfilling your lessons. Stress and uncertainty go away.

By knowing your original agreements, you actually begin to make the Game, a game. Instead of moving around like a piece on the chessboard, uncertain of your next move or outcome, from a new point of observation outside the Game, you become aware of how the entire event has evolved to this point. You observe how all the possibilities of the next move will affect all the possible futures. You become consciously aware of all the possibilities and all outcomes before any action is required.

It is important to recognize that when a new truth is experienced, it is very difficult to maintain the old truth. The value of a new truth is always found in its ease, joy and opportunities to experience a fuller life. [50]

So, that lists a lot of benefits for moving into higher consciousness. If you were feeling hesitant after reading the physical, mental, emotional and spiritual indicators in chapter 2, I hope this list excites you and makes you eager to try out the tips and tools to help you get there in section three.

> **Try this:**
>
> Go through the Life Changes list above and see which ones you are experiencing. Meditate and ask for what to do about those which you want to know more about or understand better.

I would reinforce that as you experience new truths, and let go of beliefs that no longer serve you, you may have physical, mental, emotional and spiritual symptoms of discomfort, similar to the ones in chapter two. Be aware that these are normal. As an energy practitioner, I advise you to rest, drink plenty of water and continue with any spiritual practices you may have, knowing that lower vibration energy is leaving. As Jim says above, these new truths are often a relief; bringing ease, joy and new opportunities. But know as well, these transitions come to us step by step. This is what evolution is all about. So then, you may experience *some* of the Life Changes, but not all. In time, you will eventually experience most of those mentioned above. In addition, you will increase the experiences of exciting occurrences in your life!

Summary

In this chapter I presented an idea that is radical to some; you can work in partnership with your ego. The many benefits of living in higher-conscious vibration were listed. I hope you are as excited about the limitless possiblities as I am. If your mind or critical voices are still nattering about how impossible it is for you to live the good life, don't worry. You'll learn how to manage these thoughts and eventually all but eliminate them for good.

Section One introduced you to very basic concepts about vibrational energy. We explored what it means to be awakened and conscious. You now know the benefits of living from a higher-conscious vibration and why it is critical at this time to move into higher vibration energy.

Section Two will put part one and three into context. Knowing more about what is happening energetically on the planet and galaxy helps to underline the significance of using an energetic framework to create the life we want for ourselves and others and everything that is energy.

Section Three will give you an opportunity to get to know your ego better.

Shift Happens

Why December 21 2012 is only the Peak of
an Energy Wave of a High Vibration Change
that Continues until 2018 and Beyond.

The Shift of the Ages represents a rare opportunity of collectively re-patterning the expression of human consciousness. The Shift is the term applied to the process of earth accelerating through a course of evolutionary change, with the human species linked, by choice, to the electromagnetic fields of earth, following suit through a process of cellular change.

Eric Pearl quoting Gregg Braden

"December 21 2012 is a rare and powerful window of opportunity for our collective emergence into our greatest potential"

Gregg Braden, Fractal Time

CHAPTER 5

It Is the Best of Times.
It Is the Worst of Times.

> It's exciting to wake up every day and see the world in an exciting stage of evolution.... This is not a passive process. If you fail to participate the consequence is not so good. We're being pushed into this next level.
>
> .... Bruce Lipton, Author <u>The Biology of Belief</u>

It Is The Best Of Times. It Is The Worst Of Times.

A Shift is occurring in our world. It is being referred to in many terms. Perhaps you know of it in reference to 2012 – the end of the Maya Calendar. Predictions for the outcome of this Shift include everything from a collective internal shift in human consciousness to a planetary shift resulting in total destruction of our species, and possibly the earth. Sensationalists who care nothing for the real reason that most of the 13 Maya Calendars end Dec. 21, 2012, are creating fear by saying the world will end on this day. Are these the same folks who predicted similar scenarios for Y2K (the end of the millennium)? Hmm.... We are still here.

Experts, from NASA scientists and astronomy experts, to geologists, who keep track of cycles of change on the earth over thousands of years, are telling us about earth changes, energy changes and the ends of cycles. They are saying we are at a crisis point in our existence on the planet. We can't maintain the status quo and continue to exist. We are in a precarious environmental situation, a tipping point where we can survive or destroy most of humanity.

"'The Shift' is the term Gregg Braden, (a former geologist and engineer, and now an expert on ancient wisdom and current science), applies to the process of Earth accelerating through a course of evolutionary change, with the human species linked, by choice, to its electromagnetic fields, following suit via a process of cellular change." [51] The Shift is also commonly referred to in the context of the evolution of humans to a more aware, connected, higher-conscious state, living in respect and harmony with each other and the earth.

However most of these experts are also saying that we have an opportunity to make a fundamental change and create a better world in which to live. Visionary thought leaders and futurists are reporting positive human evolutionary changes. I totally believe this is the case. This is the time foretold by ancient wisdom keepers. The Maya, the Inca, the Hopi, and other indigenous people across the globe predicted this transition. Prophets, visionaries and soothsayers, including Nostradamus and Edgar Cayce, spoke of this Shift. Ancient civilizations and Holy Scriptures such as the Bible, the Kabala and Vedic Scripture wrote of times when Peace, Love, Harmony and all Higher Vibration Consciousness values would reign.

It has been said this time is the end of an age and the beginning of the next. The Maya identified this as the Fifth World, a world of Unity Consciousness where we live and work together in harmony, recognizing our similarities rather than our differences. [52]

Unlike Y2K, the mere fact that experts from a wide variety of fields agree that change is happening lends more credence to the prophecies of a 'Great Shift into the Next Age'. However, there are differing opinions about how The Shift will occur.

My personal opinion is that we are already in the process of shifting from one age into the next. I'll provide you with some examples near the end of the chapter. This shift has been gathering strength and momentum for some time. The age we are ending had a paternalistic and controlling view that

"We, the people with power over you, know what's best for you". We have the opportunity to make the age we are moving into one where we value respect, harmony and collaboration, and recognize everyone's positive potential. The midpoint of this transition is December 21, 2012, but the window is open for about 36 years.[53] Astronomically it began in August 1987 with a rare situation, when 8 planets aligned in a configuration called a Grand Trine. It will close in about 2018. In recognition of this cosmic phenomenon, the Harmonic Convergence, apparently the world's first globally synchronized meditation was held on August 16–17, 1987.[54] "In principle, the Harmonic Convergence refers to the converging of all aspects of reality in a great, all-unifying harmony."[55] The initial moment of the Harmonic Convergence, celebrated by José Argüelles at the dawn of August 16, 1987, "was a pure prophetic enactment of being harmonically converged"[56.] According to Argüelles this period is a 26 year cycle that will end in 2013. [57]

The Current Crisis is a Good Thing Energetically

The frightening situations the media feed us focus on the terrible economy, social and systemic collapse, climate change and environmental disasters. Awakened people, living in higher-conscious awareness, realize energetically that these events are positive because the lower vibration energy inherent in these conditions is coming up to be released. If we were to describe it from the perspective of our dualistic 3D world, we would say we need to 'get rid of the bad to allow room for the good to come in' so we can create our preferred way of life. It is comforting to know that just as with other challenging situations we experience, this crisis has come -- to pass. In other words, we will pass through it; it's not going to be part of our life for much longer if we do not block its release with our own limiting beliefs.

Looking back on seemingly bad situations provides us with an opportunity to reframe them. For example, many people were disgruntled by the actions and decisions of past U.S. President, George W. Bush. However his actions provided a contrast to help us identify what we did not want in a President. Government, business and even sports scandals help us identify what our own moral values are and allow us to reflect on our reaction to them and how we live our lives.

Moving into higher vibration energy changes the way we look the global situation. It moves us out of fear, and allows us to reframe our perception of the current "crisis". Knowing "The Shift" needs to happen to make way for new healthier structures, and harmony and cooperation instead of will and power over others can result in less anxiety and fear and more insight about what is ours to do regarding the situation.

I'm reminded of a challenge that Yahweh, a master teacher channelled by Chuck Little, gave to an international audience I was part of, at a time when more and more people were complaining about then President G.W. Bush's administrative decisions. Even here in Canada I'd heard claims that the President had placed himself above the law and was making decisions without the authority to do so.

This Master teacher encouraged the U.S. citizens in the audience to become very familiar with the Constitution and Bill of Rights. Then he encouraged them to go somewhere that had a long slow line up (like the banks or grocery store), and discuss a particular section. "Well you know," one could say, "I just found out about section (X), part (#1) of the constitution. Don't you think if more people knew about it, we would be able to have better (Z)?"

Yahweh asked the participants, "What do you think the people in that line up would do?" We replied, "Spread the word." That was an example about how to create a conscious awareness or interest that doesn't push other people's political buttons or shove information down their throats. Higher vibration action could occur when they understood the importance and benefits of knowing the foundations of how their government is supposed be run. We all benefitted from the opportunity to think how we could use a similar approach.[58]

Creating An Internal Shift

We know geologically and from ancient oral tradition that physical shifts occurred on the planet during past transitions of the ages. Therefore many people are anticipating another physical shift. Tsunamis, Earthquakes, Solar Flares, and other atypical weather patterns are good indicators that this physical shift is occurring. What if this time though, the shift was more internal? What if we woke up December 21, 2012 and the great majority of the population had made a shift in thoughts, beliefs and values?... A Shift in Consciousness? I believe this is really what the shift is about. In my opinion we are moving from the Information Age to the Age of Wisdom and Intuition.

People like you and I are creating this reality. You are making this happen. Thank You!

There is an excellent 25-minute You Tube video called, '2012: A Message of Hope'. (http://www.youtube.com/watch?v=r_YOG3jMlV4). It features thought leaders such as Deepak Chopra, Michael Beckwith, Gregg Braden, Roland McCready and Nelson Mandela. It has fantastic graphics and thought provoking teachings. Learn more about the most recent research in Vibrational Electromagnetic Energy and Human Consciousness presented in an entertaining and easy to understand way.

One change that you can make that will help you, and therefore humanity, move into higher consciousness is to focus on the higher vibration aspect of all events. We are already seeing people acting from a place of higher consciousness. This has been shown in the wake of the movie "Pay it Forward," where it's become socially fun to do nice small actions for people. Some people pay for the groceries of a person in their line, or leave quarters in the pay carts; others put money in expiring parking meters. There are lots of small ways to create pleasant surprises for another, and that good feeling often results in shifting someone's vibration so they, in turn pass a nice action along to someone else. Have you noticed that even smiling at others makes a difference?

I said near the beginning of this chapter that my personal opinion is that we are already in the process of shifting from one age into the next. There are other examples of people looking outside their own little world with more compassion for others. Natural disasters are providing an opportunity for people to make a difference in the world by responding to the people affected by them. An increasing number of people are now responding even before calls for help come out. There has been a significant increase in the number of people who donated to the Haiti earthquake in 2010 in comparison with the Asian Tsunami in 2004.[59] This increasing trend appears to be ongoing. Most banks now have a permanent option for donations on their web banking sites, as well as in their brick and mortar buildings. Charitable organizations are raising large sums for relief efforts online and through text messages, so a response to the Japanese earthquake and tsunami of 2011 could be immediate.[60]

We only need to look to the internet for millions of examples of our evolution into higher vibration consciousness. Some use sophisticated video production technology, some are simple, but they have all poured their hearts and souls into their forms of service. I used to be surprised and delighted when I came across an announcement for an event such as a global meditation for peace or for the earth. Now it is common for people in cyberspace to link their energy and send it to support others they have never met. They know there are people just like them, who are innocent bystanders, devastated by natural or manmade events.

There are many new web initiatives to assist us to awaken. My body, mind and soul were thrilled when a polished multimedia event occurred that encouraged us to envision a new way of living. In November 2010, people were invited by email, Facebook and other social media, to participate in an 11-day global meditation occurring for 11 minutes each day beginning on Nov. 11, 2010 at 11:11pm. You can still see the amazing video images as you listen to uplifting music by Enya, at http://www.newrealitytransmission. com. Remember that even though the actual event is over, there is no time or space outside of the third dimension, so your energy is going to make an impact on the collective consciousness whenever you intend it to. I was encouraged to find out that this event was developed by a full time international team of physicists and mathematicians whose mission is to "discover how gravity, electromagnetism, space and consciousness are part of the same unified field...a realm of information, where consciousness literally interacts with geometry at the quantum scale to create everything that we define as reality".[61]

I was astounded by another 2010 initiative by Women on the Edge of Evolution who called to other woman across the world to co-create our preferred future. A groundswell grew from a few hundred women the first week, to having over 25,000 participants in just three weeks.

The group hailed it as evidence "that we are standing on the brink of something extraordinary that is waking up for millions of women worldwide; that now is our time to evolve ourselves and our world to the next level of our collective development--and that we are up to the task that is before us!"[62]

These examples are only a few of an increasing number of initiatives that demonstrate how quickly people are awakening and choosing evolutionary activities to shift themselves into higher vibration consciousness and help change that world. Just looking at my email every day, keeps me in a state of gratitude and expanding love for mankind. I am exhilarated by the evidence that the internal shift which will characterize the next age is occurring. I feel like dancing with undulating ribbons, singing blissfully, and soaring like a bird to spread my joy filled energy to Every Thing.

Summary

The purpose of this section is to provide you with a quick overview of common theories about The Shift so you can be well informed as you choose your course of action. In the next chapters I will present factual information based on the science of astronomy, geology and ecology. I will briefly share some of the speculation and conjecture drawn from these facts, about the outcome or effects on humanity. Then I will discuss which ancient cultures groups and religions described a world shift in consciousness. Finally I will present the views of metaphysical and spiritual experts concerning what life will be like beyond 2012.

The purpose of Section Two is to reinforce the critically urgent reason why moving into higher vibration consciousness is imperative now. I also want to share information about the wide variety of theories that are being expressed in the popular media and books.

As always, I advise you to keep an open mind, use your discretion, and feel what resonates as truth for you.

CHAPTER 6

The Facts of the Matter

The 'facts' themselves meanwhile are not true. They simply are. Truth is the function of the beliefs that start and terminate among them.

- William James

The important thing in science is not so much to obtain new facts as to discover new ways of thinking about them.   - Sir William Bragg

A great deal of confusion has occurred regarding December 21, 2012. This is the time most commonly attributed to the end of this age and the beginning of the next according to the Maya calendar and oral history. No more; No less. If the average person on the street were asked the significance of 2012, they might say that it was the end of the world (if they even knew).

I first became interested in 2012 because of my interest in the ancient wisdom of indigenous societies and their spiritual beliefs and practices. I was drawn to the Maya Culture and felt an urge to visit the Yucatan in Mexico and experience the energy of the ancient cities and pyramids. My energy healing teacher, Dr Richard Jelusich was travelling as an expert on a Sacred Earth Journeys Tour[63] Journey to 2012 when I decided it was the right time to go to Mexico. I have participated in this program almost annually, extending my stay to study with Mayan Master Wisdom Teacher Miguel Angel Vergara. I've toured many Maya sites accompanied by Richard and Miguel Angel and participated in a variety of rituals and

74

activation ceremonies. I conduct Maya solstice and equinox ceremonies live and on-line, and connect with Maya teachings and practices.

It is my opinion that the ancient Maya knew that the world would be experiencing a shift in energy at this time in humanities history. They wanted to leave information that would assist those of us alive today to make a successful transition into the next age, which they believed could be a golden age of peace, love and abundance. They were also aware that the potential existed for chaos and societal destabilization. Wisdom Teachers have been trained thru oral tradition to pass down the knowledge and practices and reawaken our memories. I have been fortunate to be involved more closely than most in this process. This is how I have become passionate about providing information to you about how to and why we must move out of our lower vibration habitual, unconscious way of life and move into the limitless possibilities for a fulfilled abundant harmonious life.

2012 has been linked to many other events. The more I researched the details, the more I realized there are often dissenting viewpoints. When we are considering the intentions of ancient cultures, emerging social trends, and softer sciences, it is difficult to state firm facts. *With that in mind, I present the following according to what is primarily accepted as fact, what is more a possibility, and what is likely embellishment.*

Fact: The Environment is Disintegrating Faster Than Anticipated

Ervin Lazlo is the author of 'World Shift 2012'. He is the founder of the World Wisdom Council, a general evolution research group and has been nominated for the Nobel Peace Prize. Lazlo says his book is "a handbook of conscious change – change that shifts today's world from the path of deepening crisis, into a kind of development that can bring peace and wellbeing to the human family." [64] Lazlo relates the urgency of the shift to the unanticipated speed of disintegration of our environment and the fact that predictions about the rate of change did not take into account how the occurrence of one problem would have a compound effect on other problems.

Lazlo also speaks of the tipping point in the system shift when there is a pause.[65] This tipping point has been linked to 2012. The Change Theory proposes that during the collapse of a system people will change; then systems will reorganize into higher levels of functioning and equilibrium. Societal values will shift, hopefully bringing more respect for nature and its resources.

Fact: The Precession of Equinoxes Cycle and Galactic Alignment occurs December 21 2012

On December 21, 2012, the earth, the sun and our solar system will be in alignment with the centre of our Milky Way galaxy. This event, called the Precession of the Equinoxes, happens every 25,920 years when the winter solstice sun rises in conjunction with the galactic centre. It is considered the end of one World Age and the beginning of another.[66] Although the exact midway point when the winter solstice is in conjunction with the galactic equator is on December 21, 2012, in actuality it takes about 36 years for the complete conjunction to occur. The effects of this alignment on our human energy began in the mid 1980s and will finish in about 2018.[67] [68]

John Major Jenkins has spent his career studying the cosmos, our galaxy, and the precession of the equinoxes. Although Carl Calleman, another Maya Scholar, states there is nothing in ancient Maya texts to indicate knowledge of the galactic alignment, Jenkins believes the Maya timekeepers knew there would be an alignment of the Milky Way galaxy with the Dec. 2012 solstice sun. He understands from the visionary shamans of the Quiche Maya, that the centre of time and space will be revealed when their major long count calendar ends on Dec 21 2012. The ancient Maya believed a cosmic centre was located where the winter solstice sun crosses the Milky Way center of the galaxy, a phenomenon that occurs once every 26.000 years[69]. Today, astronomers know the galactic centre is in the Milky Way and know the actual celestial phenomenon the Maya described long ago will occur exactly as predicted.

Mayan Calendars End December 21, 2012

The date of the end of this current age and the beginning of the next was attributed to the Maya many years ago. Many experts on the Maya culture believe that studying the cosmos was very important to the ancient Maya, who were accurately able to predict the equinoxes, solstices and other alignments of the sun and stars and our galaxy.

The Maya's accurate observation of the sun and stars provided information that resulted in the creation of **13** calendars. The Tzolkin calendar was based on a 260 day cycle. This corresponds with many events in our human existence including days from gestation to birth.[70] The Maya had timekeepers designated to track the different cycles. After learning about their calendars and culture it is my opinion that the Maya were indeed capable of calculating the end and the beginning of ages

Their long count calendar is said to have tracked the beginning and ends of cycles of 5,125.36 years. Five such cycles were equivalent to one cycle of the galactic alignment.

According to many Maya scholars and Maya Wisdom Teachers, including my teacher, Miguel Angel Vergara, the 5th age of the Maya people will begin when most of the thirteen current calendars end, on Dec. 21, 2012.[71] Others have suggested an alternative date of October 28, 2011.[72] In my opinion, although I believe the 2012 date, the symbolic meaning behind the end of the calendar and the intention held by those celebrating the beginning of a new age of higher consciousness, wisdom and harmony is the key to this event.

People across the globe celebrated the Dawn of the 5th or Unity Consciousness Age on March 9, 2011, with 2012 expert, Carl Calleman.[73] As a result of his recent studies of the Maya Tortuguero monument, Calleman believes "the ancient Maya recorded their knowledge of cycles, which revealed a Nine-Support, or Nine-Step, entity of "period endings." [74] Through extensive factual verification, Calleman says this pyramid has been shown to symbolize the nine levels of evolution the universe undergoes on its climb to its highest state of consciousness during a period or age.[75]

Although some would argue that it is happenstance, the majority of Maya scholars agree that the Maya used their knowledge about the equinoxes and solstices for their spiritual practices. They were so precise that their buildings and even windows in buildings were aligned so the sun would come through on key celestial days. Today thousands of people flock to the Maya site of Chitzen Itza for the annual March equinox. They come to see the shadow of Maya god, K'uKuulKaan (Quetzalcoatl, the feathered serpent) ascend up the side of the pyramid in the morning and descend in the evening. As a further example of their accuracy in building to significant events, the solstice sun will rise exactly along the Ball Court at Chitzen Itza and a new age of 25,625 years will start, when the winter solstice sun rises in conjunction with the galactic centre on Dec. 21, 2012.[76] The ball court at Izapa was built the same way. When they were built the sun was approximately 30 degrees below the galactic equator, so they would have had to know the conjunction of the sun, earth and center of the galaxy and believed it to be an important location.[77]

Fact: *There are Repeating Cycles in Time and Nature*

The Maya tracked cosmic cycles of time and celestial events.[78] When I was learning about 2012 and world ages, certain key numbers kept appearing. Sometimes they were rounded off for ease of explanation; sometimes there were hundreds of year's difference. Since I don't particularly like to remember numbers, I finally wrote them in one place so I didn't have to return to my reference sources as often to see if they were the same numbers. Here they are:

- **25,625 years** - the length of one precession of equinox cycle (5 ages). [79] (5 Ages for the Maya)
- **12,925 years** - the length of time the earth's Kundalini energy stays in one location (it moved from the Himalayas to Peru early this century)[80]
- **5,125 years** - the length of one age [81]
- **2160 years** (1/12 of the precession) - the length of time it takes for the precession of the equinoxes to move the spring equinox through

one constellation into another. (Astrologically and astronomically we are moving into the Age of Aquarius from the Piscean age).[82]

- **52 years** the length of time it takes for the Maya 365 day Haab calendar to mesh with the 260 Day Tzolkin calendar by ending on the same day. This was called the Calendar Round.[83]

Cycles of the ages

Bruce Lipton, biologist, epigeneticist and author of 'The Biology of Belief' talks about cycles of nature, life and evolution and presents a model likening the evolution of living creatures to the evolution of human cultures. He uses the analogy that just like the evolution from fish to amphibians to reptiles and dinosaurs, and ultimately to mammals, so human culture evolved as follows: 1) the marine culture age when humans needed to be at the water's edge for survival; 2) the agriculture age when, like amphibians, we could live away from the water and bring it to us; 3) the industrial age when, similar to the reptiles being prey to self interested carnivorous dinosaurs, small business were struggling to survive against large corporations who were only interested in their own gains and successes.

Lipton attributes the 1969 moon landing in the industrial age to the birth of a new age when the image of our planet from space awoke more nurturing people to the need to care for each other, our planet and its resources. He calls this an evolution into an age of caring, and predicts that soon, even within a year, the "dinosaur" corporations will be unable to sustain themselves and will become extinct, leaving the nurturing mammals of humanity to evolve into a new cycle. [84]

Gregg Braden believes the current physical earth changes are linked to our planetary movement through the precession cycle. His book 'Fractal Time' shows how history repeats itself in natural cycles and how we can predict what will happen by being aware of these cycles. With this knowledge we can anticipate and prepare for critical moments in our future when conditions are similar to those in the past cycles. The mathematical principles of fractals can also be used to predict our own significant personal moments.[85]

Braden reports on geographical research findings that describe the climate changes in temperature, rainfall or drought, sea levels and the depletion of resources leading up to the end of previous ages. These subsequently resulted in conditions that tended to create competition among the life forms of that time instead of collaboration.[86] We can learn from these cycles so we do not have to repeat the patterns that resulted in the downfall of civilizations. In relation to 2012, we can do more than just predict and prepare. We can choose to change our behaviour to prevent, or at least minimize, the outcomes of the earth changes and the shift in human consciousness.

As I mentioned at the beginning of this section, many experts are certain of the positive outcome of our current situation. In the final chapter of his book, Braden stresses the wonderful opportunity we have to make a choice about our future. He says, "December 21, 2012 is a rare and powerful window of opportunity for our collective emergence into our greatest potential."[87] I agree with him and I am seeing the possibilities materialize.

Fact: *The Magnetic Axis is Shifting*

The Earth's field has alternated between periods of **normal** polarity, in which the direction of the field was the same as the present direction, and **reverse** polarity, in which the field was in the opposite direction. A pole shift is a change in the Earth's magnetic field such that the positions of magnetic north and magnetic south are interchanged.[88] There is a shift occurring in the earth's magnetic axis.

I was first made aware of what was happening to the earth years ago when I read Gregg Braden's book 'Walking Between the Worlds'. He referred to a zero point in time, which was to occur because of an increased *planetary vibrational frequency and a decreased planetary magnetic field. He* explained how airport landing strips were designed in relation to magnetic fields which aircraft compass equipment relies on. He reported that the landing strips at some of the world's major airports had been repositioned in order to maintain airspace and passenger safety, because the magnetic pole had shifted enough to warrant the move. [89]

This magnetic shift continues today. You may not be aware that one of the earthquakes in Chile in 2010 resulted in a measurable shift in the poles. Business Week magazine quotes NASA geophysicist Richard Gross, "The axis about which the Earth's mass is balanced should have moved by 2.7 milliarcseconds (about 8 centimetres or 3 inches)." The magnitude 9.1 Sumatra quake in 2004, which generated an Indian Ocean tsunami, "shifted the axis by about 2.3 milliarcseconds, Gross said." [90] The shift is linked to geological changes and the earth's iron core.[91] Although it is fact that the magnetic poles have been shifting slightly, especially during earthquakes, and the strength of our magnetic fields has been decreasing, a major magnetic pole shift has been deemed unlikely.[92],[93]

Fact: There are Increases in Solar Flares, Sunspots and Solar Storms

Shifting of the magnetic poles is possibly intertwined with changes to the biosphere, or solar activities. High energy solar activity is a possible cause of further changes in our environment. I have read that the solar flare cycle #24 we are in, is supposed to be stronger than ones in the recent past. Correct information and photos regarding solar activity can be found on the NASA internet site http://sdo.gsfc.nasa.gov/ and at http://www.spaceweather.com/. Intense high energy solar flares, sunspots and solar storms can cause major power outages, interruptions in communication and GPS systems, satellites and the internet. It is possible that our computer hard drives could be wiped out. I have written about the speculated effects of the changes to the poles later in this chapter.

Fact: There are Spurious Speculations Regarding 2012 and its Impact on Humanity

A great deal of confusion has occurred regarding 2012. The end of the Maya calendar has been linked with pole shifts, solar flares, crop circles, and radiation from the center of the galaxy. There is nothing written in any ancient Maya texts about this.[94] Even though these phenomena are not linked to the Maya cosmology, some have a factual basis, which has been twisted or exaggerated into unlikely scenarios and outcomes for humanity. There are even more unlikely possibilities out there for our consideration which have no accepted scientific backing and are attributed by some to conspiracies to keep us in the dark. This includes tales of planets or meteors crashing into the earth and the earth traveling through an asteroid belt.

The fact is we *are* having increased, and recent record setting, solar flares and other celestial and magnetic earth changes. Speculation about their devastating effects on people causing inhospitable environments, disease, and slow, lingering or quick catastrophic death is being presented as fact and causing a fear based reaction among some people. I am sharing these with you as a point of interest to prevent fear, overwhelm or hopelessness about our future. I personally keep this information in mind as potential, not worrying about whether it will happen, knowing deep inside that everything is ok right in this moment, which is all there is.

If then, I truly walk my talk, how do I explain why I (and many like-minded friends and colleagues, teachers and mentors,) have items on hand which could be used in the event of a natural disaster? This is the way I personally release lower vibration energy and allow incoming higher vibration. I have set my intention not to be in the area of a disaster unless it is in the greatest and highest good for me and others. I believe my life purpose could include involvement in situations which, right now, I believe my free will would not choose. My Maya Wisdom Teacher, Miguel Angel Vergara, reminds me that when I am in a situation where I am acting from a third dimensional place, that I am human after all. Therefore, I do act and think from a place of unconsciousness at times. I may not listen to guidance and information I am given. Once I become consciously aware, I ask for forgiveness for my unconsciousness. This practice really helps relieve my acute embarrassment when I do something I would have labelled as stupid.

I am somewhat prepared for any natural disaster because I live on an earthquake fault line. Every once in a while I consider in a detached way what I have on hand, and then I release the thought.

Rather than be caught up in the hype about the end of humanity, you can choose more peaceful, higher vibration thoughts about what might happen by being mentally curious, wondering about what's happening, looking for and being aware of the awesome big picture and remembering everything is unfolding as it should and You Are One Energy with All That Is.

Reversal of the Physical Poles

One specific speculation is about a reversal of the physical poles. The information about this is confusing to sort through. One exaggerated suggestion is that there will be a physical reversal of the earth's poles, if a rapid reversal of the magnetic North and South Poles occurs. This would cause the kind of cataclysmic end to humanity predicted in popular movies and books. Geologists say this physical shift has only happened once in the history of the world.[95] A huge solar flare much bigger than anything we have experienced in modern times would need to occur for a physical pole shift. [96]

Interestingly, there was a very large solar flare two days before the earthquake in Japan. Although these events have not been officially linked, I have heard a lot of speculation about a relationship between the two.

Other Speculative Events

There is speculation that other cosmic events will destroy the earth. For instance, some books and internet sites state that there is a hidden planet in our solar system called Nibaru (companion star of the sun) with an erratic orbit which is expected to veer into the earth's orbit. Nibaru was identified by author Zechariah Sitchen, when he studied ancient Sumerian texts. Further study of these texts and of the Sumerian language suggests his interpretations were incorrect. There are many theories regarding the existence of celestial bodies and planets presently unknown because of their orbits, many based on insubstantial scientific evidence of these invisible celestial bodies.

Another interesting area of speculation relates to UFOs and extraterrestrial visitors. If you check out the internet you will find lots of information about increased sightings, and the purpose of their contacts. Some people are saying crop circles are messages from these beings. If such things exist,

I plan to be discerning, and not jump to any conclusions regarding their friendliness or lack thereof. In fact, in coming from a place of higher vibration, I will expect the best and look at the exciting possibilities using my energetic vibration and intuitive abilities to determine my beliefs about something so totally out of my range of possible imaginings. What will you do?

Summary

This chapter explored the different astronomical, cyclical and physical aspects of The Shift and 2012. It may offer incentive and momentum for you to set the intention to be part of co-creating the next golden age by simply ensuring you live for the most part in higher vibration energy.

I have seen a vision of this age and feel the exhilarating, revivifying potential to an even greater extent when I am in the homeland of the Maya, on the land, in the cenote water wells, participating in ritual and ceremony and communing with the elders and sacred energies. I believe those who make the choice will experience what we focus on.

The next and final chapter in Section Two explores the opportunity for personal evolution, spiritual growth and socio-cultural shifts that thought leaders are predicting and promoting. This is the heart of why it is essential that we release our lower vibration thoughts and habits and move into the higher consciousness lifestyle that makes The Shifts' potential a reality.

CHAPTER 7

2012 and Beyond: A Shift in Consciousness

What if this time though, the shift was more internal? What if we woke up December 21 2012 and the great majority of the population had made a shift in thoughts, beliefs and values ...

... a Shift in Consciousness? ....

I am exhilarated by the evidence that the internal shift which will characterize the next age is occurring. I feel like dancing with undulating ribbons, singing blissfully, and soaring like a bird to spread my joyful energy to Every Thing.

..... Gina-Dianne Harding

In the last chapter I focused more on The Shift as an astronomical and natural event. The most significant effect of The Shift is that it stimulates all consciously aware people to align our collective energy and create a world in which we recognize and respect our similarities and live by higher-conscious vibration values, thoughts, emotions and beliefs. I envision a world where we know we are One with all energetic matter, be it human, animal, vegetable or mineral, and therefore we lovingly and compassionately connect with All That Is. In this world we will have healthier, contented, vital and fulfilled lives and will enter into respectful, loving relationships as whole and complete partners, working and playing at doing things we love, knowing that we all make a positive difference in the world.

The Shift is Affecting Every Aspect of Our Life.

Jim Self, an expert in the field of spiritual development, personal vibrational energy management and healing, describes its all encompassing effect as follows:

The Shift that is underway is affecting every aspect of our third-dimensional reality. This Shift is so far-reaching that our limited imagination cannot begin to grasp the transition and the changes we are now in the midst of experiencing. This Shift is affecting every aspect of life on this planet – our political, social and economic structures, the environment, institutions and wars, how we view our relationships, our work. Simply put, every thought we think and every feeling we feel. It is altering time, our memory, our DNA, the wiring of our physical and emotional bodies, our beliefs, our perceptions of good and bad, right and wrong. Most especially, this Wave of Change is affecting our awareness of what is possible. It is offering us abundant, new understandings, instructions and possibilities of how to once again live in harmony with each other, the environment and All That Is.[97]

Do Other Ancient Cultures Predict This Consciousness Shift?

Myths from more than 30 different ancient cultures tell of cycles through dark and golden ages based on the precession of the equinoxes. The civilizations of Sumeria, Mesopotamia and Egypt and the Australian Aboriginal tribes, Incas, and North American Hopi Indians, predicted the upcoming shift. Early Greek philosophers and scholars, and medieval scholars, artists and architects like Leonardo De Vinci, using mathematical calculations based on sacred geometry in their designs and drawings, reached similar conclusions about the next world age coinciding with a cosmic alignment of the earth, sun and centre of the Milky Way Galaxy.[98] There is speculation that the Mystery Schools were also aware of the expected mega changes in the earth and human social structures.

What about Religions?

The Hindu Yuga cycle teaches that there are 4 ages which range from the golden age of peace and spiritual harmony with nature, through silver and bronze ages to the Iron Age, an age of ignorance, war, suffering and collapse of civilisations. The cycle then reverses and moves back toward the golden age. There are many opinions regarding which age we are in now. Recent masters like Sri Yukteswar believe we are very close to the onset of the Golden Age.[99]

The Jewish Kabala predicts a coming time of transformation and redemption when "the world is set right, a world that will be a reflection of its Creator, a world where rights and wrongs … are self-evident truths."[100] This transformation is beginning gradually at the present time. [101]

I am personally most familiar with the Christian Book of Revelations, which presents a picture of total chaos and confusion. There is both violence and upheaval, and there is also love, joy and peace during the end times. A New Jerusalem is created, similar to the high vibration energetic that is expected in the next age. During my research I was struck, as many people are, with the dilemma of fate versus free will as it relates to prophesy. Prophets (and psychics) tend to see the most likely future based on a person's current lifestyle or a society's government, social structures, etcetera. In other words, the prediction will come true if the person(s) involved continue to act in the same manner and make decisions they were making at the time of the prediction. If that person, or society, makes significantly different choices, the outcome will be very different from the one foretold. This could explain why there are two diametrically opposed visions in Revelations.

What Are the Experts Saying About Consciousness During The Shift and Beyond?

It was an interesting process to decide which experts to include since there are so many people with transformational information to share from several different perspectives. Rather than reiterate the easily accessible information from the most well known authors and speakers, I decided to focus on somewhat lesser known experts whose unique ideas resonate with the information I'm sharing with you. I will briefly mention other notables whose ideas may intrigue you, capture your imagination and move you to further investigate their theories.

Rev. Dr. Meg Blackburn Losey

In addition to being a wise woman in her own right, Rev. Dr. Meg Blackburn Losey, author, teacher, and Master Healer, is a channeller. She shares messages from ascended Masters. Her doctorate is in metaphysics and she is an ordained minister. Meg travels the world lecturing and teaching classes about spirituality, metaphysics, multidimensionality, energy, healing, consciousness and the conscious evolution of children. I got to know her during a sacred journey to Peru. She is a heart-centred, caring woman with a wry sense of humour whom I greatly admire.

Here are her comments about The Shift and consciousness:

> This is the time of shifting dimensions. What you do not realize is that while you are waiting for your shift to arrive, it is happening within and around you. Your dimension is already shifting, rolling in its infinite position to a new and different set of harmonics. It can become the world that you have envisioned. When a dimension shifts it is entirely reliant upon the energies of its interior consciousness to direct that change. You are the consciousness within your dimension. Set your intentions now. Act upon them. Where your shift lands and re-harmonizes is entirely dependent upon you as individuals and you as collective Aspects of God dictating new outcomes.
>
> Those before you became caught in egoic and self-serving traps that were causal to massive and great destruction of the world as it was then. Part of your world in this now is caught in the same kind of being. The greater part of your world is moving toward and causal to your current dimensional shift. You are there, at the crux point of all future events upon your planet. Take the wave over the top and into the reality that you have striven so greatly to achieve. You have arrived... Don't stop now.[102]

Barbara Marx Hubbard

Barbara Marx Hubbard is widely referred to as "the best informed human now alive regarding futurism and the foresights it has produced." [103]

Barbara is a social innovator, speaker, author, educator and leader in the new worldview of conscious evolution. This amazing, accomplished woman is founder and president of the Foundation for Conscious Evolution. [104] I have great respect for her as a wise elder. When you are in her physical presence her energetic demeanour and charismatic grace make her seem ageless.

Regarding the shift into a new age, Barbara believes that we need to use the lessons gained from the past 13.7 billion years to assist us through this period of crises as we move into a future equal to our spiritual, social and scientific/technological capacities.

Like me, she believes there is an internal shift taking place in each of us in which we move away from being separated, self-conscious humans and towards being connected, co-creative, universal humans. This process will be facilitated and even accelerated by our togetherness in the Noosphere- a sphere of human thought which transforms the environment around us. [105]

Pierre Teilhard de Chardin, a French philosopher, palaeontologist and geologist conceived the idea of the Noosphere in 1922. He described it as a sphere of reflection, of conscious invention, of conscious souls (the Noosphere, if you will)".[106] Barbara sees humanity shifting from "Ego to Essence," inviting the essential self to take dominion and learn to embody conscious evolution.[107] As the human mind evolves and the Noosphere becomes more aware, integrated and unified, mankind will experience a high point of supreme consciousness. [108]

Barbara describes our newly evolving selves as Evolutionaries or Universal Humans; our consciousness is awakening and growing like a child's. Individually "a universal human feels connected through the heart to the whole of life and is awakened from within by a passionate and loving desire to express unique creativity for the good of the self and the whole."[109] Conscious Evolution is Barbara's term "for the evolution of evolution, of evolution becoming conscious of itself in us, of evolution actually entering the process of conscious choice of the participants in evolution; …. We are the first species on earth to gain evolutionary eyes and realize we can render ourselves extinct by our own behaviour or involve ourselves toward an unknown future by our own creativity". [110]

Barbara envisions new social systems in the new age. Unlike many visionaries who do not articulate the how-to's, she has tangible templates we can use. She sees us giving birth to a Co-creative Society, where we will come "together as a whole planetary body with each member of the body encouraged to express their unique potential in joining with others."[111] She suggests new social templates for social synergy, such as the Wheel of Co-creation, "a symbolic representation of the whole system shift, with each of our vital societal functions seen as a sector of the Wheel,"[112] the Syncon model of seeking common goals and matching resources and needs, and the Planetary Peace Room/Synergy Engine, "scanning for and mapping, connecting and communicating what is working and, leading toward a synergistic democracy in which each person is able to do and be their best. " [113]

As we become child-like "in our evolutionary process as universal humans, we are entering the garden of co-creation. We had a long journey from the Garden of Eden however we see that through the 40,000 years of separation, individuation and civilization that the great species that Homo sapiens built and now it's turning it over to us, Homo Universalis to create the empathetic co-evolving species. What we will be experiencing as the universal humans is evolutionary spirituality. We've already begun....."[114]

Jim Self

As previously mentioned Jim Self is a leader in the field of spiritual development, personal vibrational energy management and healing. He continues to be successful in the business world and was at one time a politician and advisor to the U.S. government in the Department of Energy. Although I've never met Jim in person, I do feel his heart centred energy and enjoy his sense of humour when I participate in his enlightening teleseminars.

Becoming Aware of Becoming Aware
The "Shift in Consciousness" that is occurring is a shift in our very perception of our world. In our pressure to look successful,

"We have less time to enjoy the company of our family and friends and less opportunity to appreciate a sunset or take pleasure in the natural beauty that surrounds us. Many people have begun to feel that something is not right, that something valuable has been lost. What is really missing, whether we are aware of it or not, is that we all have lost a part of our "selves" along the way. And at the end of the day, more, bigger and better has still not been enough. We have disconnected from the things that truly nourish us and it has left us physically ill, emotionally unhappy, mentally exhausted and spiritually unclear about who we truly are.

This is now beginning to change.

As more and more of us are awakening, we are beginning to remember who we are. We are recognizing imbalances in our lives and we are asking ourselves: "What's really important to me? What truly makes me happy?" The answer isn't found through gaining more of the world outside, but in gaining more of the "me" within.[115]

Jim Reports that:
Two massive Waves of Light and Energy are moving through the Universe, through the Earth and through each of us. These Waves of change are working together in perfect synchronization, evolving everything to a higher consciousness.

One Wave is expanding outward, as an ever-widening ripple on a pond, spreading greater Light, knowledge and wisdom, opening ever-expanding gateways to higher consciousness and evolution. This Wave is shifting mass consciousness from the third-dimensional perspective, through the fourth, into a fifth-dimensional perspective.

This Wave is creating a fifth-dimensional community of higher consciousness on Earth that is realigning us with the All That Is. As this first Wave accelerates it is fascinating to observe how it is powerfully and positively affecting us. This Wave is providing us with choices and presenting us with possibilities that have not been available to us before.

This Wave is also making it possible for the second Wave to unlock all that has been keeping us stuck in the third-dimension. The second Wave operates very differently than the first. Its function is to create harmony. However, in order to achieve harmony, everything that is not of the Light, everything that does not exist in well-being and balance, is being destabilized, dissolved and cleared away. Everything that is not aligned in our lives is being loosened and released.

This Wave is releasing all dysfunctional patterns on every level. All that is lacking integrity will dissolve to be replaced with new patterns of energy, Light, knowledge and wisdom that are available in the first Wave. In short, as one Wave of Light is emptying the vessel, the other Wave of Light is refilling it. These transformative Waves are allowing all of us to re-wire, re-connect, re-align and remember who we are and what we really came here to accomplish. Like a tsunami, these Wave are significantly stepping up in intensity. We will see tremendous transitions in the upcoming months and years.[116]

What Do Other Evolutionary, Metaphysical and Spiritual Experts Expect to Occur in the Next Age?

- Peter Russell states we will move from the current information age into the wisdom age of the global brain where people will live in a coordinated way that promotes harmony.[117]

- Vladimir Verdansky says we will move into the psychozoic era of the mind. [118]

- Jose Arguelles believes that through a major evolutionary breakthrough we will move from the biosphere, where all living things on earth are seen to be a single living organism, to the technosphere, an interwoven web of electronic technology, to the noosphere. p 200 101 things you should know about 2012. [119]

- Drunvelo Melchizedek, who speaks of the changing location of earth's Kundalini energy every 12, 925 yrs, believes the energy in the next age will be heavily weighted toward more feminine characteristics of nurturing, compassion and decisions that include intuitive considerations. [120]

- Teilhard de Chardin saw the noosphere as an emerging collective consciousness and spoke of this eventually leading to christ consciousness and transcendence.[121]

- Cooperation and collaboration may take the form of smaller communities and towns with adjacent land for growing food and strong community social structures. [122]

- Mental skills may include telepathy and other energetic abilities due to incoming plasma from solar energy [123]

- Assuming we have energy for internet activity, online communities will bring together even more like minded individuals who will actively create change for the good of all humanity everywhere. [124]

Try this:

What would you like to experience in the next phase of your evolution? Write it down and refer back when you reach the how to manifest part of Section Three

---

Is The Shift In Consciousness about Ascension?

The word ascension makes most people think of a devout spiritual master, like Jesus Christ, or Confucius being taken with their body and lifted up to a higher plane which may be called Heaven. Some spiritual leaders may mean this or, they may instead mean our soul or spirit moves into a higher dimension where we do not need a body. In some evolutionary, spiritual and metaphysical circles today people use the term ascended to mean remaining on earth while living in higher vibration energy and higher consciousness, rarely interacting with people who have chosen to remain in lower vibration energy.

Karen Bishop, Jim Self and Tom Kenyon are spiritually focused Way-Showers who help us learn through guided (channelled) messages. They view The Shift as an opportunity to choose to ascend.

Karen Bishop on Ascension
Karen began her service years ago by providing valuable information in her "What's Up On Planet Earth" web updates. She explained what was happening to people and the planet as we were shifting. Rather than channel what was to happen, she validated the signs and symptoms many sensitive people and Lightworkers were experiencing as earth's vibrational frequency was increasing.

Once that information had been conveyed and her readers were able to manage the incoming energy, Karen was guided to change the focus of her articles to looking at our roles in implementing the new earth. Initially it seemed as if there was an overlay of a new earth on top of old earth. Lightworkers and higher vibration service providers were able to continue meeting with, and providing service to, people who were new to their spiritual path or needed assistance in raising their vibration as they moved into higher-conscious or higher-dimensional living. [125]

Comparing the Overlay of Multidimensional Living to Current Life Experiences
The model I use to help people grasp Karen's idea is to liken living in a different dimension from people who are not a vibrational match, to being a non smoker or a smoker. Non smokers rarely choose to spend time with smokers because of the physical effects of second hand smoke. Smokers don't spend time with someone who doesn't want them to smoke; they may feel judged, worry about being hassled and know they aren't wanted. Essentially, they live in two different worlds.

In fact, these are two groups of people who are vibrating at different frequencies on a cellular level, as well as on mental and emotional levels. Since their frequencies are not a resonant match they do not attract each other. They may go into the other's 'hang-outs' for a short period of time but they are drained and exhausted by the experience. In my experience, non smokers may go for weeks and months at a time without coming into contact with a smoker. It's as if they don't exist to each other. That is of course if they are not in contact in a relationship, work or family setting.

This is what it would be like to live in a different dimension. There is no judgement; one is not better than the other. People will naturally live among like-minded people with similar frequencies.

It can be lonesome at times when you shift from one vibratory level to a significantly higher one. You don't enjoy hanging out with your old friends and you haven't attracted new ones yet. I will list some sites I enjoy on the internet in the Resources section at the end of the book. One place to start finding them is on the net and social media sites. I will list some of my favourites in the Resources section at the end of the book. Your local community may have groups that advertise in your local paper or new thought magazines which can be found at health food and reputable metaphysical stores that sell books, crystals and other self help information.

Another way you can conceptualize ascension to higher dimensions is by comparing yourself to angels. Most of us think angels live in a realm where everything is nearly perfect – heavenly you might say. Angels have to lower their vibrations substantially to connect with and resonate with our much lower frequency. Some experts believe they are unable to maintain this low vibration for long, so despite knowing there are angels all around you, you may feel a tenuous connection, or sense them but be unable to communicate with them. As you alchemically transform and become more spiritually evolved, your vibratory rate increases and it is much easier to 'speak to' and 'hear' the angels (or other higher vibration beings). Eventually you reach a high enough frequency that it's as if you have become an angel to someone who is just starting their alchemical transformation.

Jim Self on Ascension

Jim Self is a deeply caring man with great insight and a real talent for helping those who wish to ascend. He has been studying and teaching for many years and he knew a time would come when we would have a choice about shifting into higher dimensions. Just within the last year he has begun to stress the urgency of becoming proficient with the practices in a timely manner. Jim continues providing programs (some at no cost) that are reaching out to more people.

Just as I have online seminars teaching the processes I outline in the book and more, you can listen to clear lectures and questions and answers about the ascension process on Jim's website masteringalchemy.com. We use a similar teaching method with one super benefit: the listeners practice the techniques during the sessions. You then feel confident that you are learning a new skill correctly.

Jim informs listeners about features of the 4th and 5th dimensions where there is no judgemental duality. Love as we experience it in the 3rd dimensional world, even in its most pure form, is not the unconditional love that exists in the higher 4th and 5th dimensions. There are no real contrasts like good or bad, because there are no lower vibration experiences. You can manifest very easily in the higher dimensions. You think it and there it is without delay (think carefully before desiring this skill). You live to create and do so with forethought, wisdom or consideration of the outcomes.

This is just a brief taste of the information Jim shares. If it excites you and you are a vibrational match, you may wish to continue your alchemical evolution by exploring his offerings.

Tom Kenyon, Solar Flares and Ascension

Tom Kenyon shares a channelled Hathor Planetary message regarding the solar flares and ascension on his website, www.tomkenyon.com. The Hathors are a group of energetic beings of the highest consciousness. They are not associated with the Egyptian goddess Hathor. Kenyon indicates that there is great evolutionary potential occurring because of the solar flares and magnetic storms. The effects of the solar winds will continue well into the next age, past 2012. They are made up of photons and magnetic energy, which you can use to affect your Ka body. Ka is an Egyptian concept of a life energy body similar to concepts of Chi or Prana. People who make use of the energy from solar flares to strengthen their Ka body can enhance their ascension process.

Kenyon's Hathor messages discuss what physical, mental and emotional effects will result from the solar winds, and includes specific steps for use by people who have experience in working with energy and are serious about the ascension process.[126]

Gina-Dianne Harding-- What I KNOW about The Shift
Do you know the difference between learning and actually knowing something?

You can study, and store information you have learned from books, classes with experts, teleseminars, tours and a myriad of resources, and understand something from an intellectual view point. You could take a test and get an A+ on it. That learning occurs in your conscious mind. It isn't until you take action and put what you have learned into practice that you actually know it. The subconscious mind operates completely separately in this case; it's the part that secures the knowing through habitual behaviour. This knowing can also be achieved through hypnosis.[127] Wayne Dyer explains it another way discussing it in the context of belief and knowing: your beliefs are mental exercises; your knowings are physical exercises. He says you can understand from being instructed by someone else how to ride a bike but you won't know how to ride it until you have physically sat on the bike and pedaled it and incorporated it into your cell memory.[128]

I've taken my life experiences, training and inner wisdom, as well as views from spiritual experts and teachers, and developed a unique broader knowing through integrating what I've learned into my daily life. It has all prepared me for these ongoing moments of Now. Now I can help people who are awakened and who resonate with my energy to attain and sustain higher energetic consciousness and gracefully shift into the next age.

Of course, I know the earth Shift is happening. I also know for sure that society norms and memes (collective conscious thoughts in the Noosphere) are shifting. I look for and find evidence of that every day. I find it where I work. I see the way people interact with me and my aging parents; showing care and thoughtfulness, and helping in awkward moments. I see the mental shift in awareness and wisdom in the eyes of babies and preverbal children who haven't been programmed with limiting beliefs. They know what's going on, and if you acknowledge them as a Master in a whisper, intelligent acknowledgement flashes in their eyes. I know consciousness is shifting when I connect with like minded people who help me sustain my joy and excitement as we tap into superconscious energy and "do what we are meant to do" in that moment.

I could just as easily focus on fear based events and people are unwilling to change, but why would I? I am so delighted and my heart feels so open and happy when more and more, I encounter people who feel as if something big is about to happen and are waking up and realizing they need to get involved in that something NOW.

In this moment, I do not know the details of what will happen in the world on December 21, 2012. I know I cannot be certain which way humanity will tip, whether we will survive or thrive. These still depend on the choices you and I make. I do know I can choose my thinking and I choose to believe that everything is great in this Now moment (and now is all there is). I do know I create my reality in each moment and so I feel the greatness and divine energy in everything and everyone. I know this manifests because I am in higher vibration energy and attract it to me. And I know that we all have the opportunity, and you and many others will succeed in moving into a higher-conscious vibration life.

I know what I am meant to do during this shift: that is to contribute to the understanding of the mind-body-spirit-energy relationship in a new way.

Summary

Section Two has offered detailed information to help you understand the importance of taking timely action and consciously moving into higher vibration living now. You have read about some known facts and some spurious speculations and can have clarity regarding any misunderstandings propagated by sensationalist fear-mongering folks who are doing an excellent joy of creating contrast so we can choose our preferred future. You were presented a picture of some possibilities for life beyond 2012, as envisioned by several thought leaders who have provided information to reflect on or influenced my personal evolution.

I hope you now know the urgency of consciously choosing to live in higher vibration awareness and can envision the limitless possibilities you have for a sweet life, fulfilling your passions and making the difference you are called to make.

In Section Three of this book I provide you with the tools to practice and master shifting your thoughts, emotions and beliefs into higher vibration energy so you know how to shift into the next age living in higher consciousness.

Tips, Tools and Techniques:

How to Release Energy That No Longer Serves
You And Move Into Higher Vibration Energy.

Choice is the engine of your evolution

-- -- Gary Zukov The Seat of The Soul

Einstein said we can't solve problems with the same thinking that
created the problems..... The only way out is to think differently.

-- -- Bruce Lipton The Aware Show April 2011

CHAPTER 8

Changing your Thinking:
How to Manage Your
Lower Vibration Thoughts

You may change your mental vibrations by directing your will and attention in the direction of a more desirable state. Will directs the attention and attention changes the vibration. Cultivate the Art of Attention, by means of the will, and you hold the secret to the mastery of moods and mental states.

....The Kybalion

By now you realize why we must move into the highest vibration energy we are capable of, beginning in this moment. You have gleaned some ideas about alchemically changing your vibration. This section of the book will present a multitude of practical methods for achieving this change. I suggest that you select the ones that really appeal to you and also choose one that feels just a little uncomfortable or stretches your abilities. I have found that resistance to certain methods is often a way for the ego to keep you from growing and changing.

Managing Energy Leakage and Vampires

I promised in Chapter 1 that I would provide you with tools to deal with energy leakage and energy vampires. You are sending and receiving energy all the time, although when you are not awakened you are unaware you do so. You lose energy when you live in the past or future, whether your thoughts and emotions are low or higher vibration. Think of a time when you have been extremely focused on some activity. It might have been a work project or hobby. What was your energy like? How about your emotions and thoughts? When you are focused you live in the present moment. Your emotions are often very evident and may be intense, and your thoughts are usually clear. Usually you have lots of energy- you may feel "pumped" as your adrenaline is available in greater than usual amounts. Now compare that with times when you are spending a lot of time in the past or future. If you try to accomplish anything it is a challenge because your thoughts are unclear and foggy. It can be like living in a dream; it's hard to connect with anything or anyone in the present. Most commonly, the energy is fearful, worried, and heavy and you feel overwhelmed. As I mentioned in chapter one, it's as if you are attached to an invisible garden hose with holes that leak energy as they run between you and other people, situations, memories or beliefs.

Ultimately when you live in the present in higher vibration you will be resonating at a high enough frequency that energy leaks won't even be an issue. In the meantime what can you do to prevent this? The first step is to be aware that it's happening. Notice when your attention wanders from the present moment and bring it back. At bedtime or during natural break times in the day you can also do the following: think about where your thoughts and emotions have been during the previous hours. Next, call them back to you, so your energy isn't left out and about; imagine all that energy coming back to you. Now release any attachment to it and cleanse and transform any lower vibration energy from it. You can do this by imagining a shower of white light surrounding the energy, increasing the vibrations. Visualize it returning to your physical, mental, emotional and spiritual bodies.

Now think about the energy that everyone has sent to you. You can gather it up and lovingly send it back to them. Until you are more energetically aware, you can use your imagination or ask yourself, "If someone was sending me energy or draining it, who would it be?" If you feel a strong attachment that indicates someone is draining your energy, or you are taking on someone's energy (highly energetically aware people are especially susceptible to this), you may need to take stronger action. I visualize a cord or rope connecting a client to another person when there is an energy "vampire", or if my client is a highly energetically aware person who has attached themselves to another. The energy usually goes both ways to some extent. The next step depends on your beliefs regarding a higher power. If you believe in God, angels, Ascended Masters, Saints or any beings of highest vibration that can assist you, ask them for help to cut the cords. If you prefer to call on your highest vibrational self, do so. I usually suggest to beginners that you ask your helpers to protect you and the work you are doing, and visualize yourself and the person you are attached to surrounded by divine white light and God energy. I still work with Archangel Michael who has a blue flaming sword to cut the cords and cauterize them so they won't open up and reattach again.

I believe it is important to be aware of where your energy is going, so I suggest you do the exercises above a couple of times. Once you recognize that your energy is leaking, you can prevent it by surrounding yourself with a beautiful energy in the morning. It is as if you are in an egg of shimmering high vibration light which could be pink, representing the energy of unconditional love, or it could be divine white light, whichever you prefer. This will act as a shield and unwanted energy will bounce off it. I suggest that you make it semi-permeable, so you can consciously release or accept energy. If you are in a particularly challenging situation where you know you fall into old habits of unhealthy relating, you can choose to "put on a golden shield" of energy before your encounter. You can envision this shield over your solar plexus (just above your belly button) and heart.

I will share some other energetic symbols or aids, which can assist with the process of stopping energy leaks and "vampires", in the second last chapter. I call these allies, and they include stones, crystals, flower remedies and more. They act to remind you of your abilities or, if you will, their energetic vibrations resonate with and strengthen yours.

Once you have released your lower vibration beliefs, thoughts and emotions, you will no longer need these practices. You will realize they were only necessary because of fear based beliefs. When you live in high consciousness these negative energies will no longer be attracted to you. If they existed (which they do in the 3D world,) they would flow right through you because there was no vibrational match for them to stick to. When you realize they don't exist, you can say you are living in a higher 4th dimensional energy!

This rest of this section focuses on managing your thoughts and emotions. Thought and emotions are intertwined; one creates the other. You can shift your energy using either your thoughts or your emotions, depending on the situation. Although the tips, tools and techniques overlap I will separate them because there is specific information I want to share for each aspect.

Your body, heart and nervous system function through habitual well worn patterns called neural pathways. Cell memory is laid down according to the focus of your energy. Fear is at the core of most, if not all, lower vibration thoughts and emotions. When fear unconsciously drives our actions, we protect ourselves from having something we value being taken from us, or to escape from being hurt. Our thoughts lack clarity. Our body's chemical system readies itself for fight or flight, and since both are usually inappropriate behaviours in daily life, we operate from an unbalanced limited place rather than from a position of power.

One of the most common blocks to shifting into higher consciousness is having beliefs that we may not even be aware of. They lead us to fearful thoughts which inhibit our success.

Process for Managing Thoughts and Limiting Beliefs

The following is a summary of steps to help you recognize, challenge and change unrealistic thinking patterns and manage your thoughts. *They are followed by more detailed how-to's.* Remember, realize and accept that you create your reality. Different people perceive the same situations with differing results, because they have different thoughts and beliefs.

1. **Be consciously aware** so you can identify the situation. Describe the actual event that occurred.

2. **Recognize the story** you may have created about the situation. Who might you be blaming? Write down all the automatic thoughts that entered your mind when the situation occurred and now as you revisit it. Unhook from the story and focus on the thoughts.

3. **Discern** whether these thoughts are true? Which of the thoughts are based on the facts, where true evidence exists to substantiate the thoughts? Are you absolutely sure they are true?

4. **Identify** which of the thoughts are not true but are based on negative thinking, habitual thinking, unrealistic expectations or irrational or limiting beliefs. Honour the thoughts. Is there anything you can learn from them? Breath, relax and allow insights to materialize.

5. **Choose** to replace the illogical thoughts with reasonable alternative ones.

6. **Check in** to notice if there are any changes in your feelings and behaviour that may result from changing your thoughts and beliefs.

7. **Give yourself credit** for reframing your life and situations from a different perspective.

1. Be Consciously Aware

The first step to releasing fear and other lower vibration thoughts has a huge impact on moving you into a life in higher consciousness. Set an intention to be aware of what you are thinking and feeling. Check in physically as well as mentally and emotionally: be consciously alert to the feeling of fear, uneasiness, or anxiety, as soon as it arises.

Look for patterns, themes or internal and external triggers in your lower vibration thinking. Notice if you keep repeating behaviours in your life - for example unhealthy relationships, lousy jobs, financial problems, weight gain and loss (and gain). Do you set goals that you don't achieve or even work towards? Be aware of whether you feel something is sabotaging you. If you feel victimized because someone else (such as government systems, God, your husband/wife) causes your problems, *It's because you expect to be a victim.* Be aware that you are blaming someone or something, and remind yourself that you create your reality.

Notice what situations you are in when you become aware of your negative thinking. Who are you with? Do they remind you of other life experiences? Don't judge yourself or the thought or feeling when you identify negative or lower vibration thoughts, just be the observer. There's an exercise to show you how in the Managing Overwhelming Emotions section of chapter 11.

2. Recognize the story

We also need to identify the stories we tell ourselves and focus on; those we believe are the reason we are experiencing life as it is now. It may be something someone did in the past--our parents abused us; a sibling died; our first boyfriend abandoned us for another girl. The story might be that an incident beyond our control years ago is causing what is happening in our life right now. For example, 20 years ago, because someone broke their leg in the middle of the previous hockey season just before they would have been drafted, their current unemployed status is unchangeable. Or the story might be about something that is occurring right now, such as, "I'm a single mom; my boss hates me; I have a learning disability." We allow our stories to drain the energy we could be using to focus on living our preferred life. We also allow our stories to limit what we can accomplish. You can unhook from the story by imagining yourself fishing. The fish you catch is yourself and by unhooking and releasing it you are freed to experience limitless possibilities.

3. Challenge your thoughts and beliefs

Byron Katie is a well known author who has developed an easy Thought Belief Challenging Process that is well detailed in her books and on her website www.thework.com. It results in profound shifts in changing negative thinking, challenging you to look at whether your current thoughts, emotions and actions are working in your life.

Basically you identify a limiting belief or negative thought and ask yourself four questions. .

    A. Is it true?

    B. Can you absolutely know that it's true?

    C. How do you react, what happens when you believe that thought?

    D. Who would you be without the thought?

> Then turn around the concept you are questioning. Each turnaround is an opportunity to experience the opposite of what you originally believed. To me this part of the process is a way of reframing or changing your perspective. Rather than explaining the process here, I would strongly urge you to visit her site or get her book to get details about The Work.

4a. Recognize Limiting Beliefs

When we grow up we assume the beliefs and values of our parents, teachers, and other grown-ups. [129] Until age five, we cannot tell what is true and not true, real and not real. Anything we experience is remembered in our body, in what is known as cell memory. The beliefs and values we are taught become so automatic that we respond unconsciously. I enjoy the way Jim Self explains it: "in our family we talk to these, but we don't like those and we never ever do this".

There is a stage of human development during the teenage years, when a person usually examines some of their parents' beliefs, values and actions. They may decide to choose the exact opposite, as a form of rebellion. As they mature, if they've been given some freedom and respect, they often reconsider and decide to adopt some of those beliefs and values. However, there may still be beliefs that were never excavated and examined during the teenage years.

When we become adults then, we may still unconsciously make decisions and react to situations based on someone else's beliefs and values from long ago. Before I started on my spiritual path I could identify what *I* believed. A limiting belief I had was that once people's beliefs and values were in place, they were truths that could not be changed. It wasn't until I worked with a group counsellor who helped us understand our individual beliefs and values that I realized beliefs that don't even belong to us in the first place may limit what we perceive we can and should do.

Limiting beliefs can make a big or small impact on our lives. When we encounter fear, it is often as a result of a belief that we are inadequate. When your conscious mind thinks you want something and your subconscious mind doesn't think you deserve it (or you have another limiting belief such as there isn't enough for everyone) you won't manifest. Instead you will get what you don't want because your subconscious feels it is right for you.

"A person must first rid themselves of unconscious self-limiting beliefs if they want to reach their full potential and attain the things they say they want from life". Joe Vitale in his book 'The Key' says, "inside every person are "counter-intentions" that actually attract the things they don't want and prevent them from getting those things they do".[130]

I call some of these "Sneaky Pete's"[*], because they are so ingrained it's unlikely you would identify them as limiting. I've listed a few limiting beliefs to give you an idea of the wide variation and their significance as potential blocks. It's interesting to notice how entrenched these are in the collective consciousness. People who are highly energetically aware and prone to take on others energy really need to be conscious of their own limiting beliefs as well as discerning which of the collectives beliefs they may have taken on.

Limiting Beliefs

I'm too fat, ugly, stupid, old, worthless etc.,	My parents wrecked my life,
I'm not thin enough, pretty enough, tall enough,	You can't live a spiritual life and make money,
If you want it done right you have to do it yourself,	Men don't cry,
You have to have money to make money,	Daydreaming is a waste of time,
You can't be a good mom and have a successful career,	If you eat chocolate you'll get a pimple,
Bad luck runs in threes,	You have to hit rock bottom before you will change,
I don't have enough experience,	*Monday is washing day ,
I don't know enough,	*Blondes have more fun,
I can't because of the economic downturn,	I can't walk on red hot coals,
*I can't get my whites white,	My way is the only way,
My kids never listen to me,	My husband always ignores me,
	My boss is out to get me
	I'll always be alone,

One other example that may be hard to recognize as hiding a limiting belief, lies in the phrase I'll do it when... . If you find yourself using this phrase ***I'll do it*** (go on a trip, attract my ideal relationship, go back to school, or pursue my life purpose).... ***When*** (I've lost 10 lbs, after this crisis, when I retire, when I've finished the housework, when the children are grown), look for the limiting belief at its core.

> ### Try this:
> Make a list of your limiting beliefs.
>
> Appendix 2 has more common limiting beliefs, if you get stuck for ideas.

When you check in and notice fear, anxiety, inadequacy, or resistance to change, look for a limiting belief that you can learn from for the purpose of your evolution. Realize it belongs to your old nature and no longer works according to your insights.

A valuable resource to use when you want to release beliefs that no longer serve you is the Beliefs Challenging Worksheet

---

Belief Challenging Worksheet

Write down your beliefs about:
Love, Family, Religion, Relationships, Money, Marriage and Parenting

For Example

Money   - you have to work hard and long hours to get rich
Marriage - my husband should take care of me and make me happy.
Parenting - you never stop being a parent.

Make a Statement of Belief :
I 'm divorced and don't have as much time to pay as much attention to my child as I 'should" ... so my child will grow up and be unhappy

---

Advantages of this belief	Disadvantages of this belief
I can blame my childs' Behaviour on the situation , So I don't have to try and find ways to help my child be emotionally and mentally healthy	*I feel guilty I give my child material things to make up for me not being there. My child is getting spoiled*

Belief I choose to have :
My child is happy and well adjusted. I have many easy and effortless ways to help my child be happy and well adjusted as(s) he is growing up

---

4b. Recognize your Unrealistic, Habitual Thoughts

According to various sources, we have between 40,000 and 80,000 thoughts per day. About 95% are exactly the same thoughts we had the day before.[131, 132] Isn't there a saying, "If I had a dollar for every time I…" (had this thought…etc.)?

There are different categories of habitual thoughts. I have listed some habitual thought patterns below. Naming something gives you power over it, in that you're more consciously aware and can choose to focus on the alternative higher vibration thoughts.

Unrealistic and Unhealthy Thinking

Monkey Mind: You think about too many problems at once. You feel scattered and overwhelmed.

Alternative: Solve one problem at a time. Write down a list so you don't have to keep them all in your head.

Catastrophizing: You imagine the worst-case scenario as a result of something you've done. You exaggerate the importance of things (such as your own goof-up or someone else's achievement).

Alternative: Use the same scale for everyone -- yourself included.

Use worry enhancement by blowing the situation up and exaggerating it to ridiculous proportions. Sometimes that helps you look at the light side of the situation and recognize that what you'd been imagining was unlikely. (*Don't do this* to someone other than yourself. It can really hurt!).

Mental Filter: You pick out a single negative detail and dwell on it exclusively so that your vision of all reality if affected like the metaphorical last straw that broke the camel's back.

Alternative: Remind yourself "I need to pay attention to the whole picture."

Unrealistic and Unhealthy Thinking (cont'd)

Focusing on the Negative:
You see a single negative event as a never ending pattern of defeat.

E.g. You get one negative comment in a performance review and forget all the good things.

Alternative: Tell yourself there are no absolutes.

Labelling:
This is an extreme form of focusing on the negative. Instead of describing your error, you attach a negative label to yourself (e.g. I'm a loser").
When someone else's behaviour rubs you the wrong way you attach a negative label to them ("he/she's a loser).

Alternative: Focus on the event not the person.

Ignoring the Positive:
You reject positive experiences by insisting they "don't count" for some reason or other. In this way you can maintain a negative belief that is contradicted by our every day experiences.

Alternative: Tell yourself Positives count—No excuses.

Jumping to Conclusions:
You make a negative interpretation even though there are no definite facts that convincingly support your conclusion.

Alternative: Ask yourself if you can absolutely be sure when you don't have the facts. Give the benefit of the doubt. Be alert for other information.

Personalization:
You see yourself as the cause of some negative external event which in fact you were not primarily responsible for.

Alternative: Review the event from a different perspective and reframe it.

Unrealistic and Unhealthy Thinking (cont'd)

All or Nothing Thinking:

You see things in black and white categories. Eg. "I never do what I want". Mom always liked him best".

Alternative: Choose to see where the shades of grey are.

Try this:

Since people tend to have preferred style of thought; pick out the patterns you use. Then, over a four day period, identify the ones you most commonly unconsciously fall into.

5. Identify Options You Can Shift to -- Create an Alternative Reality. When you are releasing thoughts and beliefs that no longer serve you, it is important to create an alternative reality to move into. If you don't, you will likely find it hard to maintain your shift. Seeing old friends while trying to maintain new habits is one of the most challenging and stressful things you can do. Eating healthy foods, breaking drinking or drug habits while having the addictive substances around, is also stressful. Exercising while the sloth next to you sleeps? …Well, actually a lot of people manage this.

Creating an alternate reality is an opportunity to let your creativity shine. Imagine yourself as the playwright; the script is going to have a major rewrite with the main actor now managing life experiences more calmly, easily and effortlessly, from a place of inner balance. Imagine what you can do differently if you happen to be in a situation where you are with people or objects that are part of your past unhealthy lifestyle. Remember you can always choose to stay in the present moment. There is no past or future. I've found it amazing how, when I recognize I'm in a situation or relationship that is similar to past toxic ones, if I imagine what I'm going to do differently, the past situation doesn't re-materialize. Now, perhaps I was worrying for nothing, but given what other people experience, I'm quite certain I resolved it in another reality, so it didn't need to happen for me here.

Not creating an alternate reality as a way of managing your thoughts has been demonstrated by modern-day lottery winners who have become multimillionaires. If they don't create a new reality after their win, their lives stay the same or, after a few short years, revert to how they were before the win. All of the money is gone with little to show for it. These people did not shift their perception, and their energy was not a resonant match for the new possibilities they could choose.

The opposite has also occurred. I have met millionaires who have lost their fortune but believe that making money is a skill they are great at. This perception allows them to rebuild their millions and risk them again, as if it was no big deal.

One of my fabulous, multi-talented teachers, Adela Rubio, is an expert in energy shifting. She describes creating alternate reality as opening a portal to possibilities. www.adelarubio.com

6. Check in
Notice if there are any changes in your feelings and behaviour that may result from having changed your thoughts and beliefs.

Logical Rational Beliefs

Here are some examples of *logical* thinking and beliefs I learned from a counselling course. Check in and try reading with the perspective "if this were true for me, what would my life be like"? You may wish to consider adopting some of these.

- *I can't possibly please everyone at all times.*
- It's OK not to be "perfect"
- Sometimes good people make mistakes and behave inappropriately. "I can forgive myself and others".
- Sometimes things don't go the way I want them to, but I can (a) work to change things and/or (b) accept what I cannot change.

- I am *not* responsible for *other* people's feelings and emotions.
- People can't *make* me feel a certain way.
- I am the only one responsible for my own thoughts, my feelings, my actions, my reactions and my decisions.
- I can't change anything by worrying about it. I can change some things by taking action.
- The past is over, and what happened in the past does not have to continue affecting me.
- I can accept people as they are, without demanding that they meet my expectations.
- I can't control other people and everything that happens, but I can control the way I am, the way I think, believe, feel and act.
- I accept and even like people who have different beliefs, thoughts and feelings from mine. I am curious to find out something about them and can even learn something new, which may be helpful in connecting with them in Oneness.

How do you feel when you read this? When I check in as I read this, I notice my reaction is: I breathe easier, my shoulders drop, tension in my neck eases, my stomach unclenches, I feel lighter, I experience a sense of expansion and relief. All in all, I move into higher vibration.

7. Give Yourself Credit
Celebrate your choice to look at your life from a different perspective. Know and trust that you are on a path to higher-conscious living.

> Moving into higher consciousness requires awareness and commitment, *and* it is enormously rewarding. Take some time to breathe and congratulate yourself for taking action to improve your life by reading this book.

Why Am I Stuck On Only One Thing?

If you are living in higher vibration most of the time, but you are stuck and can't seem to move forward in one aspect of your path, or there is one situation, person or area in your life that induces automatic negative thinking and responses, here is some food for thought. (See if it resonates with you as you read it). Remember, being in higher vibration consciousness means acknowledging:

- Everything that happens has been planned for us - we have our free will to decide how we will respond.
- The Universal Energy, (our Higher Power) presents us with lessons along our path, which we need to learn for ourselves. Don't forget we can choose to ask for help.
- Remember, "When the student is ready, the teacher will come."
- We need the insight, desire and strength to learn the lessons.

Other people are on their paths and have lessons they need to learn. Their lessons may not be what we think they should be. That's between the other person and Source. We therefore shouldn't rescue them, but we can be there to support them. There is a section of Iyanla Vanzant's book 'One Day My Soul Just Opened Up' called "Compassion" which I found very helpful when learning this lesson. You may wish to read it.

Wayne Dyer has a great way of looking at difficult people. He believes everyone has a "soul mate", who is here on earth to help you learn your lessons by being the one who provides them. (i.e., someone who knows which buttons to push to trigger what you need to learn). Be grateful for those lessons.

Writing in your journal might give you insight into the benefits you are getting from the negative interactions with this person. Write about the costs to you for continuing to be "sucked in".

Think about how much power you are giving to that person or situation, how you are leaking energy. You are giving them the power to ruin your day or even your life. Take back your power by recalling your energy to yourself. Feel your feelings - don't stuff them. Write in your journal, write a letter, write poetry, and use other tools to work through those feelings.

Ask; "Will this incident today be something that will affect my life one year or ten years from now"? If you're still having trouble letting go, detach from those feelings. If you don't want to detach from the problem, ask your Higher Power, (Mother-Father God, Source Energy) to help your resistance.

You can choose peace in any situation.

Remember, feelings are not good or bad. One concept in 12-step programs is that when we are dealing with a difficult situation, person or area of our life, we must stop fighting our feelings. We may be resisting the lesson. Accept the feelings or our resistance and be grateful for the lesson. Talk to the Source about what's happening. Listen and wait for an answer. The Creative Energy will show it to us in its own time.

Speaking of time, the lesson could be patience. Some manifestations are instant , and some take time. I've waited as long as 6 months to one year for clarity on some aspects of my business direction. In the meantime, I was having experiences or being guided to do or read something that was necessary for clarity, or provided me with knowledge I would need for the next steps. In hindsight, I realize I had to be patient because spirit has to get other players and situations into position for the greater good of all.

What else might the lesson be? Ask yourself if the lesson is learning unconditional acceptance. Be fully conscious that there is a part of Spirit in everyone and everything. Look for that and respond to it. If it's buried too deep for you to find it, ask your Higher Self to connect with that persons' Higher Self.

If it isn't obvious, the lesson may be to remind us to appreciate everything else in our lives. If everything were perfect we'd take it for granted.

Summary

In this chapter you learned to recognize your limiting beliefs and unhealthy thoughts, and possible ways to address them. Awareness, in my opinion, is one of the biggest keys to being successful in moving into higher consciousness living. It catapults you out of lower vibration unconsciousness and allows you to access your own wisdom and the wisdom available in the noosphere.

In summary then, one way to move into higher vibrational states is to stop unhealthy, pessimistic thinking, and practice seeing events, situations, and people as they really are, and as they could be, rather than as you or someone else believes they *should* be.

It bears mentioning that, as we change for the better, sometimes the people in our lives also change, not because we nag them or try to change them, but because they see from our example that change is possible - and rewarding. At first though, they may try to push all your buttons to get you to go back to your old behaviour, because it is uncomfortable and even frightening for them to change the way they relate to you, and they worry you will abandon them. You can choose to see this as an opportunity to practice the tools in this book. Choose to take yourself, and the situations you attract, imperturbably.

Yesterday I was reminded of how the universe likes to bring unresolved beliefs or thoughts to your attention so you can resolve them. A woman came in to the Metaphysical Bookstore where I work, and talked about a situation with a pet she had recently adopted.

It bought up uncomfortable reminders of a slightly similar situation when I had to euthanize a dearly beloved pet.

Later in the evening, I started feeling uneasy again. I smiled to myself when I recognized that the universe was giving me a chance to walk my talk. I checked in and wondered what was going on. I discovered that although I had realized I'd done the best I could at the time with the skills and beliefs I had, there was an aspect I hadn't forgiven myself for. I could have chosen to go into drama and heaviness in order to release the thoughts and emotions, but I heard my wise higher self remind me I didn't have to do it the hard, draining way. I chose a tool that best fit the situation I wanted to release, and I used it.

Knowing through experience and mastery leads us to higher consciousness. When we get out of our own way and release our lower vibration energy, new potentials we couldn't even imagine in the old energy will surface.

CHAPTER 9

Moving Into Higher-Conscious Thoughts: More tips and tools

> **Wilson:** Tim, it is not easy to change one's perception of things, but it can be very healthy. Some people might even say it's a growth experience.
>
> **Tim:** Wilson, how far does this go? How do I really know you are who I think you are?
>
> **Wilson:** Well how do I know you are who I think you are?
>
> **Tim:** How do I know you're the one who said that?
>
> **Wilson:** How do I know you heard what I said?
>
> **Tim:** How do I know you're really here?
>
> **Wilson:** Who else would have the time to come out and listen to this silly conversation?
>
> "Home Improvements" – Television show"

Now that we've talked about changing lower conscious thoughts, I want to share some strategies that will move your thoughts into higher consciousness.

Visualization

As I mentioned previously, your nervous system runs in habitual, well-worn patterns called neural pathways. When you change your response a new path forms. This is sometimes referred to as rewiring your brain. Anything that interrupts repetitive habitual thoughts can be used to break habits of negative thinking. I have heard it said that "negative" thoughts can be traced in the left brain, which is responsible for logical thinking, and that to increase your vibration you need to activate the right brain, which is responsible for creative thinking, as well as your heart space. Writing is one body-mind activity that creates new neural pathways to establish and integrate higher vibration beliefs more quickly. Singing and moving are two other activities which dramatically increase one's vibration and shift one's focus. These can act as portals to the intuitive right brain.

Cell memory is created, enhanced and imbedded through the focus of your energy and by writing, singing, dancing or other body-mind activities. Once your cells hold the memories of freedom, vitality, love, joy and peace, which you experience in higher-conscious reality, you can choose to call up these feelings at any time. These techniques have worked for me, and a number of friends and colleagues have been commenting to me lately that they are in situations where they would have been really anxious and despairing in the past, but now they have a deep inner sense of certainty that everything will be alright.

"That brings to mind a great image you can use in your visualizations. One of the benefits of using higher vibration images repeatedly in visualizations is that you can access the accompanying feelings quickly from cell memory when you are in a challenging situation where you notice that you're using habitual thinking based on old limiting beliefs. Eventually, with repeated use, these higher vibration feelings become your new set point frequency. To achieve a deep sense of knowing everything will be ok, try this.

Imagine being separate sentient drop of water in a lake. You are on the top of the water and it is rough. You are thrown about in the waves, with no control of what is happening. Now imagine you are able to become heavier and you begin to sink. As you go deeper, it becomes calmer. You feel your body relaxing and know all is well. You experience peace and serenity, a quiet mind and an ability to suspend thought. You feel as if you are able to be buoyant or heavy as you desire, you can float at one level, or go down deeper as far as you want.

Spend as much time as you can in this visualization, until you can access it easily and effortlessly. From here you can ask to connect with divine wisdom and peaceful messages or images of guidance

When the above image and its accompanying feelings are familiar, you can add the following:

As you are in the calmness of the water under the churning waves at the top, get a sense of the other water around you. Notice how it supports you, feel the buzzing or tingling energy connecting with you, until you no longer feel separate. You all have a common purpose... you are among others with like frequency and vibration. Feel that Oneness. Know the combined power you all have, the power to change the landscape, flow into a stream, then a river, gathering speed and strength, wearing away rocks, or just staying where you are and 'Being'. By 'Being' you are providing a home for the fish and water creatures, plants and bugs, a place where animals can come to drink and birds take their baths and serenade you with their gratitude."

Journaling

Writing is a form of letting go. It is useful for managing thoughts and emotions because you record both in your journal. Writing every day has the benefit of shifting your frequency and aligning your inner and outer intention to create a clear match of higher vibrational energy to send out to the universe. When you look for and find evidence of what is working, your emotions will have a higher vibration. You can write about an insight you have had, a challenge you're facing or a stream of consciousness, which often gets rid of mind chatter and moves you into the other two activities. It helps you to identify beliefs, themes or repeating patterns of behaviour in your life, which you may wish to release. When you reread your journal you may be surprised to see what you are focused on. Some people think they are being very positive and in reality are worried about the future or focused in the past. Unconscious priorities or commitments may jump out from the pages.

If you set an intention to record the good things happening in your life in your journal, you create an opportunity to express gratitude to Source, God, or Universal Energy. An increase in the flow of more good things will occur because, remember: *You create what you focus on.*

At the end of your journaling session, create your preferred day. Write your positive intentions for the day and ask for help from the highest vibration beings. Some examples include, "Today I ask to be shown the next step. Today please help me be more aware of _____. Today I feel courageous and speak clearly as I ask my boss for a raise". You can read more about this in chapter 15.

Sometimes people who I work with resist journaling. I find there are three common reasons given and I've included the suggestions I offer in response. Do you have a reason I haven't listed here? Ultimately of course, it is your choice but if you want to give journaling a try, here are some suggestions.

a. But I Don't Like to Write.
If the idea of writing is foreign and uncomfortable, I urge you to try it for 3 weeks. That's the minimum length of time it takes to establish a new habit. You may want to start on a long weekend or vacation. Set the positive intention that you are willing to take 20-30 minutes to sit, reflect and doodle, draw pictures and write in any form. Don't worry about spelling, punctuation or grammar.

You can also audio record instead of writing a journal, at least until you feel comfortable knowing what to say. The advantage of writing is that it's easier to review and see changes in your thinking and behaviour patterns, and other clues that might enhance your evolution to higher consciousness.

b. But I Don't Know What to Write!

I find journaling really makes a difference for people who are experiencing overwhelm. It gets all the low vibration mind chatter, clutter, what ifs, ands, buts and maybes out onto the page, leaving room for clarity and allowing higher vibration thoughts and possible solutions to replace the chaotic ones. I can personally testify to its effectiveness as can many people who use this technique.

Some people find it difficult to know where to start. Write about how it feels to be sitting there not knowing what to write about.

You can start with that observation. "I don't know what to write I feel stupid sitting here, what will I say? Oh this is dumb. How dumb is it? It's so dumb that... it feels like, for example, when I used to try and write a paper in school and I couldn't think of a thing to write. I hated wasting time when I really wanted to.... Right now I'd rather be...; and you start to identify some of your likes and activities. Without realizing it you just started a list of what to do when you are stressed or overwhelmed. Just write stream of consciousness, whatever else comes. Commit to being in one place for 20 minutes and sincerely intend to journal.

If you really believe you are stuck, reread the visualization section at the beginning of the chapter to get ideas for building neural pathways. Writing may flow more easily if you move or sing for a minute or two, with the intention of accessing your creative brain. You may decide not to read what you have written right away. Whatever works. Just Journal It

c. But I Don't Have Time

Another reason people give to avoid journaling is they don't have time. Although I enjoy journaling, when I'm "too busy", I often neglect it for too long. When I start to slide back into the tarry muck of overwhelm, and have depressed or discouraged feelings, I journal. I sit for 20-30 minutes a day, and write down my stream of thought. In the end I save so much time because I find it much easier to change my thinking and choose higher vibration thoughts and emotions.

When we are overwhelmed our energy is chaotic, incoherent and cannot flow smoothly or connect to another's energy. If you have a situation that pushes your buttons, remember you have a choice about how to respond. If you know in advance that you will be with people who challenge you, are very needy or manipulative, write about it. Write down what you are telling yourself in your head. Tell the story as you are imagining it will take place, including your feelings and your responses. Write from your own perspective -- what's happening, how you are feeling and why you think it's happening. Writing about it will allow you to release your emotions and the other person's energy (which you may have taken on). You can identify some limiting beliefs that may be driving your response and look at the situation in a clearer, detached, higher-conscious way, instead of with a knee jerk reaction. Then, you can choose how you want to respond. You may come up with a creative solution or be open to more possible ways to approach the situation. It allows you to do so in a way that feels in integrity. Another benefit is that the other person may be surprised and thrown off and may not know how to respond if you don't react with the behaviour, the emotions or intensity she or he has come to expect. The situation may be diffused or dissolved easily.

Reframing

a. Change Your Perceptions

When you realize you have fear-based idea, a limiting belief or you recognize that you have an unreasonable thought, remember; you create your reality. As you believe, so it will be. You may remember Bible stories that talk about this principle. There is the story of the woman who was continually bleeding and was healed just by touching Jesus' hem. Another story told of a captain of the army whose child was dying. As he met Jesus on the roadway, messengers from his home arrived to tell him that his child had died. The man said to Jesus that just as when he commanded his army he knew they would follow his orders, he knew Jesus had the same authority to heal his child. The third story involves a blind man, whom Jesus healed by spitting in the mud and putting a mud paste on the man's eyes. All these people perceived that their healing by Jesus was within the realm of possibility.

Jesus warned some of the people he healed to go away and not tell anyone what had occurred. He told them "Your faith has made you whole". What occurred when some of the people did tell others of their healing? It seems that the healing was reversed because of the disbelief they were met with when they told their story. Those people thought it was a magic trick that only appeared to have healed them. In a way they were like some of today's scientists; if it wasn't logical, it wasn't possible. This disbelief and scorn caused the belief and faith of those whom Jesus had healed to waver, their perception of what had happened changed and they were drawn back into the realm of third-dimensional, limited perception, despite the evidence of their healing. This demonstrates the importance of changing your perception, and reframing what you think is evidence that supports your beliefs regarding what is possible.

b. Evidence is Not the Whole Story

A key part of changing your perception is to look beyond the evidence we observe. We need to realize that evidence does not assure us we have the whole story, and we also need to realize that we may not even understand the significance of what is occurring. We can take the opportunity to check out whether we are engaging in either/or thinking and look for shades of grey.

I have heard Wayne Dyer tell the following story on several occasions. He speaks of his encounter with a man on a subway train whose child was behaving wildly, and the man wasn't paying any attention. Wayne held his tongue but thought what a dreadful father this man was and how his child must be neglected. When the man was getting off the train, he thanked Wayne for being patient and said he was distracted because his wife just died and he and his son were coming home from hospital.[133] What a huge shift in perception Wayne Dyer made in that moment!

c. Consider Multiple Explanations for the Actions of Others

In addition to asking yourself if you are absolutely sure that what you think is true, another way to live in higher consciousness is to shift from the habit of jumping to negative conclusions, to being aware of the possibilities that can result from reframing. When you encounter someone who does something that might ordinarily push your buttons, challenge yourself to think of possible reasons besides, 'He's a jerk'. If it is someone you work with, for example, consider whether he might feel misunderstood and is reacting to all the staff negatively. What if she has a sick parent she's thinking of and she wasn't really ignoring you in the hall. How about recognizing someone may be behaving in a certain way because they are feeling undervalues?

Shift the way you look at situations. Check in to see if you're reacting to a reflection of your own feelings of being ignored or feeling invisible because someone didn't acknowledge you. You may be attracting that experience for a reason, so you have an opportunity to consider how you are doing that in your own life.

d. Don't Take it Personally!!

Don Miguel Ruiz lists this as one of the agreements in his book, 'The Four Agreements', an easy to read guide which, in my opinion, is required reading for people on a personal growth path. If you think about how often misunderstandings occur because people unconsciously jump to the conclusion that another's actions are deliberately done to annoy them, and then look realistically at that assumption, it often takes on the flavour of being ridiculous. Suppose you are shopping at a shoe sale for your child. You see a lady taking the last pair in your child's size. Your child believes she won't be popular without them. Well, you think as you see her later, trying to get to the checkout before you. I'll show her.... and you just manage to get ahead of her and take your time, getting the clerk to check a price........ Of course as an awakened person, you wouldn't likely do that. But you get my point. Why would she want to ruin your day and make sure your child was an outcast? She was focused on her own needs and not even thinking about others.

I have always tended to imagine reasons for why other people act in a rude uncaring way. I imagine their side of story and give them the benefit of doubt. People sometimes told me I was too understanding and didn't stand up for myself. I think I was so aware of other's feelings and had such a good imagination, and dreaded hurting anyone's feelings. I did not realize that deep down, I was thinking I had the personal power to ruin or make their life.

As I got older, I wondered if indeed this response was a weakness. I eventually began to take it personally and sometimes felt resentful and angry especially if I was under other stress. Since I stopped taking things personally again, with new beliefs and healthy boundaries, I don't leak energy to people or issues that were never mine to begin with. I now tend to stay calm, feeling unaffected by most people's behaviour.

e. Others Actions May Be a Mirror to Gift You Insight.
When you notice behaviour in another person that irritates you, look carefully to see where you are doing something similar in your own life. This is called Mirroring. Someone might be infuriated when they are cut off in traffic and the person cutting in doesn't even seem to notice. If they look to see where they are metaphorically 'cutting in' on someone in their life, they may notice that they interrupt when people are trying to express themselves, and they don't acknowledge what that person said.

When I realized that other's behaviours could be a mirror to give me insight into an area I could change or develop, it reinforced my awareness that I needed to recognize their role as a teacher in my life. I also learned that if I started to take things others did personally; it was a signal for me to evaluate the stress in my life and do something to take care of me!!!

f. How to Reframe Worry
People are often amazed when they become conscious of their worries and realize how much energy they lose to this low vibration habit. We may worry for a whole weekend about whether something we said in a meeting Friday was the right thing or if our actions will result in disaster. While we need to spend some time considering the future, we often leak energy by worrying and engaging in, "What If This Happens"?

If you spend time worrying about what if bad stuff will happen, here are some suggestions:

A couple of techniques I learned for managing worry so we can live in the Now were suggested by Rev. Canon Geoffrey Dibbs, an Anglican minister at the church I attended as a young person.

- Set aside ½ to 1 hour at the same time each week as worry time. Any time a worry comes up, mentally make a note to think about it on the next worry day. (*Most of the time, myself, family and friends could not remember what we wanted to worry about*).

- Write down all your worries and put them in a jar. The purpose of this activity is to track how many of your "What Ifs" really happen. Once every 4-6 months empty the jar. I bet you'll be surprised at how few came to pass.

"What If it's Something Good?" game

Many people immediately jump to the worst conclusions in any situation. It's a limiting belief I had to really work on releasing; it resulted in poor money management because I was afraid to open my mail. I had an unreasonable fear that was not based on any experience in my adult life. I would worry, "'what if I really owe a lot of money"? "What if they made a mistake and I haven't been charged the right amount for years and now I have to come up with it right away"? When I finally opened the bills, they weren't as big as I'd imagined and I paid them and had money left over; but I was paying a lot of late fees.

So I decided to cultivate a new habit of expecting good things by playing the "What If It's Something Good" game. When I got mail from the government, the city, credit card companies, or anything that I worried might be demanding my money, or making other demands on my time, or hassling me in some way, I would start thinking: "what if it is a refund check? It's probably just a notice about something". I opened the letters right away and 99.9% of the time it wasn't something bad. In addition, I also think "Well, I've always been able to manage before; I have more than enough to pay my bills; I am grateful for having money to buy the things I have purchased." Then I pay the bill coming from a place of gratitude that I can pay it.

Another situation to play in is if you worry constantly about a family member who is living on their own. Your imagination can create mega disasters if you can't get in touch with them. So, think about the good things that could be happening. He could be busy enjoying himself with friends and forgot to check his answering machine. He could be working extra shifts so he can get married and give you the grandchild you've always wanted. She might be tired of interacting with people and just want to have time to herself. Her cell phone might be misplaced, have fallen out of her purse, or run out of power and is misplaced and she can't call. You could think really big, like she's won the lottery and had to fly to another town to pick it up and she wanted to surprise you. You could think small; maybe he had to wash his hair. Maybe your parents decided to check out the senior's complex and took advantage of their weekend trial package. Maybe some old friends picked them up and took them out. See all the possibilities I came up with?

These optimistic thoughts keep you in higher vibrations and may bring a smile to your face, which also keeps you in higher vibration. It recognizes the strength and capability of your loved ones, and it has the benefit of improving relationships because they can sense your confidence in them.

When I'm in high vibration I attract matching good stuff. Ideally, I am always in the present moment, but if I do stray out of the Now, into past or future worry, I can choose to playfully shift the tension and fear even slightly. If that doesn't work I can choose something to focus on that moves me into high vibration. Having a pocketful of high vibration generating thoughts that feel good is worth its weight in etheric gold. Personally, I think of a picture of my son taken within one hour of his birth when he was still awake and had a real smile. Other "thoughts I feel" are imagining petting my cat and feeling her purr, and remembering dancing in the rain in a tropical storm in the Maya ruins. I also use inspirational quotes or messages. Here is one I came across recently. It's from a site I subscribe to that sends me regular messages from "The Universe".

> "The trick with courage, Gina-Dianne, is realizing that it isn't so much about overcoming fear, as it is about not settling for less. And then, it comes as effortlessly as a midsummer's night breeze.

Whhhhhhhhhhhhhh-a-a-a-a-a, who-o-o-osh -

The Universe,[134]

g. Reframing Register

When your journaling raises an issue, or when you want to reframe a challenging situation, there is a tool you can consciously use. It has a more structured format that serves the purpose of deliberately challenging and changing your perceptions of a situation and identifying some possible choices for action.

Draw a table with 5 columns and the following headings:

What's happening?	What you would be your ideal experience? How do you want to feel?	What are possible solutions?	What do you want to energize within yourself?	Action

During the day, check in, and if you notice feelings of discomfort, use the reframing register. Take two minutes when you are experiencing a contrast between what you want to feel and how you actually feel, and really focus on it; focus on how you would like to feel and what you want and write about it for future reference and evaluation. Then move back out into your day with shifted energy. **Remember - We create our reality based on our thoughts and emotions. Focusing on possibilities helps you raise your vibrational rate so you can attract the matching solution.**

> ### *Try this:*
>
> Do you become frustrated when you slip back into old lower vibration habits or thoughts?
>
> Use that as a cue to check in. Are you under greater stress? Do you need to take care of yourself?
>
> Try getting more sleep, have protein snacks and eating smaller more frequent meals. Get outside and connect with nature or pick an activity from the stress busters section of Chapter 11.

Make Friends With Your Critical Voice

You know, that voice that tells us we are too fat, too skinny, too ugly and too stupid, that we are no good and who do we think we are? It may be the voice of someone from when we were growing up, our parents, teachers, ministers, or from someone in our current life: boss, partner, child and our self. Generally they have good intentions; most don't want to hurt you. They did the best they could. To blame them would be to indulge in lower vibration energy and ignore the opportunity of letting go and living in higher consciousness.

That critical voice may be one or many. I call the many a committee. This critical voice lowers our vibrations, discourages us from change and drains our energy. It is often the source of our "shoulds". When you become fully aware of this critical voice and recognize it as part of you, you have the same power as it does. You have the ability to make the negative voice reveal everything about itself. You may be surprised at what you learn when you get to know the critical voice or committee that sits in your head. I know I was blown away.

a. Don't 'Should' On Yourself

I found several ways to work with my committee. I suggest you play with these and see what works best for you.

b. Remember you are the landlord
You have power - you allow the voice to talk to you and give you all these messages. So respectfully listen to what it's telling you, and thank it for its opinion. In many cases you'll choose to ignore it or challenge what it says with facts.

c. Establish New Neural Pathways
I have written about how your nervous system runs habitual well worn patterns called neural pathways. Cell memory is laid down according to the focus of your energy.

The following activity interrupts the old pathways, and using your non dominant hand challenges the brain and embeds cell memory more successfully. *Read this whole section before you begin. Set aside a few hours, since you may really let go of a lot of thoughts and emotions and understand the origin of some of your beliefs.*

- Take a page and divide it into two columns.
- If you are right handed write as many put-downs you tell yourself that you can think of in the right column.
- Then, with your non-dominant hand, write positive responses.

There is a second part to this exercise. <u>If you have been through traumatic experiences in your relationships with parents, partners, or others, and have not had counselling for it, please skip this part.</u> It can be powerful and can open areas that are best worked through with an expert.

At the beginning of this section, I explained that thoughts and feelings are intertwined, but for the sake of clarity I separated them. Since it's important to let go of your energetic cords and attachments when working with your critical voices, let's continue the exercise you are doing. Allow yourself to feel as you are doing this. You may experience anger, tears of sadness or hurt or other unexpected feelings. Stop and Breathe and drink water throughout. This activity will allow the messages embedded in your cell memory to surface in your conscious mind so you can release them and experience the lightness of moving into higher vibration.

- Write all the negative things people told you from when you were growing up until now (your classmates, parents, teachers, friends, spouses, authority figures).
- Respond with what you would have like to have told them.
- Reflect on any changes to your responses as you progress down the page.

Now with your non-dominant hand write what you wish they had told you, what positive messages you wish you had received.

Then, imagine, using all your senses, that this is the way it really happened. (Refer to the section on Visualization if you need help doing this).

Ideally when you are imagining this you will take a bath. Water is an element associated with emotions. Many highly creative people I know get inspired ideas and messages when in water.

Prepare your bath area before starting this activity, with candles, quiet relaxing inspiring music, bath oils or bubbles. Put out a fluffy towel, your robe and slippers. Have a bottle of water nearby. When you have written what you wished you had received, have a quick shower and visualize all the energy you have released being washed away. Ask that it be transformed or transmuted into high vibration energy for universal use. Then fill the tub, breathe, consciously relax your body and visualize receiving the positive messages. It doesn't matter if you don't remember them all, make up some more. Imagine the setting, use all your senses, *See* with your minds eye, feel your emotions, feel what you are sitting on, *feel the touch* if you get hugs. *Smell* the setting you are in, trees, water, a person. *Taste* the water you have set out. Imagine it cleansing internally and enlivening every cell. If there are any foods in your visualization, taste them. Notice your mouth water. *Hear* the background sounds in the setting of your imagination. Hear the person say what you would have liked to hear.

Next, say the positive messages out loud to yourself, from yourself. Breathe. Imagine your higher self is saying them to you in a loving caring way. Believe that your higher self really means it, because it does. Feel the words. Open and try to accept them. If this is challenging, ask yourself, "What would I feel like if this were true"? Feel that.

When you feel ready, come back from that place. Open your eyes. Relax in the quiet, warming up the water if needed. Don't expect anything, but note any ideas, messages, feelings that arise. Rise from the tub, dry yourself, put on the robe, and go snuggle in your favourite chair with some more water or herbal tea. You may want to have a nap. Leave the cleanup for now and pamper yourself. You have just made a huge leap forward in being able to live a higher consciousness life.

After you do this activity, if you have any Ah-Ha's you'd like to share with me and others who read this book, I'd love to have you share them on my blog, http://gina-dianneharding.com *or on* facebook. com/GinaDianneHarding

d. Know Your Authentic Desires
If you consciously know what you like and want, and what your life purpose is, then when your committee starts to natter you will have a better idea of your true self and you will be able to make some reasonable decisions about whether to say no to the 'should's' that don't fit.

Make a list of what you don't like or want. Don't worry, you won't attract what you don't want if you are detached and have little or no feeling when you are making your list. It serves as a contrast to help you identify what you do want.

Next, list what you do want. If you know your life purpose, include it here. Include your hopes and dreams.

Review the lists and pick out what's there because of external approval - cross them out. If you decide to do something that you "should", change it to "I want to". This will decrease the power of the 'I should' message and give you back the power, and *you won't be 'shoulding' on yourself.*

e. Confront Self Doubt and Negative Voices

Talk back to them - tell them to go away, express disappointment with them for being unsupportive, and refuse to buy into their negative messages. I would playfully tell mine to go to a nearby huge rose garden and count all the petals on every flower, or give them instructions to count all the cars downtown.

The voice and committee are afraid of change. They will be very loud when you want to contemplate doing something in a different way or making changes in your life. When I was considering making a change, I reassured them that I was just playing with the idea and wouldn't be making any decisions just then.

f. Ego and Your Critical Voices

Some people say their critical voice is the voice of their ego. They talk about how ego hates change and needs to be crushed or eliminated. I prefer to look at ego from the perspective of how useful it really is. Ego is what carries out the automatic or semiautomatic activities you do during the day. Have you ever driven home from somewhere and realized you don't remember what you did from the time you got in the car? Ego got you safely home. Ego allows us to complete higher functioning activities and be creative while it does more logical, routine things. Although we don't want to have ego rule us, it is a part of us we want to integrate and collaborate with in order to make the best use of both our strengths and abilities.

Once you know what your inner critic says, it's time to make friends with it. By making friends with and understanding your critical voice you will be able to put its opinions in perspective. You will be able to respect and integrate it lovingly as part of your whole self.

g. Making Friends With Your Voices Meditation
The following meditation will assist you in getting to know and befriend your critical voice(s). I will interchange the use of it and them because the criticism comes to everyone differently. Allow yourself to hear whichever term is most appropriate for you.

You may want to record this or have a friend read this to you.

> Begin by getting comfortable, sitting up or lying down. Take three deep breaths and as you release them, ask the muscles in your body to relax more and more. Allow them to become heavy and warm with relaxation.
>
> Close your eyes and imagine you are in a favourite safe spot, one that you know or one you create. Know that any sounds you hear such as traffic noises, sirens, people calling their children, dogs barking, phones ringing, will not be a distraction. In fact, they will act as a trigger to make you feel even more relaxed.
>
> Imagine you can see the sky. It's a beautiful blue with clouds floating slowly out of sight. As the clouds drift by, any thoughts and worries drift and disappear from your mind. You feel peaceful, warm and relaxed.
>
> Ask your critical voice to come to you. Imagine what it would look like if it was to take a form. How big is it? What colour? Who or what does it sound like? What else do you notice about it or them? What feelings does it generate in you? Do you experience any sensations inside your body?
>
> Thank them for coming and tell them you want to get to know them. If you feel discomfort or lower vibration energy in their presence, you can turn them into another form. You could make it small enough to fit into your pocket and choose to morph it into something you feel comfortable with, like a child's stuffed toy or a miniature dog whose bark can barely be heard. Or just accept them and allow them to take whatever form they first came in.

Then begin a conversation, without any expectations. Ask it why it says what it does. Don't be defensive, but feel free to give examples that demonstrate that its perception are inaccurate. If it says you are stupid, you can calmly reply with facts. "I graduated from school with an above average grade, or, I am able to tally the cash at the end of my shift, or, I am very knowledgeable about X, Y, Z. They may have a comeback. If so, state some more facts, but don't have any expectations about them changing their mind.

Then ask "What are you afraid will happen if you don't criticize me?" When they raise concerns you could let them know that you realize these internal critics probably want what they think is best for you, or that they are truly afraid right now. Part of that fear is that you will no longer pay attention to them. You can tell them you appreciate their concern but that you are still choosing to do this. You might want to reassure them that what you are doing isn't a forever change. (Remember there is only this moment.) Tell them you are just playing or experimenting right now.

At the end be sure and thank them and let them know you are grateful that they came to talk to you and that they care about you. Let them know how valuable they are for trying to keep you safe and that you would like to communicate in a new way. Perhaps you will ignore them when they criticize but listen when they express their concern directly. Perhaps you'll listen and thank them for their opinions but you will make decisions consciously.

Perhaps you'll just agree to know they are voices from the past and you don't intend to pay attention to them. What you don't focus on disappears eventually, and in the meantime, stating your truth will remind you to consciously empower your Real Self.

Rituals and Ceremonies for Letting Go and Manifesting

Another tool I have found to be effective in many areas of my practice are rituals and ceremonies, perhaps because ancient traditions have power in the collective unconscious. People are moved by the careful, conscious, thoughtful way they are performed. Another reason behind the power of ceremony is that it's mysterious and connected to the unknown, a Source of creation in a way people are not even aware of.

I have noticed that people are more open to releasing old energy, limiting beliefs, lower vibration thoughts and emotions and attracting new beliefs in a ceremonial environment when the intentions are synergistically enhanced by group energy.

I often use the following releasing and attracting rituals with classes. I include them during the equinox or solstice ceremonies I offer live or on line. I addition, I use it personally every New Year's Eve, utilizing the information I gathered in my preparation for the December 21 Solstice ceremony.

You can do this yourself in a personal ceremony. Here's what you need:

- An energetically powerful area which you resonate with.
- Markers to designate the boundaries of the space (e.g., stones or flowers).
- A cloth to use as sacred or high frequency space for ceremonial tools. If you are making a fire in a pit, put the cloth beside it.
- Tools to build a safe small fire outdoors or in an iron pot or fireproof bowl.
- Sand to extinguish the fire.
- Kindling wood to start and feed the fire. A couple of sticks will likely last long enough if this is a ceremony just for yourself.
- If you are unable to have a fire, use a fireproof bowl with enough sand in the bottom to anchor a candle, so paper will be able to burn to ashes.
- Matches.
- Paper and pen.
- A special item that represents your connection to nature, the highest vibration and the highest consciousness. Put this on the

cloth with any other ceremonial items you are attracted to (bells, a picture, offerings for mother earth, animals, birds, guardians).

Before the ceremony:
You may wish to make a list of everything you want to release: beliefs, habits, people or experiences you are still energetically attached to: whatever you need so you can be purified to allow energy of the highest vibration to move in. Make a second list specifying the new beliefs, energy, habits, relationships, personal goals and desires, health and experiences you want to attract to your life. Be very specific and descriptive, using the information from chapter 14 regarding how to write intentions.

When you have found a space that resonates, be sure to ask the energy of guardian spirits and ancestors of that place for permission to hold the ceremony, and check in for an answer. The guardians' energy is often in a large natural object such as the biggest, oldest tree, a body of water or something near or at the entrance to the area.

Ceremony:
Breathe deeply three times and focus your thoughts and energy before you enter the ceremonial space.

Enter quietly, contemplating the energy of this place. Using your senses; notice what the environment is like. Is there a breeze? Which way does it blow? How strong is it? Can you hear any birds or animals? Look up. Is there anything remarkable in the trees or the sky? Notice the scents. Be aware of this so you will notice if anything changes during or after the ceremony. It may be a signal that other energies are with you. Connect with the energy of everything around you, above and below. Express and feel gratitude for this connection and all you are experiencing. Add any other things you are grateful for. If you are in a place where you can speak aloud, this will add power to your ceremony. If you feel uncomfortable, then ask for protection as you do this work. You can ask for any high vibration energy Source you believe has power to do this. It may be God, Jehovah, Allah, a prophet or saint, Goddess, angels, or a master teacher alive or ascended.

Sit comfortably in the space. If you wish, you may choose to contemplate and make your lists here rather than having prepared them before the ceremony. When you are ready, start the fire or light the candle. Fire represents destruction of low vibration energy. Thank the fire for assisting you at this time. State that it is your intention to release all energies that are keeping you from living consistently in higher vibration consciousness. Read aloud the list of what you want to release.

Fold the paper, and put it into the fire ensuring that it burns to ashes. It seems that almost every tradition I have studied or experienced has a way of signifying or sealing the action. It may be by saying 'Amen' (which means 'so be it'), or, "So it is. It is so. It is done". Select one that feels best and end this part of the ceremony. Remove the ashes and if they are small enough to scatter or blow away do so. If not, put them aside and bury them after the ceremonies are over so they continue to disintegrate until the energy is no longer present.

Notice what the environment is like, just as you did when you entered the space. Has anything changed? Has anything new appeared? Did anything leave or move?

The second part of the ceremony is similar. If you haven't already, prepare your list of what you want to attract. Rekindle the fire if necessary, and again express your gratitude to the fire for joining your energy for this ceremony. This time, the fire represents the light and energy of the sun, which brings the power of renewal, growth and strength, and symbolizes co-creation with the universe. State that it is your intention to call in energy of the highest vibration to further purify you so that you are a vessel for ongoing higher-conscious energy. Further, that it is your intention to pursue your life purpose, co- creating with Divine Source, and ask for the universe to help you stay aware and awakened, and maintain clarity and strength of purpose.

You may wish to add "I know this higher vibration energy is always with me and my intention is manifested by the power in the words I have spoken, through grace, easily and effortlessly. I release these words now for action by the universal laws". Fold the paper, stand and put it into the fire ensuring it burns to ashes. Say the words to seal the action from the example above.

Remove the ashes, and if they are small enough to scatter or blow away, do so. If not put them aside and bury them separately after the ceremonies are over. These ashes symbolize the seeds of your intentions being planted and nurtured by the soil and rain and sun, so the energy in them continues to expand.

Notice again what the environment is like, just as you did when you entered the circle. Has anything changed? Did anything new appear? Has anything left or moved? I often notice the wind will pick up as an acknowledgement that there is energy present, to validate the intention. Sometimes the fire will suddenly burn brighter or faster. I may see a hawk or an eagle circling overhead; a bird will start singing at the end. Any number of signs may occur that indicate you are in the flow. I occasionally ask for signals and get them. For example, I was in a grove surrounded by three somewhat young trees, working with Mary Magdalene energy. During the ceremony an acorn, a leaf, and a branch fell from the trees as I was thanking the guardian of that direction at the end of the ceremony. I went to physically connect with the trees after the ceremony and each had a one had a similar mark in the shape of a heart on their trunk.

Try this:

Remember the importance of sincerely believing what you say on every level. Feel free to add or subtract words so what you say is your truth.

Summary

When we are living from old energy minds we can't perceive new energy potentials. In this chapter I offered four dozen tips and tools you can choose from to let go of your limiting thoughts and beliefs. I included a great visualization exercise that moves you from separation into the energy of the whole. I told you how to get over the three common reasons people don't journal. An important tool was provided, for changing or reframing your perception with regards to looking beyond the evidence, seeing limitless possibilities and considering a variety of causative factors for someone else's behaviour.

Remember there are both positive and negative reasons for what is happening in your life and in the world around you. If you fuss with your human worries and mental issues, your old mind energy will get stuck and you'll experience brain lock and energy gridlock. Since worry is such a big challenge for many people, I also presented three tools for you to play with: a specified worry time each week, a worry jar to track how many worries came to pass, and the reframe game "What If It's Something Good?"

I also shared tools for creating new neural pathways through releasing lower vibration energy from your inner critic, and told you how you could make friends with your inner critic. The chapter finished with directions for doing rituals and ceremonies to free you from beliefs that no longer serve you and help you manifest your desires.

As long as we hold on to lower vibration energy we cannot even get a glimpse of the limitless possibilities of the energy in the upcoming age. You now have the knowledge to let go of low vibration thoughts. Practicing will bring proficiency. As mentioned in Section One, the energetic changes we are experiencing are enhancing and quickening the speed of integration of these new practices into our cells, body-minds and spiritual bodies. To create and integrate these new responses, I suggest you pick one that resonates with you and consciously use it as often as you can until it becomes second nature. Then move on. However, as always, go with your intuition. There may be a better way for you to get the results you want.

The next chapter discusses when you may want to consider consulting an expert, various energy modalities you may want to investigate, and offers tips for how to select the best person for you to co-create with.

CHAPTER 10

Working with Body-Mind Experts

> Education is a lifelong experience. Experience is a lifelong education. Education plus experience equals expertise.
>
> Michael Bugeja
>
> The supreme end of education is expert discernment in all things--the power to tell the good from the bad, the genuine from the counterfeit, and to prefer the good and the genuine to the bad and the counterfeit.
>
> thinkexist.com

If you have practiced the tools and tips in this book for few months and you find there are one or two beliefs that have not shifted, I would recommend consulting with an expert energy worker, coach or counsellor. There are other body - mind energy work techniques that can help to release stuck limiting beliefs that have dense, thick energy. Working with an expert you trust can allow you to experience the bliss of being in highest consciousness. When you have the experience of being in this energy it can be easier to re-experience it on your own.

There are people like myself who can work with you remotely, in person or via telephone. This is possible because there is no time and space outside of 3D reality and everything is energy. It really helps if a person is open to limitless possibilities, but it works even if they don't really believe.

I have provided information below about some of the many techniques that are offered by experienced expert providers, and also given you some advice for discerning appropriate healers and teachers who are a good fit for you.

Guided Visualization

Guided visualization is a process where you relax your body and follow the words of a helper who may intuitively create a scenario that addresses your needs, or uses a script designed to achieve a predetermined need. You may be taken on a journey, go inside your body to be healed, or assisted to manifest a desire. You can be helped to release stuck limitations and habits and replace them with new habits. You may meet your guides or angels, who will help you by activating strengths and skills you need to do your life's work.

You can experience fairly personal guided visualizations by listening to CDs. There are several great CDs that have the participant release their lower vibration energy and move into higher consciousness by imagining themselves in various situations, feeling and using all of their senses. You can walk up a mountain and find a wise guide who leads you to a beautiful location where you receive a message or a gift. In other CDs you can ask a question and receive an answer, or step into a circle and be surrounded by beings of the highest vibration who will help you or provide you with any qualities or attributes you desire. Sometimes you arrive and just explore, being free to create any setting and free to do anything you want. Another favourite of mine is walking up coloured steps (chakra clearing and strengthening) and increasing your vibration as you experience the different colours. When I reach the top, I'm met by angels. Just listening to these CDs in the morning or evening will put you into joy and bliss.

I find this tool so valuable I use it in almost every encounter with my clients. I specifically tailor the experience to the individual or small group I am working with. I prefer to use this as a first step to meditation because it keeps the mind and thoughts busy and prevents ``monkey mind chatter``

Visualization Research

Visualization experiments have demonstrated outcomes of people who actually worked out on a treadmill or engaged in other strenuous physical activity compared with those who imagined they were doing their chosen sports activity, fully engaged with just their mind and emotions while sitting on a comfy couch. At the end of the experiment the people who had visualized their training were in the same good condition as the ones who actually did the physical training. Physiologically the same chemicals and hormones are released during visualizing. New neurological pathways are also established.

I can create a state of physiological balance, perfuse tissues with oxygen and totally relax my client's whole body using guided visualization. In addition, I may guide my clients to release old cell memory and re-pattern new ones, reframe past experiences, then experience them as if they lived them and shift beliefs

The field of sports uses this technique extensively and their research supports the findings that physical performance is improved when the mind imagines the desired outcome. To the same extent that attending to the health needs of the body are the foundation of a good training regimen; mental focus, concentration and visualization are keys to physical success. Most people are familiar with the saying that sports are 90% mental and 10% physical. Why is it then, that so many athletes fail to give attention to mental training? That 90% figure should be pretty hard to overlook, yet it often is. By studying transcendent athletes and sports stars, it becomes apparent that the common edge they have over competition does indeed begin mentally.[135]

A study conducted by Dr. Blaslotto at the University Of Chicago is an intriguing example.

The goal of Dr. Blaslotto's study was to determine the effects of visualization on sports performance. As a performance measure for this experiment, the researchers chose the free throw percentage of a group of basketball players. First, to establish a basis for the study, the current free-throw success rate of each of the subjects was tested and recorded. Three groups were then established, and the athletes were assigned to one of the groups at random. After 30 days of testing and retesting, the results were as follows:

- The third group, who neither physically practiced nor visualized shooting free-throws, showed no increase in percentage.
- The first group which physically shot free-throws for an hour daily, collectively improved their free-throw shooting by 24%.
- The second group, which practiced daily by visualizing shooting and making free-throws, collectively improved their free-throw shooting by a shocking 23% without having physically shot a basketball!

There are other studies with a greater number of subjects, which validate these findings.[136]

Hypnosis

Hypnosis is another technique that you can use if you're experiencing challenges to shifting your beliefs. Clinical Hypnotherapists can help you to move from lower to higher vibration and awaken and raise your level of consciousness. A very creative colleague and friend of mind, a certified hypnotherapist, has a unique technique she uses with clients on a spiritual path who wish to experience ultra-height vibrational energy. This is an amazing experience, which has the added benefit of making you feel like you just got back from a two week vacation. I use a tip I've learned from her when helping someone relax during a guided visualization. That is to suggest that any noises are a cue to become more relaxed.[137] So when the phone rings, people talk in the hall, the toilet flushes, the client sinks deeper into trance. You may want to use this idea when you meditate or do your own visualizations

Sometimes people are afraid a hypnotist will put them into a trance and make them do something against their will. This is a myth.[138] Another common misconception is that you won't know what is going on. I used to worry that I was not really in trance because I knew what was going on around me and thought I was making it up. Not so. *I really couldn't have imagined some of the things I came up with.*

Massage

Massage helps relax the body and increase energy flow, removes toxins, improves circulation and can drain lymphatic tissue. It can help release any low vibration energy that is ready to leave a person's physical, mental, emotional and spiritual bodies, especially if the intention to release old stuff is set by both the massage practitioner and the client. I use Sacred stone massage and energy work to help my clients release cell memory.

Emotional Freedom Technique (EFT)

EFT (Emotional Freedom Technique) is a form of energy therapy that you can use to release limiting beliefs and form new ones. Tapping with your fingertips on meridian points on the body is a technique derived from acupuncture, which can release energy blockages that cause negative emotions. It's simple for anyone to master. One key part included in every tapping round is incorporating the message that you love and accept yourself exactly where you are right now. You begin by checking and rating your chronic pain, emotional problems, disorders, addictions, phobias, post-traumatic stress disorder, or physical diseases, on a scale of 1-10. Then you say, *"Even though I...* [eat too much chocolate, have cancer, or whatever the issue is], *I completely love and accept myself."* After the first round of tapping, which takes about from one to 5 minutes, you check in and see where you are on the scale. You can use EFT with other energy techniques to enhance them. [139] [140]

There are many more energy modes I haven't touched on. The About.com site had 60 holistic therapies listed. There are little tidbits about some types, and more extensive information about other methods.[141] Since 'Everything Is Energy', one could call all of them a form of energy healing

Here are some of the possibilities: crystal readings, acupressure, chakra balancing, reiki, shamanic healing, aromatherapy, sound and color healing, healing touch, magnetic healing, biofeedback, dolphin therapy, dreamwork, huna, kinesiology, NLP, reflexology, ayurveda, herbal remedies, homeopathy, acupuncture, naturopathic medicine, prayerful intention and Chinese medicine.

Other 'New' Energy Techniques

There are other relatively new energy techniques, which trained energy workers can do in as little as 5 minutes or less. I have included them below. Because they are relatively new, there is not as large a database of successful outcomes as for the more established complementary or alternative modalities. I cannot give a satisfactory explanation in the context of this book. If any of them call to you, please check them out in your community or do online research regarding the positive and less positive evaluations of the techniques and the practitioners.

Matrix Energetics

Richard Bartlett is the "inventor" of *Matrix Energetics,* He teaches an

Easily reproducible, verifiable and results-oriented healing process, using subtle energy physics, and consciousness. Matrix Energetics starts with a gentle light touch and the power of focused intent and builds into a new and joy-filled state that can affect life changes. It's about transforming beliefs concerning healing, disease and the structure of reality. You are creating and transforming reality at the quantum level and observing the macro effects of that change. It's a natural extension of changing your way of perceiving; your old reality collapses and new possibilities materialize instantly. Physical and emotional conditions can be resolved with the speed of thought. Often you will see and feel a wave like motion when Matrix Energetics is applied, as the person being worked on experiences a smooth wave of transformation. What seems to be happening is that the unconsciousness and the biological physical field matrix is rearranging itself. [142]

I experienced a session with one of his students. I wanted to transform my attitudes about clutter. I did achieve a rapid lasting result from the experience.

Theta Healing

The theta brain state is associated with REM sleep (dreams), hypnosis, meditation, lucid dreaming, and the barely conscious state just before sleeping and just after waking. Theta is the border between the conscious and the subconscious world.

A trained theta healer moves her clients into theta brain waves, which "releases negative emotions from the subconscious and changes limiting beliefs to belief systems that work. It deals with longstanding issues in a series of sessions but each session is brief".[143] "It not only heals illness but it can heal finances, love and the way you work your business".[144]

Reconnection

Another relatively new energy system that dispels limiting beliefs is Reconnective Healing.

> It is a sub-system of The Reconnection which is the umbrella process of reconnecting to the universe. These evolutionary frequencies are of a new bandwidth and are brought in via a spectrum of light and information that has never before been present on Earth. It is through The Reconnection that we are able to interact with these new levels of light and information, and it is through these new levels of light and information that we are able to reconnect.[145]

> "The Reconnection is about connecting our personal energy grid system (i.e. acupuncture lines and subtle anatomy, including chakras) with the energy grid system of the greater universe. When we connect with the greater energy grid, we receive an influx of light and information that completely transforms our body-mind-spirit. ... You are now able to receive light and information that your system was not able to receive or process before. ... The Reconnection is about restoring yourself to spiritual wholeness. It's about releasing or removing the blocks or interferences that have kept you separate from your intrinsic perfection. It's about the restructuring of your DNA and your reconnection to the universe on a new level."[146]

My story... continued

As a practitioner, I use energy to assess balance, remove low vibration energy, strengthen weak energy and restore a person's balance, physical, mental, emotional, spiritual and etheric health. There are many people who are gifted with this skill and many teachings and methods of delivery, with varying results. My first introduction to healing energy was in the late 1970s when I graduated with my Bachelor of Science in Nursing and became a registered nurse on a medical ward. I attended a day seminar where a fairly new technique was being demonstrated. It was called Touch for Health. I practiced Touch for Health only on night shifts when there wasn't a lot of other nursing or medical staff around. I used it with people who were in pain but were not due for medication. I found that my patients often fell asleep or became deeply relaxed as I was working with them, and many slept through their next scheduled pain meds.

Over 20 years later, when I left my formal nursing administration position because of health problems, I began to examine my career expectations and to mourn. At that time my unhealthy thought was that I had failed: I had not been able to make a difference for nurses I managed who were doing an outstanding job with what I considered to be less than ample equipment under difficult working conditions. I felt that in addition to this, their happiness was my responsibility. (I have shared the story of the depression I experienced concurrently, earlier in the book).

When I began to live my life anew, literally re-examining every activity and opinion I held based on a conscious assessment of whether it was true for the real me. Looking back, I realize that my beliefs about being responsible for the professional happiness of the nurses was tending towards catastrophic thinking based on limiting beliefs. I have given some tips for managing unhealthy thought patterns in chapter 7.

I began to reframe a new perspective about alternative medicine practices, which I had previously considered successful only because of the placebo effect and the power of the mind.

I have a belief that nothing is impossible. There is so much we haven't known about ancient wisdom and indigenous healing practices which is now being corroborated by current research. I already believed in miracles, having experienced one or two, and I knew there is something greater that guides and supports us. I have always experienced synchronicities in my life and had a response to prayers that asked for what I wanted to happen, if it was in my own and others' greatest and highest good.

I don't remember how I got started offering "healing" services to friends and family, and I didn't realize how intuitive I am. I just offered to help someone feel better-- maybe get rid of a headache or pain, or relax, to clear their mind or soothe anxiety. I would get an idea of how to do it. That would work, and a bit later I would read about some healer doing what I had intuited. Another way my intuition was validated was when occasionally I would go to a gathering of like-minded individuals and see a healer there doing the same unusual technique that that I had done. I gradually helped more friends and acquaintances and was guided to more tools and techniques. I heard serendipitously about Carolyn Myss, a medical intuitive, and went to hear her speak. I was quite captivated by the stories she told and decided I would check out medical intuitive courses.

Well, as has happened frequently in my life, when I, the student, was ready, the right teacher appeared. Dr. Richard Jelusich is a reputable, incredibly powerful, intuitive healer who has a professional background in engineering and is a teacher, author and former Dean of the California Institute for Human Science. Not only did he help me develop my intuitive assessments, he also taught energy healing based on a unique framework he had developed. I learned the rationale behind the techniques I had intuitively used prior to taking his classes. I also learned some very advanced techniques. One of the greatest gifts I took from that course was to trust my intuition.

Everyone has their own way of receiving information, and mine is often in metaphors or other odd symbols. In the very last class, I experienced something I never had before. I kept coming back to an area near my client's shoulder blades that felt different. It didn't feel like low vibration energy, just a disturbance in the field. Near the end of the session I received a message that it was her angel wing buds. Just as the branch of the tree is a bud or bump before it comes out, her angel wings were budding. Well, I was in a dilemma. It was the last class. My teacher had repeatedly told us to be complete in our reporting. I was in a lower vibration space of fear. Would I end up not graduating if I told this? Was I totally imagining it?

I reported what I'd found in the assessment and the core reason for my findings. I paused, took a breath and at the last moment decided to describe what I had intuited about the angel wing buds. When the woman reported what she, as the client had experienced, my statement seemed to be ignored. However, when she seemed to be finished with her report she added; "Oh and by the way, I do have angel wings." I felt like doing an end-zone touchdown victory dance. I had evolved from a purely research based scientific practitioner to a higher level energy specialist, more open to limitless possibilities.

Be aware then, that as you move into higher consciousness, you too will strengthen your intuition. It will become clearer as you eliminate your lower vibration energy. The people I work with and support also initially report that trusting themselves is a real challenge, but I encourage them and you to be patient with yourself, and if you feel guided, record your messages and look for positive evidence that you are indeed receiving higher vibration information. In the event you feel guided to take Dr Jelusichs' course for healers, I have included contact information in the resources section.

How to Find Experts to Assist You and Red Flags to Run the Other Way

It is getting easier to find people who offer energy-based assistance than ever before. If you go into a health food store or even in the organic food section of some grocery stores, you will likely find a local magazine that features stories about complementary healing, ecological issues, and metaphysical, spiritual and inspirational articles. People advertise their services in these. You will also find excellent information in specialty stores that sell crystals and books about channelling, metaphysics, spirituality, ESP, eastern philosophies. The staff in these stores usually know reputable experts who have had successful outcomes with their clients. Many of these healers don't need to advertise because their clientele is based on word of mouth recommendations. When you ask for a recommendation, most people will offer you at least a couple of names. This takes into consideration the importance of a finding someone who is a vibrational match or with whom you resonate. I also listen carefully to the first few names; since I think there is a tendency for people to list the people they feel are the best practitioners first.

As more people are awakening, they are coming to realize that they have healing gifts and they sincerely want to offer them. Unfortunately, some of them do not have the insight or maturity to determine their abilities or to offer service as a clear vessel, unimpeded by energies they need to clear. It is important to discern whether the person offering their services to you is safe, has practice standards, and is ethical in terms of confidentiality, honesty and integrity. They should be willing to tell you about their training and experience, and the risks and benefits of the energy work they offer, and advise you when the treatments have done as much as they can. You can expect them to conduct themselves appropriately in practitioner-client relationships. Check on their willingness to refer to others, and their financial practices. It is your responsibility to then make an informed choice based on logical and intuitive responses and energetic resonance. As in any field, there are energy workers who should not be providing services no matter how much training and experience they have, just as there are some people who are truly blessed and innately understand the ins and outs of being a professional energy worker or change agent.

Most good energy workers want to ensure that your working relationship will be a good vibrational match, so they will gladly speak to you or even offer a short consultation. Ask about their training - where they went to school (was it a licensed or accredited school), the format (distance, correspondence, live classroom), what practical hands on experience they had (if applicable), and what courses they took. There are different rules in every country regarding professional designation and qualifications of practitioners vary.

At this point, I'd like to offer a tip about using your intuition to select your healers. This also applies to teachers and even the learning material you choose. It is very important to trust your intuition and be aware of what your body, mind, emotions and spirit are telling you. Do you like and trust the person? Are you attracted to that person on an energetic level? Check in with your body and see if it feels tight or open and comfortable. You may consider working with a healer or teacher who has a great reputation for wisdom and healing and connection to highest Source information. If however, you do not personally feel comfortable with the person or their beliefs and practice steer clear. Everyone resonates with certain practitioners in a way that is perfect for their learning. Sometimes you second guess yourself, thinking you must be wrong if everyone else is enthralled with the energy master. It may be that person has been clear in the past, but changes in their beliefs, perceptions and clarity in receiving the messages are not accurate in the present. It can sometimes be confusing because their intent is very sincere, but they are not able to detach from what is occurring in their lives. They may have started to believe the hype from their followers, the media and others who would make them a guru. Or they may sense they are not clear and have gone into fear.

It raises red flags for me if a teacher says his is the only truth and you must follow her way or if your practitioner takes it personally when you choose to work with another.

You may not resonate with a practitioner for any number of reasons. Perhaps it is not in your greatest and highest good to work with them because someone with a better vibrational match is coming.

Once you are working with a helper, check in regularly. If the information they present or care they give do not resonate, and you want to discontinue your relationship; be discerning. First, see if this is a pattern for you. If you change helpers often it may be that you reach a certain point where the stuff coming up is too uncomfortable and you are using your practitioners or teachers as scapegoats.

If you have had the experience of working with a less than "ideal" helper, remember you attracted it for a reason. Sometimes your intuition may encourage you to choose to stay in a situation or relationship, take the information and help that resonates and discard anything that does not feel in integrity.

Remember, put out to the universe the qualities you want in a healer, teacher, or other helper and when you are ready the appropriate one will appear. You can go to the section on how to place an order with the universe now, if you want to play with this more.

With the information you gather when seeking an expert, the discerning intuitive comfort you feel, and the continuing awareness you have as you interact and co-create with the expert, do the work, and allow it to work, you will experience shifts that *blow your socks off.*

Summary

There are many expert practitioners and many new energy techniques which can help shift your thoughts and feelings and beliefs. In this chapter, I shared some tried and true processes, such as guided visualization and hypnosis, massage, and EFT. I also informed you about some of the many exciting new techniques that you may wish to select if you find your intuition is guiding you to consult with a practitioner. I also provided advice about how to find the energy worker and teacher who can assist you to shift in a way that was for your greatest and highest good.

In the next few chapters we move from working with our thoughts to working with our emotions. I'll explain a process for letting go of lower vibration emotions that don't serve you. Do you know someone who can't identify what they are feeling? I'll share some possible reasons. Of course I'll include more techniques for managing emotions and moving into higher vibration frequencies, including some fun "quickies".

CHAPTER 11

Changing your Emotions:
How to Manage
Your Lower Vibration Emotions

"The curious paradox is that when I accept myself just as I am, then I can change."

....Carl Rogers

Several years ago, before I realized I was suffering from clinical depression, I felt overwhelmed, anxious, hopeless and uncertain. Physically, I was chemically unbalanced because of the stress I'd been experiencing. Depression is a very common mental illness, and if untreated it can result in a very unfulfilling life. It can be dangerous. Although I have said in this book that it's important to know we have choices in every situation, I believe you can't choose to ``get over`` depression, or choose to be happy when you are acutely depressed. But you can choose to get help, and keep on trying until you are successful. In Appendix 1 there is a questionnaire you can use to determine if you might be depressed. **It is imperative... if you are experiencing these symptoms, I implore you to check with your doctor and get help instead of judging yourself and trying to stuff low vibration emotions or fake higher vibration ones. I can testify: Life can be so much better.**

Lower vibration emotions such as fear, uncertainty, anger, depression, disappointment and despair seem to be the norm in western society. I am surprised when I walk down a busy street or through a mall and see so many people who appear distracted, frowning, or at best with a neutral expression on their face, no sign of light or happiness in their eyes. If they notice me they seem surprised that I am happy and smiling. I remember recently when I was out with my mother and we stopped at the shoe repair man's busy counter. He looked at me and said "You - why do you look so happy". I said, "It's a beautiful day and I'm out with my mother. I'm glad I can enjoy time with her".

There is a lot of fear and despair in the world as I prepare to send this manuscript for publication. U.S. politicians have been fighting over how to deal with their inability to pay their debt and there has been rioting in the streets of London England. We feel fear viscerally as lumps in our stomach, headaches, sore jaws from clenched teeth and muscle soreness. It eats away at our energy. Chronic fear leads to high blood pressure, heart disease, hormonal imbalance, and many other disorders including depression.

Process for Managing Your Emotions.

If you suffer the normal ups and downs of our stressful lifestyles, the following process can help you manage your emotions. When you use this process you will shift into higher vibration and you will think more clearly without the clutter that comes with low vibration emotions.

a. Know that no one can *make* you feel anything. Realize and accept that you create your reality. Different people perceive the same situations with differing emotions.

b. Identify the emotion as specifically as you can. Some people have stuffed their emotions for so many years they don't even realize they have feelings. When you can consciously name an emotion, you are able to release it more easily. My *free* e-book "What are you Feeling?" will be available early in the new year on my website http://gina-dianneharding.com

c.   Recognize the story associated with the emotion. What do you think has caused you to feel the way you do? Who might you think you should blame? Unconditionally accept yourself and release the story, remembering that you created it to help you learn or strengthen higher consciousness skills and abilities. Keep the emotion without the story.

d.   Honour the emotion by connecting with it and feeling it. Check in and see what physical sensations are attached and where you feel them. Are there any limiting beliefs behind the emotion? Since checking in is a very important practice, I provide information and detailed tools about it in several parts of this section, especially chapter 13.

e.   Is there anything you can learn from it? Breathe, relax and allow insights to materialize.

f.   Is there any action you need to take? Sometimes it is important to share your emotions with a counsellor, especially if they are related to a significant relationship you wish to maintain and nurture.

g.   Create an alternative reality. State a belief you want to have. Use the manifesting process and accompanying tools, as well as other "how to" techniques and strategies, to have this belief materialize in your life.

Connect with Your Emotions

A basic technique that is crucial to understand and practice in this book is checking in. I tell you to check in as part of many of the tools and techniques I share. You need to establish a habit of being aware of how you are feeling, and how that is affecting you physically, mentally, emotionally and spiritually. You might, for example, notice you are close to tears; a physical manifestation of the emotion you are feeling. Your chest might feel tight; your stomach might be in knots. Mentally, your thoughts might be about a loss you are experiencing. By checking in further with your emotions and thoughts you might realize you are feeling hopeless and abandoned by people in your life and by your Higher Power.

Another time when you check-in, internally, you may start from a physical place. Suppose for example, you are stroking the family pet. Your pet is adoring the attention and nuzzling closer into you, looking at you with loving eyes. In addition to using your senses to physically experience this precious time, you may notice a warm feeling in your heart, relaxed muscles, and slow even breathing. You might call the feelings you are experiencing loving and peaceful. Spiritually you might be moved to feel gratitude and unconditional love for your pet.

It is also important to check in externally, noting who and what is around you.

Checking in externally, for example, might involve becoming aware of the energy of people around you. If you are a highly energetically aware person (HEAP), you may sense or take on lower vibration energy from those in your immediate environment. Some HEAPs` can even feel energy from people and disaster situations on the other side of the globe. It is important to also be aware that you can take on the energy of the collective conscious. In this time, where most people are perceiving systemic chaos, disaster and fear, it can be a real relief to understand that if you are experiencing feelings of lower vibration that seem unrelated to anything around us or within us, we may be taking on these other energies. You will be able to process them and transmute them into higher vibrations with the tools you learn in this book .

Something essential to be aware of when checking in is your breathing. Very few people I know, myself included, take in enough air. As a result our bodies and brains are deprived of the vital oxygen necessary to think clearly, connect within and ground our energy in physical form. We might feel spacey or unclear, our emotions may be influenced because our bodies cannot manufacture and process the body's natural chemicals, like endorphins and serotonin, which help manage and elevate our moods. I recommend taking three deep belly breaths each time you check in, and developing an awareness of your breathing until deeper breathing is a habit.

When you are aware of the energy in your immediate environment, it may be easier to understand the experience of your inner check-in. You can also determine whether your surroundings help you to be in higher vibration energy.

Manage Your Emotions

By managing your emotions, you can gain a clear vibrational signal of what you want. This is how to get clear so your conscious and subconscious minds agree, and you achieve a vibrational match.

- Know what you don't want, (it's ok --just don't attach emotion to it and don't dwell on it).
- Choose what you do want. Be specific.
- Let go of the inner roadblocks to your desires.
- Feel it already accomplished.
- Let go but show up so the universe can provide.

Does this process sound familiar? Yes, it's the process for manifesting.

a. Why Some People Don't Express Their Feelings

We sometimes make assumptions about our feelings and so we don't express them. I was the queen of repressed resentful, annoyed feelings. As a highly energetically aware person, I felt not only my own, but other's feelings. As a child I cried when my goldfish died. As an adult I would cry when the young beavers in the scouting movement walked by in a parade. I cried at happy endings. I sobbed at sad endings. I stopped going to movies because I always left with a headache. *Crying was the only acceptable (to me) way I expressed my feelings.* But I almost never felt angry, or had other negative feelings, because at the age when my beliefs and values were being formed, I'd learned at church that it wasn't nice or forgiving or understanding. At home I never wanted to worry or burden my parents by letting them know I was less than good.

I had definite rules that kept me from expressing feeling. It got so I only knew whether I was feeling happy or sad. And as I worked with other people, in the beginning I found the ones I was most comfortable with, didn't express their feelings either.

I've listed below what I believe are some of the most common fears that prevent people from expressing their feelings. I suggest possible ways to reframe them. You can apply these to any relationship you want to maintain and nurture, including personal, family and business.

Common Fears and Limiting Beliefs about Emotions

If they really cared they'd know how I feel.

Reframe: Not everyone is as highly aware as you. They really *can't* read your mind.

What if I tell her my feelings, and she doesn't tell me hers; they won't care how I feel anyway; they won't change.

Reframe: It is healthy for me and for the relationship to express my feelings. I'm not doing it for them. I may learn something about myself, even if I don't have an effect on anyone else. It may help me clarify the issue. Although it would be nice, I don't expect anyone to say or do anything when I share my feelings.

My feelings come from what other people say or do. Other people make me feel.

Reframe: Your feelings come from within. Feelings can come from objects, pets, nature and beauty.

I'm afraid they'll be mad, or put me down or leave me if I say how I'm truly feeling.

Reframe: I can say things in a way that is true and diplomatic, not blaming or critical. Maybe I'm strong enough to listen to them and hear what they really mean.

What if I hurt their feelings or crush their spirit?

Reframe: People generally are a lot stronger than what we give them credit for. I can't make them feel something, either.

I'm a bad person if I share negative feelings. I might act on them.

Reframe: Feeling and acting are two different things. It is normal to have positive and negative feelings. Feelings aren't something to judge.

My feeling is pretty unimportant in the big scheme of things.

Reframe: Trivial feelings can become bigger over time. It's like an iceberg; energy that's below the surface and incomprehensible to someone who runs into it.

Try this:

Identify your common obstacles to expressing your feelings. Can you reframe them into healthier perceptions?

When we learn to express our feelings in a non-blaming nonthreatening way (by saying such things as "I'm feeling this way in this situation)", it becomes a healthy outlet. Sometimes we need to journal the intense emotions to get them out so that we can manage them before we discuss them with others. When I allowed myself to experience emotion during the healing process, I knew I was feeling angry, but I felt really uncomfortable saying it or pounding pillows or doing anger expression exercises. Living in higher-conscious awareness doesn't mean we will never have lower vibration feelings. We'll just be able to recognize and process them more quickly from a peaceful center that knows everything is truly okay.

Are You Overwhelmed?

Life is moving very quickly and we are being inundated with so much information (a lot of it useless.) If you are discerning, you may wonder if you need to know what's happening in the far corners of the world in such detail. Although my heart aches for the family of a woman who was run over standing next to the driver's side door on the freeway in Toronto, Canada, I find myself wondering how that is important in the lives of the people hearing the news report in Vancouver. I have to be aware and manage my energy so it doesn't leak out from my field, so consequently I am very selective about how I get the news. I tend to listen to an all news radio station headlines at the top of the hour when I am driving. The driving serves as a distraction and I am emotionally distanced from the energy of the stories. I highly recommend you consciously assess and choose what is best for you. You can always change your mind.

Information overloads our energy and adds to the demands we place on ourselves at work, in relationships, and everything we do while striving for success. Although I see signs that society is shifting its values, it seems many people still view success in relation to being super achieving humans with the most material goods such as big status houses, cars, boats and knowing the "right people". It's no wonder that one of the biggest challenges people deal with today is overwhelm.

Everyone experiences "negative" emotions. In addition to the reasons I've already mentioned, they may occur during a personal crisis. Sometimes we feel our life is a soap opera. People in our family may become ill, we may lose our jobs, and our relationships may dissolve. People often feel overwhelmed and afraid, sometimes paralyzed and unable to act when challenging events occur. But if we have a lot of general stress, sometimes something seemingly insignificant can tip us into overwhelm. I've asked people to look back over a period of months or years to look for the same situations that repeat with different people. Often they realize that what started out as small challenges they chose to ignore because they felt overwhelmed, repeated and gradually became more significant, until they became forced them to take action. So the information here and in chapters 8and 9 is vital, not only to increase your vibration, but also to help you avoid pain and the physical, mental and emotional results of stress.

a. Assess How You Respond to Overwhelm
You can assess your experience of overwhelm by asking yourself the following: Am I consciously aware of what it is in my life that overwhelms me? Am I aware of how I respond? Do I withdraw, put up walls and focus mentally on one area I feel comfortable or skilled in? Do I give up? Do I keep on pedalling as fast as I can, becoming more exhausted and burned out, experiencing more frequent illness? Do I have a favourite coping mechanism---overeating, drinking, using illicit or prescribed drugs, watching TV, reading or exercising to extremes, or helping everyone else so I can avoid looking at my life? These are just some of the avoidance activities I see in people whom I provide service to, and ones I have used at various times in my life. What about you?

b. How to Deal With Overwhelm
There are several simple tools you can use when you are overwhelmed.

 i. First do the self-assessment above.

 ii Become the 'watcher watching the watcher'. One exercise I teach to help people detach and move out of overwhelm is that of becoming the watcher. When your thoughts are confused and chaotic, if you are feeling short of breath, or just unable to cope with the situation, imagine that you are watching your 'self'. As the *watcher*, you are standing across the room and observing your 'self's actions, compassionately, in an unconditionally accepting manner. Notice how you feel *as the watcher*. Check inside your body: is your stomach tight? Is there a lump in your throat? Is your body tense? Are your teeth clenched? Is your breathing shallow? Your *watcher* may or may not experience these symptoms. If it does, it is emotionally attached to the situation. In that case, become the Watcher watching the *watcher*. Observe that first watcher and notice the physical changes it is experiencing, and then check in with yourself as that second Watcher watching the watcher. At this point, you will probably notice that, as the second Watcher, you have no sign of anxiety and are able to be an impartial viewer.

This is one tool to overcome overwhelm, to calm yourself, achieve clearer thoughts, then move into higher vibration energy.

self ← *watcher* ← Watcher watching the *watcher* (twice removed and detached)

iii. In addition to getting to know ourselves and clarifying our feelings, another way to manage our emotions is to see each big or small challenge as an opportunity to change, to grow and to evolve. We can use the energy and adrenaline our bodies create, to propel us from our daily routine into a new level of functioning, a level of higher-conscious action.

iv. By consciously choosing to detach ourselves we will be using our age old flight or fight reflex in a new evolutionary manner.

Some Experts Say "Get Organized"

Does it work to get organized, have a plan or decide how much time you want to devote to life areas such as work, relationships, personal time, rest and relaxation when you feel overwhelmed?

Not for me. Although many articles recommend this strategy, if I'm overwhelmed, trying to do any of the above tips me over the edge. I need to replace the energy I have used up. Energy is like a bank account. You have a finite amount and when it is all spent, you need to earn more. This can be achieved by resting, doing light exercise such as walking, and by doing activities which connect you to nature and Source Energy.

So yes, you can get organized once you have more energy reserves and feel comfortable with examining your lifestyle. It sometimes helps to have a supportive coach or counsellor work with you individually, or in a group setting. This is where having a helping relationship with a reputable person with good assessment skills and a variety of tools can make a huge difference. They can assist you to manage old and integrate new emotions with ease so you can move into higher consciousness habits.

Affirmations

a. To Use or Not to Use?

I Am using (*positive*) affirmations more and more every day.

Another tool, which I often recommend for managing emotions, overwhelm and thoughts, as well as for manifesting what you want, is the use of positive affirmations. Are you aware you are already making affirmations? Often we are affirming our limiting beliefs: "I'm so stupid", "That coat is to die for", and "Just looking at a piece of cake makes me gain 5 pounds".

Many people would define affirmations as positive statements that declare what you want to experience in your life as if it is happening now. There is a real art to understanding and crafting positive affirmations. If you haven't researched how, you may do what many people do and create an affirmation such as, "I have 3 hot cars, a home in Hawaii, I make 5 million dollars a year and I have a partner who is tall, dark, handsome, a good dancer, rich, and makes me laugh". Even if you say this affirmation with feeling, the chances are you cannot achieve the inner vibrational match to make it so. Louise L. Hay's book 'You Can Heal Your Life' (the expanded version) has a very good explanation of affirmations. She also provides readers with affirmations for physical, mental, emotional and spiritual healing of very specific health issues.

Affirmations are most successful when you truly believe and feel what you are saying. If your conscious mind is saying something and you have a limiting belief that is subconsciously saying "Oh yeah and I believe in the tooth fairy too", then (unless you sincerely do believe in the tooth fairy) you will not manifest what you want. When you do not have a vibrational match between your affirmation and belief, you will experience a loss of energy. This lack of energy contributes to overwhelm and poorly controlled emotions and the energetic cycle spirals down instead of up.

You may be making unconscious affirmations about being overwhelmed, such as: "I can't take this any longer", "I don't know what to do next", "I'll never get this all done even if I don't sleep for the next week", and "I can't get out of this bed to face the day". These thoughts are associated with feelings of overwhelm and a vicious downward spiralling cycle can occur.

Instead of unbelievable affirmations, you can create ones that feel true. Perhaps one of these would work for you:

- I know my life becomes simpler and I attract the right resources to bring me into a state of balance and calm.
- I release my feelings of overwhelm and move into higher vibration, knowing that I experience clear thinking and decision making, and that everything in my life flows easily and effortlessly.
- I have all the time I need to accomplish everything I want to get done.
- I am confident I will accomplish what needs to be done in perfect timing.

Remember, what you think and feel is what you'll experience. What you speak with feeling will make the experience even stronger. This ancient knowledge has been recorded in the Jewish and Christian Scriptures. You may remember reading or hearing that, "In the Beginning was the Word" ...and so began creation.

Science of Mind and Law of Attraction teachers often say the spoken word is more powerful than thoughts. Those who are familiar with true ancient wisdom will also tell you that feeling is the most critical power with which to imbue the manifesting process.

Now you can appreciate why managing your emotions and feeling the joy and freedom that comes with higher vibration thoughts is a vital skill to practice so it becomes second nature as we move into the next great age.

b. Do you Doubt your Affirmations?

If you don't feel the above statements resonate, instead of making a positive statement you don't feel is true, I recommend trying the following:

Look at the area you want to make a change in. What are you experiencing in that area now?

Recognize:

- I create my reality.
- I can create an alternative reality in any moment.
- I have limitless possibilities I can choose to shift to.
- If I move a bit at a time then I'll end up in my preferred place.

Your subconscious mind accepts a **slight shift** to an adjacent reality better than to a totally opposite one. It resists if you say affirmations that are at the other end of the spectrum because it doesn't feel like the truth. For example, if someone runs out of money before the end of every month and makes the affirmation, "I have more than enough money to live like millionaire", their conscious and subconscious minds would not be in alignment. In addition to an affirmation needing to feel truthful, you need to believe you're worthy and deserve it.

Modified Affirmations (MAffirmations©)

I'm going to share a little known alternative to affirmations that works for the naysayer in me. I discovered it while taking 'The Advanced Spiritual Business Building Program' (www.coachingfromspiritinstitute.com) and have modified it for myself and for use with my clients. Instead of writing affirmations, I learned to write what I actually believe. It also works by describing what you want to feel and what you are willing to receive. I call these MAffirmations©: for modified affirmations. The capitalized MA represents a Mastery of Affirmations achieved by having learned and practiced a creative way of manifesting your desires by taking graduated steps towards a belief that is a vibrational match between the subconscious and conscious mind.

For instance, to continue with the issue of emotional overwhelm, I'd start by writing: "I believe I can deal with the overwhelm in my life", or to be more specific, "I believe I can trust the universe to help me release overwhelm and move into and maintain higher-conscious vibration".

I'd check in, and if I felt disquiet, I'd reflect and see if I believed this statement: "I want to believe I can deal with the overwhelm" or "I can trust the universe".

If that didn't feel right, then I'd add another qualifier;

"I want to believe that I can believe I can deal with the overwhelm" or "trust the universe..."

Finally, "I want to believe that maybe someday I will believe I can deal with the overwhelm or trust the universe...." might be the affirmation which I'd feel most comfortable with in the end.

I could also say "I want to feel confident and certain that I manage my life easily and effortlessly".

Or, "I allow myself to feel trust, certainty and confidence flow in me in everything I do", and move backward from there if necessary.

This technique has been really helpful to me. I step back and qualify as far as I need to go to be hopeful and feel good. I write this day after day until I feel a shift, and then I go ahead a step to a higher vibration affirmation. Eventually I do get to the place where I can say with sincerity and positive emotion "I now release all overwhelm and move into and maintain higher-conscious vibration." At that point I feel open, trusting and in higher vibration instead of tight and shut down. I therefore attract something or someone to help or it becomes a *no thing* and I no longer feel overwhelmed.

This is such a powerful tool. It has allowed me to love and accept myself at whatever point of the process I am. I am able to move more quickly and easily into my highest vibration, feeling confident, "in"powered, and connected to Source Energy.

Quickies

Here are some more simple ways to manage your emotions and increase your vibrations.

a. Stress Busters

You may be familiar with stress busters: exercises you can do to relieve stress in the moment. Ten years ago, when I developed my Simple Pleasures Stress Reduction Classes, I found a fun, and at that time, a somewhat unique, way to increase the energetic vibration of participants. I didn't really understand energy at that time, but I knew everyone felt better. Before I tell you what they are, I want to add: now I start by having participants do a check-in like the one listed above, '*Connect with your Emotions*,' prior to a stress busting activity.

I still often do an exercise where everyone brainstorms what you can do in 1, 3, 5 and 15 minutes to reduce stress and revitalize. We also look at what you might choose if you can carve out 30 minutes, an hour, half day or more from your busy schedule. I have some quick things my participants try. There are common ones (like breathing, stretching and drinking water), and some fun ones like energetically selecting and sniffing essential oils that shift your physical, mental and emotional vibrations. The mixed blends have names such as Retreat, Refresh, Peace and Joy, Goddess and Immunity. The power of the words in the names begins the shift, and then the energy vibrations in the oils cause the body to align with a vibrational match. We also use single oils to help with physical stress symptoms such as peppermint for sore muscles, eucalyptus to aid breathing, and lavender for headaches.

Another fun thing you can try is to apply cologne to your pulse points. Buffing or painting your nails can be a fairly quick activity. Turning on the radio to your favourite station and singing or dancing along with one song before you return to your task at hand can also quickly shift your energy.

b. Move

When you find yourself caught in negative feeling or thinking, *move.* Change your position, walk around the room, into another room, dance or sing. The result is an instant shift to a higher frequency. It also opens the heart, which makes it easier to move into higher-conscious awareness.

c. Meditation On The Go

When you are feeling anxious and experiencing mind chatter, you are almost always focused on the past or future. Try using this tool to get back to the present. Look around at your environment. (If it's like mine, ignore the clutter). Connect with something of beauty, art or nature and ground yourself by describing out loud what you see for two minutes.

> I see a beautiful picture of an amber carved, translucent jaguar, the light catching its sinewy stalking motion. I see my computer in the corner surrounded by books and paper, crystal orbs, and essential oils. I see my serene orange cat sitting motionless, looking out the window. I see the gorgeous evergreen trees and a grey sky.

Then be quiet. You'll notice you are fully present in the moment. Most people find they experience more mental clarity as well as a more peaceful state. '

d. Cleanse Your Energy Field

Here are a couple more quick tools for changing your energy by cleansing.

- When you wash your hands imagine that low vibration energy is leaving your body. Feel it draining away. This can be helpful if you are in a tense situation and you choose to disengage for a couple of minutes to manage your thoughts and emotions. You can also do this when you are taking a shower, before or after a stressful day.

- Imagine cleaning off low vibration energy from your body while standing under a beautiful refreshing waterfall. See yourself with a comb, and as you run it through your hair, all energy of disagreeable thoughts or fears are removed from your mind. Now feel the highest energy of the water, mother earth and the cosmos, energizing and revitalizing you as you visualize your body and mind becoming clear and purified.

This is especially useful when you are in an environment where there are a lot of unconscious, lower vibration people and you feel your energy is being drained.

Chapters 13-15 also have activities that you can use when you choose to move into higher vibration after having released low vibration energy.

Try this:

Make your own list of quick fun stress busters or quickies, leaving about two inches between items. Cut them into squares, fold them and put in a little bowl. When you feel overwhelmed or want to increase your vibratory frequency, pick one and do whatever it tells you.

Summary

This chapter reviewed the process for managing emotions, especially overwhelm which, next to fear, is the most common lower vibration emotion today. It examined seven limiting beliefs which prevent people from expressing their feelings, and how to reframe them. I explained how we all use affirmations unconsciously, and when we wake up and become aware, we realize why we are creating our life as it is.

Many people find it challenging to believe affirmations, as they are taught to create them. I offered an alternative; MAffirmations©, modified affirmations. In addition to dispelling the myth that creating and using a good affirmation will always result in manifesting, I also challenged the "get organized" myth as a first step to managing overwhelm. I replaced it with the practice of regenerating energy for your energy bank.

This part of the "how to" section of this book has provided you with a number of tips and tools for letting go of low vibration energy so you can move into higher vibration. When you use them, you will become much more skilled at managing your energy and have a clearer vibrational signal so you can attract your preferred higher consciousness life. You can then explore what you want to co-create, paying particular attention to the feeling associated with the outcome you desire.

Just as it takes practice to build muscle, it is important to practice new skills so you can use them easily, efficiently and effortlessly. My intuitive healing teacher, Dr. Jelusich advises us to go to the Chakra Gym. I like to think there is a part of the gym for the mind and feelings, too. When you train your mind to think in a higher vibration way, and your feelings to move into an uplifted state, you will rarely experience being overwhelmed and fearful or stay focused on what is not working in your life. Remember, it's really about retraining your mind and your neural pathways. Like any new skill, it takes time. In the long run, you will become almost instantly aware of your feelings, identifying where you are focusing, and shifting your energy to where you want it. You will also become much stronger and more capable in managing your energy. When an issue appears, you'll have developed a habit of thinking, `` OK, here are the circumstances. How do I want to experience this? What solutions could there be, or how could the end result be even better?"

CHAPTER 12

High Vibration Emotions

> You may change your mental vibrations by directing your will and attention in the direction of a more desirable state. Will directs the attention, and attention changes the vibration.
>
> Cultivate the Art of Attention, by means of the will, and you hold the secret to the mastery of moods and mental states.
>
> The Kabalyon

You have almost certainly been in high vibration energy at many points in your life, perhaps remaining there for long periods of time without realizing it. When you first fall in love, the world seems rosy and your lover is perfect. You accept them unconditionally; your energy is in a higher frequency.

If you are thrust into a dangerous situation where you fear for your life and live to tell the tale, or if you have a life threatening illness and recover, you feel so grateful to be alive. That too is higher vibration.

If you have been following your path for a while, you may consciously move into this natural high. However, it's discouraging when you cannot maintain a higher vibrational state consistently. It can often get frustrating because you understand the power of emotions and thoughts and recognize that these create your reality.

If your goal is to live in higher consciousness and align with your life's purpose, you need to shift from unconscious reaction to intentional consciousness. Since you are still reading this book, it's likely you are consciously awakened and aware. If you have begun to practice the tools and tips in the earlier chapters, you have probably let go of lots of limiting beliefs already!! You may notice that you feel lighter more often, the churning in your stomach and contracting of your throat has decreased, you can think more clearly, you are risking speaking up and being your true self more. I still feel thrilled when someone I've been working with tells me the muscles in their face are sore because they have been smiling so much!!!

Accomplishing the Shift into Higher Vibration Energy

There are two main ways you can accomplish this shift. The first is by releasing your lower vibration energy; the second is by increasing your vibration. Shifting each of these requires changes in your physical, mental, emotional and spiritual energy systems, and the creation of new neural pathways by choosing new desired thoughts and actions more often than old ones.

There are some basic underlying principles that are important to know so you can accomplish this alchemical transformation. I have made some reference to them earlier in the book but want to put them together in a framework for your consideration. Perhaps you will decide to choose one or two as new beliefs to incorporate into your higher-conscious life.

Principles

1. Be in this world but not of it.
2. Live in the now moment.
3. We create what we focus on.
4. Energy is a cycle.
5. Choose 4th dimension or higher thoughts, emotions and lifestyle.
6. Manage your physical, mental, emotional and spiritual bodies

Principle One: Be In the World But Not Of It

This overarching principle encompasses the philosophy of living in higher vibration consciousness.

Although this is a teaching from the Bible, it is originally from more ancient wisdom. When we choose to live in higher-conscious vibration, we are following this teaching.

When we live in third dimension energy, we are surrounded by fear; our own negative lower vibration thought forms, and those of our family, friends, and the collective consciousness. We live with a polarity viewpoint, where we judge and label concepts as good or bad, positive or negative, stupid or smart, rich or poor. We feel driven by time and deadlines. We relive the drama of our yesterdays thinking, "I should have", and we worry about tomorrows and "what ifs". People realize they need to stop and smell the roses – a reminder to enjoy the present moment, but that somehow gets neglected amidst all the other stuff.

When we are *in* the world but not *of it,* we are not attached to past or future; we are calm, peaceful and we know that everything is ok no matter how it looks. We know that everything we need will come in the right moment.

Principle Two: Live In the Now Moment

Living in the now moments eliminates regrets, worries and helps us focus on being present to create dynamic outcomes in whatever it is we are undertaking. When we are in the 'right now', we're aware of our surroundings and can connect with the energy around us. We are able to use all our senses including our intuitive sixth sense to discern what is occurring and choose our best response to the situation we are in. If we are not ``in the now moment`` we may be losing energy thinking about the past, worrying about the future, or not even be in our body. Another way to describe this is we are not grounded. What do I mean by that? People go out of their physical bodies for a variety of reasons. Sometime it's because their minds are so active, they really aren't aware of what their body needs. They ignore urges to drink water, go to the washroom, and even breathe deeply to ensure an adequate oxygen exchange and clear thinking. At times my mind used to be so focused on what I needed to do on the other side of the room, that I would already 'be' there while my body banged into furniture and people in an attempt to catch up. People also leave their body to escape a traumatic situation such as abuse. Metaphysically, people may leave during a meditation and find their etheric bodies floating above their physical body. They may be intensely focusing on a scene in a guided vibration, they may be going on a shamanic vision quest, be remote viewing or one of many other remarkable happenings.

I think this principle is familiar to most people, partly as a result of an innovative internet education program offered by Oprah which featured, thought leader Eckhart Tolle. Hundreds of thousands of people participated In weekly sessions in which Oprah and Eckhart discussed the concepts in his book `The Power Of Now` regarding why focusing on the present is a key to living successfully

Principle Three: We Create What We Focus On.

Reading this now may not create as much of a reaction as it did the first time you read it. Hopefully, you have a better understanding of how we are creating everything in our lives. A common heart wrenching misconception is that you are somehow the cause of an illness or injury to someone important to you. I particularly remember one young woman who had heard this principle and believed she had caused the crib death of her newborn. This is most definitely *not* true. Everyone – every soul, creates their own life and our worries about them do not affect the universal metaphysical laws.

Although I have covered this concept in the first part of this section about releasing lower vibration energy, I now want to consider it from a higher vibration perspective.

This principle evolves from the universal law of attraction- energy vibration attracts a vibrational match in energy. You get what you *think and feel intensely* about. Remember, thought is a force, a manifestation of energy; it's like having a magnet attached to your brain and solar plexus. You might think you need to be very serious and concentrate to get what you desire. The good news is that doing fun activities increases our vibration and connects us to the matching higher vibration Universal Energy!

Here's an aside that may help you understand my outlook about this; I believe we create a plan before we are born, which has general objectives or things we want to focus on. These are not detailed and can be changed, because we have free will. However, members of our soul group, who are alive during our lifetime, have agreed to play a certain part to help us accomplish our life purpose. They can help or hinder us, according to our agreement. In the end though, they really are helping. I have learned over time to reframe the more challenging people's actions by considering what a good job they are doing of pushing my buttons and how they are even improvising, and going beyond what we had set up and recognizing what a masterful job they are doing.

Our outside reality depends on our inner beliefs and thoughts and feelings. The key here is not about controlling them but about guiding them. Controlled energy is tight and blocked, whereas guiding is about accepting your thoughts, beliefs and feelings, allowing them to flow and choosing to refocus on a higher option.

Your attention must be on what you want to be, do or have - not on the lack of it. Setting intentions is one of most important ways of ensuring you attract what you desire; it is a critical tool to have as you go along your life path. Another helpful tip is to know that the more relaxed you become, the more powerful your energy. If you are clear on what you want and willing to show up and do what it takes, in an easy and effortless way, you can trust that it will materialize.

The emotions that accompany your thoughts are the key to achieving what you desire. If you are not attracting what you intend, it is an indication that you are not aligned with the Creators energy and being a vibrational match. You can use this knowledge in many kinds of situations; if you want to materialize a desire, concentrate on seeking higher vibration energy when you are experiencing emotions like joy and fun.

Practice non-attachment. When you want to create something, state what you desire but without any attachment to the specifics of how it will happen or what it will look like. Just playfully put it out there. I always ask for 'This or something better' then release it like a balloon of fun to the universe to do its thing. It will arrive in a way you often don't expect. It has to! It's The Law!

You'll notice I write about the universe almost as if it has human attributes or like it's a big Genie just waiting to grant our wishes. In reality I think of it as a creative energy that we can work with. Please keep in mind that it isn't personal, as you try out the tools in this book.

> **Try this:**
> Take a moment to reflect;
> What messages do I give myself if I *don't* Consciously create?

Principle Four: Energy Is Cyclical. Everything in Creation is Part of a Cycle.

One aspect of the cycle of energy is about receiving--giving—receiving. Energy is in Everything. Therefore it is important to give as well as receive. You have to be able to receive energy in any form so that you can use it and pass it along. If you don't give energy away you'll back up energy being given to you, it will stagnate and no more will come to you.

I'll use a common situation as an example.

This principle is quite evident when we examine the energy of compensation for the work you do. Many self-employed helping people feel uncomfortable about charging for their services. They don't realize that they are actually doing their client a disservice if they do not permit an energy exchange. Their client's energy will not flow easily and their abundance will be limited. If you don't know how to receive, you are giving the universe a message that you do not need to its offerings. If you can't graciously accept an offer of help, or a gift, or even a cup of coffee without feeling that you have to repay, you are limiting your abundance. Self-employed persons will probably find they have fewer clients, and their cash flow decreases, if they have not learned how to receive.

Inherent in this principle about cycles and flow is the knowledge that there is more than enough for everyone: there is no lack. The more you give, the more you get.

Remember, when you integrate this principle, be aware to consciously ask yourself "What am I doing? How am I helping others? What am I supporting? How am I contributing to betterment of others or the planet?"

Principle Five: Choose 4th Dimension or Higher, Thoughts, Emotions and Lifestyle

Once again I ask you to suspend disbelief and open your mind to "What if"...

We can tell if we are living in fourth dimension energy when we know and trust that everything is happening exactly as it is meant to, for our greatest good. We know there is energy greater than we are that we can access and co-create with. This is how we can change anything we don't want to experience.

In the fourth dimension, there is no time or space. I find it fun to play in no time. When I have a commitment scheduled that I need to drive to, and especially when I'm running a little late, I ask the universe to ensure that I arrive at the perfect time. I don't look at the clock in my car, and I eagerly anticipate and wonder how the universe will accomplish this. This playful anticipation takes place in higher vibration energy. Some "times" I get all green lights. Other times, the program I'm attending has been delayed, and I arrive just as it is about to start. As I was writing this paragraph, I had a thought that I haven't played in space. Then, I realized that when I do remote or online energy work, I access and connect with my clients' energy in no space. When the work is done, I bring the energy into the three-dimensional world and the clients' body.

a. Duality in the Higher Dimensions
Duality in the third dimension is largely a contrast between lower and higher vibration energies like good and bad. Duality in the fourth

dimension is nonjudgmental. Day and night, up and down are examples of 4th dimensional duality. Abraham-Hicks states that we have duality in this life to provide contrast-- to help us see what we want and don't want. In higher vibration, The Universe doesn't differentiate. It can't conceive duality because the Truth is, *We Are All One Energy*. There's no good-bad, happy-sad, rich-poor: there is only high vibrating energy.

If we consider materializing abundance again, the universe "thinks" 25 cents is the same as 25 dollars, $250, $2,500, $25,000, $250,000, 2.5 million, or $250,000 million.

Don't limit what the universe can give you! By asking for money so you can travel or buy a new car, you are limiting abundance. If the universe is free to provide in whatever way it creatively can, amazing, unimaginable things can happen.

b. Alternate Dimensions

Here's another *Woo Woo* idea to add to the mix. When we want to move into higher vibrational consciousness, we can create an alternative reality in any given moment. There are dozens of adjacent options we can shift to. If we move a bit at a time, then we'll end up in a different place. I was once practicing a new meditation I had received in an email. It described how to move into parallel dimensions where a preferred reality was occurring. My cat had gone missing a few days before, so I decided to meditate on being in a dimension where my cats and I were all together, living healthy happy lives. As I was meditating the phone rang and I decided to answer it (not my usual practice). It was a neighbour saying my cat had just gone past her window and was hiding in the bushes there. *WOO woo WOO woo!*

Principle Six: Manage Your Physical Body

I have referred to managing your beliefs, your mental and emotional body earlier in Section Three. Although it is possible to be in higher-conscious vibration without your body being in the best health it is capable of, there is a drain of energy that takes away from your energy reserves. Managing your physical body to maintain its balance and health is a multimillion dollar industry but basically comes down to good nutrition, getting enough sleep and moving the body to keep it strong and flexible and the internal organs functioning well. It is important to maintain an awareness of the body systems and how they function, so you can provide the appropriate care it needs. There are many easily accessible sources of information regarding managing physical health to assist you in this area.

These principles are the framework for you to construct a higher vibrational conscious life.

The Process—How To Be In High Vibration

If your life isn't flowing, you are in old energy. New energy is very dynamic. It is full of synchronicities; resources or helpers appear the moment you need them. *Each moment* you need be aware and awakened. The process of being in higher vibration is fairly simple.

1. Breathe.
2. Connect with Source, Your Inner Self and the External World.
3. Choose Your Preferred Thoughts, Feelings and Beliefs in the Now Moment. Remember the Power of Gratitude and Love Yourself
4. Make a conscious choice to be in high vibration conscious living and choose to act accordingly.
5. Accept the Process, Be Patient and Allow.
6. Trust your intuition and the Universal energy.

1. Breathe
   Being aware involves checking in and opening to receive. You have to breathe. Breathing is a way to shift energy and create a dynamic flow. You have to connect. This is how you get new ideas; this is how you magnetize like-minded people for relationships or collaborations.

2. Connect
   Connecting with your inner self, the process we described as checking in, involves being aware of what's going on in your body–mind, emotions and intuition. Are your body's signs related to positive thoughts (like being with a new lover) or are they connected to a

limited belief? Are you connecting the current situation with a past one and re-experiencing those old emotions? Checking in gives us an opportunity to notice how draining our story is and whether we are in higher or lower vibration energy.

Connecting externally involves being aware of your environment, other people, the situation, symbols or messages from other energetic essences, such as nature or spirit guides. It encourages awareness of whether your intuition is being sparked by an external Source. Another key to connecting externally is being aware of your choices. It also reminds us of our Oneness with the Energy of Source and All Our Relations, the trees and plants, rocks, sky, seas, all the creatures that live in or on them, Mother Earth, the Cosmos, the wisdom teachings of our ancestors, and more. To me, because I know everything is energy, I also connect with the parts in my car, my appliances, and other things that are manmade, which you might not think of sharing energy with. And of course I connect with the oneness of every human on the earth, knowing we share so many similar thoughts and feelings. When you think of how almost every parent is proud if their child graduates from college, of how common it is for people to cry at weddings, or how almost every culture has a form of baby talk, we realize how much we share as a human race.

3. Choose in the Now Moment, Be Grateful and Love Yourself
Managing your beliefs, thoughts and emotions is another key to being in higher vibration. As you will see, gratitude is one of the highest vibration emotions. It is essential that you believe you are worthy and deserve love. You must love yourself to be in the full experience of higher consciousness.

4. Accept and Allow the Process.
Although you choose high vibration energy, even the savviest people I know who live in higher vibration say they experience times of lower vibration. They know that 'what you resist, persists', so they just recognize it, accept it and themselves, feel the feelings and move back into higher vibration when they are complete with the experience. It's

as if you are peeling the layers of an onion. The same things continue to come up to be released but they last for shorter times and are less intense. It gets to the point where it's a bit humorous. You greet the situation with the attitude of *"Oh, are you here again? Nice to see you here (*maybe not at this moment but...*). Thank you for coming to help me let go of what's not really me. What choices will I make as an outcome of what you bring up? "* The technique of continually reframing your thoughts and shifting your perceptions of how you view and interpret your immediate situation will be an ongoing part of the process, until you automatically detach from the situation and don't take it personally.

5. Choose to Live in Higher Consciousness and Act Accordingly
   Whenever possible, choose fun, freedom and childlike attitudes of wonder and limitless possibilities. Play differently, and unanticipated, remarkable and perhaps enchanted happenings will occur. Creating or participating in fun events is an excellent way to be in higher vibration. Choosing higher vibration words when you speak also helps you reach and stay in higher consciousness.

   Remember you can choose what action or inaction to take. Since this can be overwhelming, I advise you to take baby steps. It's ok not to have the whole picture, not to know all the steps you need to take. In fact, it is a benefit not to know. Because the energy right now is shifting so fast, it's easier to be more flexible and go with the flow when you don't have a definite plan.

6. Trust
   Allow the universe to create without expectations, knowing you have been clear about your preferences. Trust that it will happen in the best way without your on-going supervision and interference.

Summary

This chapter presented six principles to be aware of when living in higher-consciousness vibration. It briefly summarized six helpful steps to use, as a framework. In the following chapters I will expand on these principles and steps and offer more tips and tools, providing examples of how to use them. Soon you will be experiencing the feelings of assurance and well-being consistent with living in higher-conscious awareness.

CHAPTER 13

Tips and Tools to Live in Higher Vibration

> **Try this:**
>
> Live in the present. The past is gone; the future is unknown - but the present is real, and your opportunities are now.
>
> ...... Maxwell Maltz, developer of Psychocybernetics

Now that you are aware of the principles about Higher Vibrational Living, I am going to share some practical ways to do just that. They are simple, and one of the most important first steps is just being aware. Check in. Are you doing it or not? If not, be grateful for that awareness and go back to developing neural pathway to create this new habit. You will be getting double value for your actions, because you will also be creating the habit of connecting and checking in.

Live In The Now

You can only experience higher consciousness by being aware in every now moment

As I mention in the last chapter this is a key principle of higher-conscious living. This practice offers a challenge for most people. We tend to focus on the past and the future. We worry whether we did the right thing. We worry about the future, and play "What if?" and we combine that by worrying about whether what we've already done will blow up in our faces in the future! That is why it's helpful for coaches to remind us to imagine and affirm that our desires are happening in the present, when visualizing and manifesting our preferred future,

Living in the now involves allowing thoughts and feelings to come up, be felt and reflected upon; then you can choose what you want to do with them. I remember hearing a speaker say that what was occurring in our lives had come to pass. In other words yes, it was happening, but the situation would end and pass out of our lives, it wasn't there forever. This reminded me of an idea I had when my son was going through the terrible twos. I had read in a childhood development book that a two year old would move out of their challenging behaviour in 4 – 6 months.

This seemed to be the pattern for development in general; a challenging stage followed by a peaceful stage. Well, on the days I was finding my responses to his behaviour hard to manage, I'd say "Gee, you've been in this stage for quite a while now. The books say it will end soon. When do you think it will be over?" At 2 ½ he said, "Soon, mommy."

Each stage he went through I'd do the same thing and as he reached 3 years and older he'd say "It's just about over Mommy," and sure enough, within a few days life was smooth again.

Another reason that the feelings and thoughts, and situations that evoke them, are coming to pass is that the purpose the energy coming into the planet with the Shift, is to help you let go of what is not really yours; in other words, all the beliefs and behaviours you learned from your parents, teachers, pastors, friends and their beliefs about you. This includes messages from the media, marketers, books and 3rd dimension lower vibration thoughts and feelings such as fear, jealousy, anger, envy, frustration, conditional love and conditional acceptance, all of which lead to stress, poor health and violence.

Even people who have been on their path and live in higher vibration energy most of the time are experiencing the release of what they are carrying that is not really theirs. We are sometimes hit with a feeling that throws us off balance. I have been more reactive to experiences lately and have to make a great effort to choose a higher perspective. The stronger than usual energy of the solar flares is contributing to this. But, by living in the now, really feeling what's coming up, accepting it and detaching from it, at least we can love and accept ourselves as we manage these experiences.

The belief that situations in our lives have come to pass has allowed me to maintain equanimity and get through some of the drama I have created. This concept reminds me that I can choose how to experience an event, learn from it, change my perception of the situation, and then let it go. I check in, and usually consciously choose not to resist the circumstances, because I know from experience that the situation may stick around until I grasp its meaning or relationship to my life.

Mindfulness

Another part of living in the now involves the practice of mindfulness. This Buddhist meditation practice, called Vipassana is the subject of many books, classes, and online resources you may wish to check out. Although I am really oversimplifying the practice, I find it most workable to think of being mindful as essentially living every moment in awareness. This is partly accomplished by using your senses to consciously and fully experience whatever you are doing. Here's an exercise to try that will allow you to experience mindfulness.

Take a grape or a cherry tomato. In order to experience eating it mindfully, begin by expressing gratitude to all the energy that brought this tasty tidbit to your table. These include the sun, rain, soil, water, planters, pruners, harvesters (whether human or machine), truck drivers, trucks, gasoline, people who built the trucks, manufactured the materials, shippers, other handlers, the produce sellers who displayed and culled the fruit, people who took your money as an energy exchange for all of the above, the water you washed the fruit in, and so much more (especially if you use a plate or napkin during your experience).

Now look at the grape or tomato as if it is something you have never seen before. Don't label it as a grape or tomato; just be aware of it in its essence. Be mindful of your reason for eating it – perhaps to nourish you, to take care of and nurture yourself, for enjoyment, and/or, so you can sustain your own energy for the work you will do. Now use all your senses to appreciate it. Feel its texture; smell the aroma; look at its colour, notice any markings. Try rubbing it next to your ear to see if there is any sound (perhaps a squeak like a balloon?). Play with it; try bouncing it and rolling it and do any other creative experiment stimulated by being in this higher vibration energy.

Thank it for its gift of life and nourishment. Then, as you bring it to your mouth, notice your body's response. Don't bite it yet! Is your mouth watering? ...Your stomach gurgling? Feel the texture on your lips, in your mouth. Does it taste stronger in one area of your mouth over another? If you inhale the way you would a fine wine in your mouth, what is the smell like? Now! Notice what happens when you first bite it. Does it pop out its pulp? Chew slowly. Is it refreshing? Can you smell its bouquet? What does it sound like inside your head when you chew? Does it taste sweet or sour? What happens in your mouth as you swallow it? Is there an aftertaste? How far can you feel it going down your throat and into your digestive system?

Next, check in with what's happening in the rest of your body. Connect with the cells, the bloodstream, and the organs. You also might notice some signs of being in higher vibration such as feeling expanded in your heart area.

I've found this mediation is really powerful to demonstrate how being mindful keeps you in the now moment. There is less chance to wander into the past or future.

Being connected to the energy in this way also ensures you are living in higher consciousness.

Now that you know how to be deeply mindful during meditations, you can simplify the process and use this concept in everyday living. Try being mindful when you do ordinary everyday tasks, such as showering or doing dishes. Use all your senses. Take all your activities, whether meaningful or mundane, and reframe their purpose in the context of accomplishing your life's purpose, providing service to yourself and family, engaging in an ecological earth-friendly action, or whatever comes forward during the mindfulness practice. Being aware of whether being mindful will move you into higher vibration energy, and practice for short periods of time to create a habit that keeps you in the now moment more often. You will eventually realize you are spending greater amounts of time there.

Connect with the ONE SOURCE ENERGY, Other People, All Our Relations and Your Higher Self

Connecting is quick and easy when you know how. It becomes an automatic process. Here are the steps to practice until it becomes as natural as brushing your teeth.

1. Be Aware

Being aware is one of the most powerful things you can do if you want to live in higher consciousness. If you are aware - you are awakened. When you are awakened you can't go back to sleep (choose to be unconscious again). Have you ever noticed how the word beware is actually be (a)ware? It's not really a warning! You might as well choose to go forward along your path, because you really can't go back. The flame within has been stoked.

When you are aware, you think about choosing actions that are for the greatest and highest good of all involved. When you consciously set that intention your actions will be guided when you check in. I am reminded of a young mother I saw who desperately wanted to create an environment for her daughter to grow in that honours and respects her daughter's gifts. She has some fear that she might unconsciously force her daughter into a mould because she wants to look like a good parent to those around her.

As we spoke, I believe she came to realize that even if she slipped into habitual behaviour, it would not be long before she would be nudged by her Higher Self and reminded of her higher intentions.

2. Check In Internally and Externally

As I mentioned before, this is a crucial habit to develop. Part of being aware involves the habit of 'checking in' to see what's happening physically, mentally, emotionally and spiritually, inside.

a. Take three deep breaths. This allows us to think more clearly, access the bodies natural chemicals which uplift our vibrational frequency.

b. Ask yourself, 'what is happening inside me at this moment.' You might notice physical changes first. Your heart might be pounding; your throat might be dry. Your pupils may be larger. Mentally you might find it hard to concentrate, your mind might be drawn to one thing. You might feel blissful as if all life is perfect.

c. Decide what is the emotion you might be experiencing? In this case, when you check in, and gather this information, you could realize you might be involved in a budding romance!

d. Check externally, noting who and what is around you, including Source Energy and All Our Relations. See if your surroundings help you to be in higher vibration energy. Most people find they experience higher vibration if they are in a place surrounded by nature, green trees, and running water. Re-creating nature indoors with plants and fountains or photos of natural scenes can help you shift into and sustain higher-conscious energy. This can also occur when you appreciate art, music or any other creative pursuits.

e. Continue with the rest of the process.

Try this:

Identify what internal and external triggers you are aware of that assist you to create and maintain higher vibration energy. Write them down and plan how to incorporate them into your daily schedule. Use these ideas to create a high vibration energy space at work or home.

---

3. Trust Your Intuition

Part of checking in spiritually (or metaphysically if you prefer), involves trusting yourself and your intuition. Clients often confide that they get clear guidance, but then don't trust that they could have the ability or gift to really get it. It is important to check in with yourself and be discerning, especially with external teachings. If you receive information that feels uncomfortable, ask yourself if it's pushing a button about an issue you need to learn to deal with, or whether this discomfort is coming from your Higher Self. If recognizing your intuition is not part of your routine practice at this time, I would suggest you begin by becoming aware of what parts of your body react when something positive enters your energy field, and when something lower vibration enters your energy field.

Trusting your intuition may be challenging if you are fearful about whether you are getting the guidance coming through clearly. People wonder if lower vibration energies are coming through, or if their ego is urging them into a certain action.

I advise my clients to notice the feelings the energy brings. If you are being put down or if the message doesn't feel loving, it is not an intuitive knowing. Even if the message is one you would prefer not to hear (such as the person you are dating is incompatible, break up with them), it shouldn't come with the feeling of "You are such a loser; you'll never learn".

Higher vibration energy is unconditionally loving and accepting, no matter what you do. I have found that one situation in which you need to be especially discerning is when you feel you have to do or say something right away. Sometimes urgent action is required, but I have found it useful to take a few moments to check in. More often than not, my ego is the one who feels that what I have to say is so important it must be spoken; that the group will be forever hindered if the wisdom I want to share doesn't get expressed and used. I have learned to wait, and if it needs to be said someone will speak. If after a minute or two I feel intuitively guided to share, I do. When I don't follow my own advice, I usually end up with egg on my face and what sounded so profound in my mind comes out in a way that I wish I could take back. I feel like carrying a sign that says, "That wasn't really me".

4. Connect
4a. Connect with All That Is

After I check in, I align with something that puts me in contact with the highest vibration consciousness possible.

I think of something I feel rapturous about and take a relationship to it. It seems to work best if it is a thing, as opposed to a person, as there is less chance of becoming enmeshed with a thing. It can be a scene or object in nature, a piece of art, a poem, whatever you conceive.

When I am connected with All That Is, I feel lighter. My heart feels open and bigger than the Grinch's at the end of the Dr. Seuss story. I have lots of energy and look forward to my day. My mind feels clear. I know what to do; I listen to my intuition. My life unfolds easily and effortlessly, and I have more than enough of everything I need. I am happy and want to interact with other people.

When we are connected to higher vibration energy, we move out of third dimensional duality. We live multi-dimensionally, and we can access information and energy from a wider range of frequencies -- from our higher selves, other people, from Divine Source Energy and from All That Is. All That Is includes everything on the earth, in the earth and in the cosmos. We can work with the All That Is, because Everything Is Energy. Many of these objects are called allies. They includes crystals, objects in nature, totems, fetishes and beings of the highest vibration such as angels, saints and ascended masters. I consider them allies because they agree to work collaboratively with me for the greatest good for all. I ask Divine Source to filter any aspects of myself and the allies that would limit our effectiveness.

I also work with helpers; sound vibration, aromatherapy, essential oils, flower essences and colors. They have specific vibrations, but *to me* don't have the sentience and flexibility that the allies do. There is more information in chapter 15 about allies and helpers including specific ones you can use to assist in shifting and maintaining higher consciousness.

i. *Ways to Access Information and Energy*

You can access information and energy in many ways. In meditation, for instance, you can ask a question and wait for a response from the small still voice of your Higher Self, or from Source Energy. It may come at a later time or in a form you don't expect, such as symbols. If you are attuned to nature and the symbology of animal totems, your answer may come when you see an animal that is not common to your everyday experience. You may see a feather, a flower or some other natural object in an unusual place.

You could see the answer on the back of a bus you're following or hear it on the radio or TV. At one time I regularly got answers to questions I thought of during the week at a weekly meditation group I attended. Sometimes the answers would come through during a meditation, but just as often, they came during the silent time following the meditation. I would open a book I felt drawn to and the answer would be on that exact page. It still excites me to see the wonderful ways I receive my answers.

You may receive the answer in a dream, either clearly or again, as a symbol. You can use Oracle cards, resource books or other objects that stimulate your intuition. However, the most important tip I can give you about using the external resources is that you first use your intuition about symbols you receive. For example, if you are selecting an oracle card, look at it and go with your immediate intuitive reaction. Then you may choose to look at the explanation, but if it does not resonate, go with your intuition. Always listen to and trust your intuition.

Another way to access information is by participating in guided visualizations, where you set your intention, breathe deeply and rhythmically, connect to energy of the highest vibration, let go of the outcome, allow the information to come to you and be open to receiving it.

4b. Connect with others

You can connect consciously with like-minded people by working in collaboration with others. In our patriarchal society, will and power have been valued and competition has been encouraged. As more and more people evolve into living in higher consciousness, values of harmony and cooperation are replacing the aforementioned energies. You probably know about the concept of synergy: how 1+1 does not equal 2, that a much greater, more creative outcome is produced. Connection and collaboration are important keys to quickly effecting greater changes during this critical time of enhanced evolution in those of us who choose to move forward into the next great age of higher consciousness.

It is so easy these days to connect and collaborate through the internet and social media. You can find people with a common passion. Living your passion and sharing it increases your vibration significantly. Just notice how a person, or even yourself, perks up when they are asked about an interest. They speak more quickly, sit forward in their seats, and often connect by touching you. You can see their radiance as they come alive and the energy flows through them.

Another fascinating way to connect is by intently listening to someone as if they are the most important person on the planet and what they have to say is of utmost interest and importance. Even people who feel inarticulate speak clearly and passionately when listened to in this way. I experience this personally in a group I play with exploring quantum awareness, multidimensionality, and superconsciousness and beyond.

A simple way to connect with a group of like-minded people is to stand in a circle holding hands and have each person receive the energy from the person on the right and pass it on to their left, along with their high vibration energy. The energy will be going clockwise in a circle. After a few rounds, stop and feel the energy in the centre of the circle and around you. You may feel drawn towards the centre if you created a vortex. You will likely feel lighter, perhaps spacey and your chakras may feel more expanded. You will probably have more energy, and be in a space of higher vibration.

Quickies

I have offered many tips and tools that you can play with in this chapter. I wanted to end with a couple of quick and easy ways to be in higher vibration.

- Frequently during the day take a relationship with whatever feels rapturous for you. This accesses high vibration cell memory. Then take three deep breaths, connect with Source Energy, relax and focus on the now moment. Check in with how you are feeling and gauge where you might be vibrationally, (use low, medium, high, - nothing complicated). Remember what being in high vibration feels like.

  Using this technique can remind you about being instantly in high vibration.

- Some fun alternative ways to play with energy include the following: Imagine you have a light inside in the area where your high vibration energy comes from. That light has a dimmer switch on it. Imagine you are turning the dimmer switch to increase the brightness of the light. The light represents your higher vibration energy. Feel yourself move into higher and higher vibration; keep turning the lights up higher, as far as you can. Now focus on maintaining that light. Be aware of how it feels in the different parts of your body. You can turn it up in any areas that aren't fully illuminated. You'll find you can increase your frequency in less than a minute, once you have tried it a few times.

- When you are able to maintain the energy in a quiet state, try getting up and walking around and keep the lights turned up. Practice this, increasing your exposure to people and activities a little at a time.

- A variation of this involves visualizing a mixing board, used by musicians to edit their music. It has a lot of sliders on the board, which allow you to combine different instruments and generate the sound vibration you want. Assign your thoughts, emotions, physical energy and spiritual energy to one slider each, then imagine you can combine the vibrational output to have the perfect highest vibration resonance you are capable of achieving in that moment.

When you have established new neural pathways by habitually practicing activities that result in higher vibration, they will be quickies you can use too. For instance:

- One way is to think about what you are grateful for upon waking up or driving to work in the morning.
- On a rainy day check in, breathe and connect with Mother Earth. Feel her gratitude for the water that sustains the plants, helps them grow and turn into sweet corn.
- On a sunny day, be grateful that to feel energetic and ready to get up and take action.
- Go through your day alert for anything that enchants or amuses you.
- Joyfully undertake your activities, eagerly anticipating the next wonderful occurrence.
- At bedtime, reflect on the rapturous moments, and express and feel gratitude for the events of the day, including the bliss of taking a deep breath and feeling your body sinking into, relaxing and being supported in your cosy bed.

Summary

You now understand that living in the present moment allows us to process whatever thoughts and feelings that come to pass that are not of our true self. We are not able to sustain higher vibration energy until this process is complete. You've had a yummy taste of being mindful; can connect with All That Is by using the tools of being aware, checking in, connecting, learning to trust your intuition and avoiding egoic egg on your face. You know some ways to access higher-conscious information. I shared several quick ways to connect with higher energy and ways to feel good in any situation.

In the following chapter, I will cover more tools for moving into and sustaining higher vibration, including a powerful one that many thought leaders and energy shifters personally use to begin their day.

CHAPTER 14

Manifesting:
The Basic Process

> You wouldn't call Sears every day to make sure your catalogue order was correct, check when it was coming or verifying they had your address recorded properly. Once your order to The Universe is placed, surrender your attachment to the process and trust that it will be delivered.
>
> ....Gina-Dianne Harding

One of the great benefits of living in higher-conscious energy is the ability to manifest what you want and need - physically, mentally, emotionally and spiritually. Yes, people can and do manifest when they are not in higher vibration. We create everything in our lives. Anyone who knows the technique or has a natural ability and belief can manifest material things, but often these people are not able to create happiness. When you are in high vibration frequencies, your desire is for the best for *all that is* including yourself. You understand the energy cycle of giving and receiving that is needed for manifesting. This chapter describes the manifesting process and several tools you can use to have fun while creating your heartfelt desires.

Order From The Universe

You can use higher vibration energy practices to attract anything you desire. Since I described ways to connect with like minded people in the last chapter, let's consider how to attract a collaborative business partner. You could also choose to manifest a life partner. Once you see how to do this you can use it to manifest whatever you desire. A fun way to do this is by using a tool called "placing an order to the universe". Approach this activity with light, playful wonder and be unattached to the outcome. When you have a light energy signature you become very magnetic, so try to sustain this manner all the time. Start by getting clear about what qualities, attributes and skills would be a good match with your skills. It's like ordering from the Sears catalogue, or shopping on the internet.

First, connect with the Universe by increasing your vibration, using any of the tools you prefer. (it's like going online). Next, figure out why you want a partner. This will help you to state a clear intention and visualize your daily life with your partner. Then determine your specifications. Write out what you don't want and what you do want. Don't be afraid of attracting what you don't want. A key to manifesting, which most people forget, is the intensity of your emotional attachment. In this process, you indicate what you don't want for a short period of time, and you are likely to be coming from a more objective, less feeling place.

It is also important to write what you want to feel when your partner appears, how they will feel working with you and how your clients will feel and respond. Remember to write this in the present tense as if it has already occurred. Then send the order off into Universal Energy (or cyberspace if you prefer). Feel just as you would if you had ordered from a catalogue. Be confident, and know and trust that it will be delivered at some point in the future. Surrender the process. Let go and let the Universal Laws do their thing. You wouldn't call Sears and say "I just wanted to make sure you got my order for a blue dress"; then the next day call and check up on how the order is coming, and then the next day call with the excuse, "I wanted to sure my credit card cleared", just to reassure yourself they are doing their job. Once the Order to the Universe is placed, surrender your attachment to the process and trust that it will be delivered as ordered.

Part of the process is being aware of and acknowledging your power to co-create, and the power of the Universal Laws governing manifesting. I usually make a statement when I am sending the order off. "I know the power of these words, thoughts and feelings and release them to the

Universal Laws, knowing they are manifesting in this now moment."
I then express gratitude that I have this knowledge and gratitude for
everything good in my life, finishing with "And So It Is".

Learn How to Manifest

Many people on their spiritual or metaphysical path were pleased when
'The Secret' and 'What the Bleep Do We Know!?' were released. Although
much of this information is well known to people who have studied
ancient wisdom and mystery schools teachings, they were a big first step in
getting information to the general public about energy, universal laws and
living in higher consciousness. Unfortunately, one concern expressed by
the metaphysicists was how 'The Secret' focused so much on manifesting
material things. In addition, the general public, who were excited by Law
of Attraction secrets, tried to manifest their desires and often had difficulty
- especially when trying to manifest bigger things. So people in the know
started sharing "The Secret Behind The Secret". One such secret is the
importance of emotion. Another, perhaps not as widely shared, was how
limiting beliefs block manifesting. So on one hand, the public may have
been ready for this information, because over the last decade or more it
has been more common to hear about athletes using visualization before
competing in an event. A runner, for example, will visualize running the
race, using all his or her senses to experience the event in great detail. This
is proven to improve overall performance. On the other hand, the interest
may have waned somewhat when people started to believe it didn't work.
You, however, now know about feeling and letting go of beliefs that no
longer serve you.

Visualizing
Visualizing is one part of the process of manifesting. *Research demonstrates
that doing something or visualizing doing it has the same effect on the brain.*
It creates neural pathways that instill physical, mental and emotional
behaviours. There is more detailed information about guided visualization
in the section on how to move out of lower vibration.

I provided an example of using the 'order form to the universe' tool for manifesting. I want to review the complete basic manifesting process I use and go over significant details I didn't mention above. I will use the example of manifesting a new job, as it is a bit more esoteric than manifesting material things (new car or house).

When I first began to practice manifesting, my teacher and I had a discussion about co-creating material stuff that was for pure enjoyment as opposed to something with a more "spiritual" use to benefit others. She pointed out that one way to know I had been successful was that something material was created.

The Manifesting Process
This is the process I have my students use to materialize their desires.

a. Connect: Acknowledge your connection with the Universal Energy (God, Spirit, Creator of All That Is, Higher Self - however you see this).

b. Gratitude: FEEL grateful for all good in your life, for others, for animals, nature, earth and more.

c. Intention: Be very clear. Write it down

Identify what characteristics you want generally. Don't limit yourself. For instance, if money were no object would you work? We want the universe to create the spirit and intention of our desires. Feel what it is you really want, but don't describe it in definite terms. This allows for creativity. The universe often sends something great - a perfect match that you never would've thought of. So avoid saying ``I want to be a _____`` or, ``I want to work at _____ as a _____``.

> ### *Timely Tip*
>
> **A** secret to consider when setting your intention is to explore what benefits you might be getting by not having your desire materialize in your life? What fears arise as you visualize having it? Gently and gradually release your resistant thoughts using MAffirmations, the alternative to affirmations tools in chapter 11. -- Pick an intention that feels better and matches a higher vibration. If you notice mind chatter (what you don't want to happen; what you don't want to feel), write it down as if you were Ordering from the Universe, with as little feeling and attachment as possible.

Sometimes people who have been on a spiritual path for a while, understand that things come to pass, are able to detach from drama and accept that 'Shifts Happen" in unanticipated ways. They will include in their manifestations the intention that, "whatever serves the greatest and highest good for myself and others". They also add that it "happens easily and effortlessly" and actually feel the feelings they want to have when their desire materializes.

> ### *Timely Tip:*
>
> There is one caveat; the intention for my greatest and highest good can mean the end of things or challenging situations so you can move on. There is a wonderful phrase to include in your manifesting process. That is: "this or something better". For instance, I put this at the point when I say, "I know there is power in these words and I release this now to the universal laws knowing "this or something better" is manifesting now. And so it is."
>
> ### *Try this:*
>
> Try trusting the universe with something simple a few times and see how it works for you.

d. Believe: It can and will happen. If your belief wavers, go through the process again, or use some of the other fun ways I mention below, to refocus for yourself. *Be aware that* you are not doing it to remind universe; it knows.

e. Desire: Choose it to happen. Feel what it's like to have it now. Envision having it.

Use all your senses. It is important not to get bogged down in visualizing the steps it takes to get to the end desire. That can actually hinder the process.

The most important part at this point is the feeling you generate as you see yourself living the lifestyle as if it was occurring in the Present Moment.

f. Release/ Surrender:

Know the power of your words. The universe listens or resonates to positive, specific Words. Release them to the Universal Law for manifesting now (there's no other time than the present).

g. Allow Allow a feeling of well being; time for delivery; Be patient and don't dwell on how and when it's going to happen. The best thing to do is to forget about it. If it comes into your thoughts, choose higher vibration thoughts. If you see someone with what you want --feel good for them. If health is your desire— remember the perfection of your etheric DNA blueprint.

If you don't feel trust and faith or when you lose your sense that your order is being filled in the ethers, it may be helpful to remind yourself that things take time. If you ordered a new job for instance, you need to be living in the energy that will resonate with the job you want. That means you have to find something about your current job that you enjoy and focus on the feeling that brings. Also the person in the job meant for you needs their life to be arranged. There are a series of events that need happen in the 3-D world. It may take time, so you get to practice being patient, and being open to receiving the good that you are attracting right now.

h. Receive: This can be a challenge for many people. The metaphysical bookstore where I work attracts many heart centred awakened souls who love to give. When I offer them a compliment or suggest they pick up a little something to nurture themselves, or if one of the staff feels guided to offer a free energy session of some sort, they refuse to accept it.

One of the crystals we recommend for our clients and customers is rose quartz, the stone of love. It is not only for opening your heart to give love to others and yourself; it also helps one to receive love.

There are lots of reasons we find it hard to receive. Limiting beliefs about our self worth and feeling obligated to do something in return are two of them. The old saying "it is better to give than to receive" is stuck in our cell memories, playing a loop over and over.

It helps to reframe any limiting beliefs by considering the cycle of energy. In order to be abundant we have to give and receive. You are not only blocking your own abundance by not receiving, but you are also blocking that of the person who would like to give to you. You are depriving them of the pleasure most people get from giving. I know people who don't like to be the centre of attention. I remember when a regular favourite customer at a coffee place was fairly certain the staff was going to acknowledge a special occasion. He had developed a great relationship with the young staff, and they always went out of their way to make sure he was comfortable. Because he didn't like to be embarrassed with extra attention he decided beforehand that he wouldn't go in for a couple of days. I pointed out how disappointed the staff would be because of the fun they would have had planning a little surprise to show how much they considered him to be almost like family and an important part of their work lives. Unfortunately he was unable to overcome his discomfort and allow the energy exchange and the benefit to those whose generosity and affection were stifled.

Did you know that you can give intangible gifts like energy healing back? If you lose faith, begin to question possibilities, and believe nay-sayers, you hinder the energy's integration. This is what occurred for a friend who received a healing from a few healers I knew. He noticed an immediate shift, had more energy, could breath more easily, his heartbeat was stronger, and he could negotiate stairs more easily. However, within a couple of days he had an accident, his heart, lungs and stamina deteriorated again and he required assistance again. His conscious and unconscious vibrations had not matched when he was 'healed', so he unconsciously created a situation that would allow him to 'return' the healing.

So be aware of the power of thoughts and feelings.

i. Gratitude: Express gratitude again to the Universe for providing for you (it is already beginning to organize it.)

Try this:

Incorporate the process for manifestation into all your Intention statements to create a higher vibration energy match.

Sample Powerful Intention Statements

Lets use the example of the intention "I want a new job", or "I want a career change". Here is a fill in the blanks example that may assist you in constructing your own manifestation.

I know I am one with the divine energy of the creator, and all of creation (living or inanimate, in form or in spirit.) I am grateful for all that is good, beautiful and (holy) whole in my life. I am grateful I have a job and I have income. I'm grateful I have a bed, a roof over my head, enough clothes, ample food, supportive friends, _____ (add other things you are grateful for).

Intention Statement

I work in a friendly, compassionate, supportive environment, close to home, at a salary of $ _____ or more. The manager is _____. My colleagues are _____ and the people I provide service to are happy, enjoy the service, and are unconditionally accepting and grateful.

I have time and energy to pursue my dreams. I live a balanced life - physically, mentally, emotionally and spiritually: full of joy, love, peace & _____ .

My health improves daily and manifests my body's etherically perfect DNA blueprint.

I deserve it and claim this or something better.

I am grateful that the universe is providing this and I know there is power in these words. I release them to Universal Energy, knowing they are manifesting as I speak (write). And so it is.

Tools That Increase Your Vibration

There are several fun activities that focus your energy and high vibration emotions on what you want to manifest. There are guided meditations that take you through the process simply and effectively. You can create a vision board or collage, write a story, create a picture or write a poem. These methods all encourage creativity and allow energy to flow.

a. Creating a Vision Board

When I wanted to manifest a relationship I used all of the above tools. I'll share how I made a collage, so you can try it out. I went through magazines, cutting out pictures of men involved in creative and fun activities like playing with a pet, walking along a beach and painting. I used pictures of myself and pasted my head on women I found in magazines who were doing things I liked to do. I cut out words and phrases that represented interests and attributes and personality traits. I used a foam board that had two sections, which unfolded exposing the middle. I put the men on one side and the woman on the other side. I decided to do this to show that we each came complete and fulfilled in our own lives, and would choose to be in a relationship to *add to* our lives, not to fill a need. I found pictures of couples working playing and loving together and created word art that described what I wanted in a relationship. I pasted pictures of the couples in the middle section. I really enjoyed the *process*, taking my time, consciously considering how it fit together and focusing on it as a now moment occurrence. When it was done, I spent time each day enjoying it, taking a scene and seeing myself and my partner in it, feeling the wonder and love. I wasn't focused on the where or when it would happen, I trusted in Divine Timing.

b. Writing a Story

I wasn't consciously trying to manifest a relationship when I started writing a romance story. I'd asked the universe what I could do to stop focusing on a past relationship. I wanted to take my attention off a broken relationship with a man I had been deeply connected to. I was really enjoying writing the story and developing the hero's character.

One morning a seemingly unrelated event occurred and I got some information that convinced me there was no hope that I would get back together with the fellow I loved and whose soul I still felt connected to. As I felt the wind knocked out of me, I turned to Divine Source and pleaded for help to let go of my connection with this man, so I could get on with my life. I felt guided to go about my business in a different order, and at the end of the day, during my last errand, got into a conversation with a man whom I agreed to have coffee with. We began seeing each other. It wasn't until a co-worker remarked that this man I was becoming friends with was a lot like the hero of my story that I realized I had manifested someone with the same job, dreams and even very similar looks and traits to that character. I had focused on my writing so deeply with such open high vibration that I had magnetized him, in form, in the 3rd dimension. I have no doubt that the energy I generated in making the vision board helped too.

c. Gratitude

One of the steps in the manifesting process is "Be grateful". Gratitude itself is also a tool which maintains higher consciousness. Gratitude has been identified by many human energy experts as the most powerful emotion for shifting people into their highest vibratory frequency, (even higher than love). Dr. Daniel Amen says an attitude of gratitude is one of the seven "programs" we need for the brain to work right.[147] I have heard it said that gratitude is the highest vibrating emotion in our 3D world, since our ability to love unconditionally is challenged. It is easier to get our conscious and unconscious energy to be a vibrational match when we align with the energy of gratitude. This powerful energy can be used for healing and balancing people, and it can be sent to any part of the earth to provide support and encouragement to its inhabitants, be they people, or All Our Relations.

d. Heart Coherence

There is a well-known organization, the Institute of HeartMath, which has studied many aspects of heart coherence, an important part of mental, emotional and physical health. There are several wonderful tools on their site to assist you in increasing your vibrational frequency. I strongly recommend visiting the HeartMath website, www.heartmath.org.

The Global Coherence Initiative's Global Care Room, a project of the Institute of HeartMath, at www.globalcarerooms.org is a virtual room where people can spend a few minutes focusing on a place or group of their choosing, and the global coherence focus area. You can see the location of all the other participants in the care room, because the room has a globe with little lights that show where the other people live. It really brings a sense of cooperation and solidarity that we can work with others around the world to make a difference in the world. "The Global Coherence Initiative is a science-based, co-creative project to unite people in heart-focused care and intention, to facilitate the shift in global consciousness from instability and discord to balance, cooperation and enduring peace".(http://www.glcoherence.org/about-us/about.html). This site also has solid research about earth changes such as earthquakes, natural disasters, and solar flares, and reports from monitoring sites across the world, which tell of significant pre-warning signals. Check it out at http://www.glcoherence.org.

Timely Tip:

Before I continue with more quick tools in the next chapter, here's a tip: Remember energy is a cycle. We need to give and receive. When we increase our vibration by conscious connection to our inner self and the external world, it radiates out and benefits not only our personal beingness, but raises the vibration of mass consciousness.

Anecdotally I know that many people gravitate towards people with higher frequencies and feel better just being in their presence without them having done anything.

This explains how you can affect the world around you by Just "Being" and allowing the energy to radiate from you.

Summary

This chapter brought you a very detailed description of the steps involved in being in higher consciousness while manifesting.

I shared some fun techniques to help clarify and focus your intentions, including placing your order with the Universe, which low-techies can think of as catalogue shopping, and high techies can relate to shopping in cyberspace. I emphasized the step of expressing gratitude in the manifesting process, because it is such a key step in sustaining higher vibration. Finally I recommended that you check out 'The Institute of Heartmath', which focuses on gratitude as a way to express love and get into higher consciousness, and the Global Coherence website, which provides a place for people to gather individually or at a designated time to focus on sending love and gratitude to the world.

CHAPTER 15

More Tips and Tools

> To destroy an undesirable rate of mental vibration, put into operation the Principle of Polarity and concentrate upon the opposite pole to that which you desire to suppress. Release the undesirable by changing its polarity
>
> .... The Kybalion
>
> Pick up the other end of the stick.
>
> .... Abraham, via Ester Hicks

This chapter describes in more detail how to increase your energy to a higher vibration and sustain it. It takes the steps listed in chapter 9 and offers one or more substantial techniques to put it into practice. Many are unique ideas I've discovered as I found ways to live in higher energy.

Have you ever read a book where the author says how successful they have been at overcoming a hurdle and then, here and there, the text is worded in a way that makes you wonder if they're still enmeshed? I'm finding that it's more difficult to avoid giving that impression than I expected. To be clear then, I do still have times when I experience lower vibration energy, feel overwhelmed or take on other people's stuff. I still seem to have issues I thought I'd let go of again and again. So do other savvy higher-conscious people I know. It's the way we handle it that is different. So, if my writing seems inconsistent, please keep these comments in the back of your mind.

Pick the Thought that Feels Better [148]

I find this idea fun and use it if I find myself occasionally wallowing in self-pity or fear. A straight-forward example is when you have a cold. You feel physically miserable, and you may think, "I hate this cold. I have so much to do and I just want to go to bed. My nose is plugged and I can hardly breathe or talk. Colds always last twice as long in me than anyone else I know, and they always seem to turn into bronchitis or even pneumonia." This is obviously lower vibration energy.

As soon as you recognize this, pick a thought that feels better, "It's been 4 years since I had a cold, I'm very fortunate, my immune system must be really strong. Maybe I've been burning the candle at both ends a bit lately. This is a good reminder to take better care of myself. I'll start right now by taking the day off, resting; drinking plenty of fluids and listening to my body tell me what it needs. I know I'll get back on my feet more quickly if I do that. Oh it will feel so good to let my body relax into that bed. Oooh yes that feels better – Ah". That is the other end of the stick, as Abraham calls it, the opposite or positive polarity. Abraham also offers another option if this isn't working; that you pick up an entirely different stick. In other words distract yourself with something that does raise your vibration. It might be petting your dog or cat, listening to your favourite music or other ideas you resonate with as you read this book.

Using the Language of Higher Consciousness

Another aspect to be aware of when living in higher consciousness is the power of your words. Listen to what you say in conversations. We are so accustomed to using words that have a lower vibration that they often slip out if we aren't really paying attention to our choice of words. There are common words that we don't even associate with lower vibration. For example if we are speaking about following our path we will often label ourselves as seekers. We seek enlightenment, peace, joy, love and more. Seeking implies never finding. It tells the universe that we lack knowledge, wisdom and whatever else we desire. The universal laws give us what we focus on, so we are presented with more and more opportunities to seek. If we reframe our perception and operate from the perspective that we are finding something, the universe aligns with that energy and our desires show up. As I first wrote this sentence I used the future tense - the universe will align and our desires will show up. The problem with using the future tense is we never, ever get to tomorrow, because when tomorrow arrives it is today. Speaking in future tense makes manifesting much more difficult. Another common word to think carefully about using is 'want'. Want implies lack. If I want a new car it means I don't have one right now. I lack a new car. Many words that begin with 'un', 'dis', and 'de' also imply lack.

I have a couple of colleagues who love playing with words, just as I do. It keeps me on my toes and makes me more aware of what I choose to say. You may want to cultivate word play with some of your like minded friends, or even ask people to remind you if they hear you speaking the language of lack.

It is important to be aware of how words affect our bodies. For years I have been trying to be grounded, a sense of being in my body. One day I happened to be sharing how difficult this was with my coach. She asked me what I felt inside when I used that word. I checked in and told her it felt like my heart was being squeezed, it was hard to breath and I had an image that my leg had a ball and chain around it. *No Wonder* I had challenges being grounded. We brainstormed and came up with the word embodied. When I use this word I can feel my etheric body, (which tended to be stuck outside my body half way up), move right into my feet and I become fully physically present.

The following are high vibration words to play with.

Timely Tip: Choose Higher Vibration Words, Feelings, Thoughts and Beliefs

Try picking one word a day and see how many times you can experience it, even if it's by watching someone else experiencing it. Add other high vibration energy inducing words to the list.

joy, fun, peace, innocently wise, compassion, care, patience, limitless, unconditional acceptance, open minded, recognizing there is no one right way, love, light, courage, generosity, abundance, nature, brilliance, potential, prosperity, sharing, giving, receiving, trust, allow, kindness, focus, clarity, attentive, listening, community, forgiving, self love, self respect, self acceptance, connection, universal energy, divine energy, superconsciousness, open, ascension, honouring, wisdom, our favourite activities, laughing, creativity, serving, supporting, contributing, reflection, Truth, responsive, responsible, life, soaring, affection , enough for everyone, trust, collaboration, depth, awakened, conscious, freedom, harmony, wholeness, One.

Another aspect of language is when you are consciously aware and focusing externally. Pay attention to what you choose to focus on. Be very discerning regarding your choices of how you receive news, the words of songs you listen to and what you allow into your inbox. This awareness can also be useful to help relieve overwhelm when you observe how changing this shifts your energy.

You can shift your energy quickly using language. Choose a quote, affirmation or mantra that inspires or acts as a symbol of higher vibration. Connect with your body. I feel my heart open up and expand to fill my chest, I breathe easier and I actually feel as if the sack of cares and woes I may carry if I'm unconscious lifts from my shoulders.

Creating your Preferred Day

I promised to share a tool many thought leaders use to establish and sustain higher consciousness. When you live in higher-conscious vibration you can create your day; the flow, the experiences, the outcomes, as you want them to be. I have heard many influential and highly productive men and women share this as a secret of their success. They begin each day using the power of words to write and focus on how they want to feel in each situation, project and opportunity.

This practice combines looking at your *inner* self -how you want to feel - and your *outer world* - as you go about your day. It aligns your conscious and unconscious vibrations so they match and the Universal Energy is triggered to produce your desires. This practice uses the process of intention setting described above.

Creating your preferred day is one of the *keys* to manifesting all the things you say that you want, using higher-conscious vibration.

- Begin by connecting with your Higher Self and Source Energy (think of and feel something rapturous),

- When you have a focused clear mind, set your intention.
  It is most beneficial to write this in a brief sentence or two, since the action of thinking and writing creates new neural pathways to establish and integrate higher vibration beliefs more quickly. As a result, old pathways with limiting beliefs are not used and disappear. Additionally, cell memory is created and enhanced when you concentrate and use your body and mind together.

- Look for signs that verify your intentions are being met. It could be going into a store having asked the universe to help find the perfect item and seeing it as soon as you enter; traffic that clears at the right time; pouring rain that stops just when you need to go outside; helpful people who efficiently take care of your needs - whatever is verifying your intention is being created. Start to notice all of the things that are working, feel great, and you will start activating that higher vibration more and more.

- It's a great idea to write a quick summary of these verifying signs during or at the end of the day. It helps you focus on what you are thinking, feeling and doing: what you want and what is super about your life. If you happen to skip a day, use it as an opportunity to compare how your day flows. You can refer to your notes on days when your belief is wavering or you are feeling challenged to sustain your vibrations. When you find yourself feeling less than great, don't beat up on yourself, just find the best thought, feeling, or action *in that moment*, hold the intention that you are working your way up the vibrational ladder, and be gentle with yourself!

There are further examples of how to raise your vibrational level using this process in the chapter dealing with journaling and affirmations.

Creating your Preferred Day intention examples:

- I want to express myself effortlessly, have all my conversations clearly understood and result in the best outcomes for everyone involved.
- Today I ask for and will act on clear guidance about how the posters for the workshop can be distributed.
- Somehow, Someway, Someday I will believe I can learn to manage overwhelm.
- Today I want to feel life unfold easily and effortlessly. I want to feel everything will work out when I talk to the bank manager.
- Today I want to attract people who I can best serve for all our greatest and highest good.
- Today I want to experience and appreciate each moment in its fullness – to stop and be aware of the beauty around me.
- Today I want to be in the flow and amp up my energy to the highest vibration consciousness.

- Today I want to believe I can feel renewed and refreshed after going to the mall to shop for Christmas presents.
- Today I need major help to 'amp' up my energies so I can deal respectfully and lovingly with my energy draining neighbours and achieve a win-win solution.
- Today I really want to _want to_ go to the dancing classes.
- Today I want to serve others in ways that feel good for me and for them.
- Today I want to expand time so I can accomplish what I need to do.
- This morning I really need help getting out of bed.
- Somehow, Someway, Someday I will believe I can appreciate my sensitive nature.

Helpers and Allies

In addition to using internal methods to increase our frequency and sustain higher consciousness, we can also use helpers – external material or immaterial high vibration energies, to assist us to entrain and sustain our own frequency. In other words, by aligning with the vibration of an external higher vibration element you can bring your own vibrations up higher.

If you were to poll energy workers about whether their preferred tools are helpers or allies, you would probably find different viewpoints. From my perspective the difference lies in whether or not they are sentient – if I can communicate with them to set an intention, if they can discern and co-create the focus of their energy for the greatest and highest outcome, then they are allies?.

I would likely categorize the next six as helpers, but I'm certainly open to changing my beliefs.

a. Sound and Colour
For example, sound waves can elicit emotions. One pianist learned how to make people cry by playing one note, just by putting a certain pressure on a piano key and holding it for a certain length of time. [149]

A lot of research has been done in this area. It has been determined that different areas of the brain can be affected by sound waves. Your brain can be entrained into an alpha state in which you are relaxed, meditating or reflecting; a beta state of alertness and active engagement in mental activities; a delta state where you are in a deep dreamless sleep; a theta state in which you daydream or perform any repetitive task and generate great ideas; or a gamma state, which is considered to be an optimal state in which your memory and self awareness are enhanced, you have higher levels of insight, you can absorb and process high level information more efficiently, you are more focused, experience more positive thoughts and feelings of compassion and have higher physical and mental energy levels. [150]

You can purchase CDs or Google "brain waves" and find music that stimulates the area you wish to entrain and enhance. I have two CDs that help me focus when I write. My concentration is better, I write for longer periods and I feel more in the flow.

The frequencies of colours also affect our vibrations. One of the ways they do this is by aligning with our chakras, helping to balance them. If you want to enhance your creativity, for instance, wear orange. Dress in yellow if you are working on issues of personal power. If you are deficient in your heart chakra, wearing green will strengthen it. There are colour essences designed to enhance the flow of the chakras. You may find yourself drawn to a certain colour much of the time. If you find out which chakra that colour is energetically matched or attuned to, you may unearth issues you wish to deal with.

b. Flower Essences

Flowers have special energetic or vibrational qualities. The energy pattern of every flower is unique, and it has its own special characteristics, which perform a specific action. Flower essences alter the subtle emotional, psychological and spiritual energy levels and filter down to the physical body. They were first intuitively developed in the mid 1930s by Dr. Edward Bach a British physician and homeopath.[151]

Flower essences each have a very specific vibration, which balances your energy system by addressing often subtle aspects of a challenge. You'll notice this in the example below. Some flower essences release negative moods and emotions. Others help us to recognize and let go of behaviour patterns that create negative feelings. Some affect the physical body by strengthening various organs or the immune system, or by preventing reactions to stress in the home or work environment. Many flower essences work in the spiritual realm, helping you know you are following the path that is right for you and helping you feel you have a real purpose and meaning to your life.

Essences enhance the connection between body and mind and your spirit. Depending on which essence you choose, your response may range from feeling a sense of contentment and wellbeing, to feeling joyful, having lots of energy or a clear, focused mind. Even during interaction with others, certain flower essences assist you to maintain a calm presence. You may feel safe and secure from fear, and you can be in the present moment.

There are excellent reference books on this subject such as the 'Flower Essence Repository', which lists essences from many reputable sources. If you are interested in pursuing flower essences to enhance the work you are doing as you read this book, I recommend working with an expert to achieve the greatest benefits. An expert will understand that there are many remedies for fear, for example, and assess the subtleties of your specific fears.

There are remedies for emotional blockages and letting go; non-attachment; general fears, specific fears and fears of the unknown. Bach's safe rescue remedy is useful in any traumatic situation, or to stabilize and calm a person or animal in a stressful situation.

There are some essences with fewer subtleties that will *shift your energy into higher vibration.* These include:

Inspiration: Iris (flower essence society FES)
Spiritual growth: Scotch broom (FES).
Inner harmony: California poppy, star tulip.
Perception: sage brush, Shasta daisy [152]

c. Essential Oils.
Essential oils are extracted from aromatic plants. Their properties are different from flower essences; their vibrational qualities are not identical although the

same type of flower may be used to create both. In other words, the effects of jasmine flower essence are not the same as those of jasmine essential oil. Usually the vibrations of flower essences are higher and primarily influence our thoughts and emotions, then their effects shift into the body. Essential oils tend to work on a physical level, although they can have some psychological benefits. For that reason, it can be useful to use essences and oils together to form a broader band of vibrational energy.

d. Oracle cards.

These helpers represent almost anything you resonate with. There are cards with messages from angels, ascended masters, saints, mermaids, fairies, power animals, spiritual teachers and authors. There are psychic oracles, wisdom of ancient cultures, indigenous cosmology and beliefs, affirmations and more featured in Oracle cards. You may ask a question or shuffle the cards and pick one that calls to you for a general message. Once you get clear, focus and set an intention, the messages from the cards are usually synchronous. All the cards come with instructions and many can be purchased from your local metaphysical stores. Even mainstream and online bookstores carry them.

Timely Tip

Any book you find interesting, inspirational, metaphysical, spiritual, or read for self-help can be used as an oracle. Simply think of a question and open the book. Let your eyes rest where ever feels right and you'll be amazed at the message you get.

For example if you want to know which angel or power animal to ask for help, select an appropriate book, connect with the energy and open the page. If you want guidance about a specific challenge, focus, stand in front of your bookshelf, see which book draws your attention, and open it. I still relish the delight I experience at the appropriateness of the response.

You'll sometimes hear people say the book with the information they need calls to them or falls of the shelf. My coworkers at the bookstore have literally seen this happen! WOO-WOO? SINCE YOU'RE STILL READING, I KNOW YOU HAVE AN OPEN MIND AND MAYBE EVEN GIVE ENERGY ITS DUE.

e. Mother Nature

Nature can be a Helper, and an Ally. To use it as a helper, bring nature inside. You may wish to have a fountain, so you can be around running water, which is a symbol of cleansing. It creates negative ions, which are a positive way to increase your vibration. Plants release oxygen and absorb carbon dioxide so breathing is easier. Sun produces natural heat and warmth, and gazing at a natural scene from your windows can be relaxing, stimulating, inspiring, uplifting and energizing.

Using the Energy of an Ally

Allies are somewhat like helpers, but to me they actually have personalities, are sentient and interact with us, supporting our intentions. Many indigenous cultures work with animal totems that represent the wisdom of the animal you are connected with. Shamans interact with animal allies and get messages and guidance for their work. Shamans (and Shamanic practitioners who have studied with Shamans), also connect and get messages from all energy including trees; the elements of wind, fire, earth and water; rocks and crystals. People who are waking up and realizing there is more to life sometimes do so because they are making these connections with all energy –All Our Relations as well. Whether you believe allies support us literally or symbolically with their energy, they still represent possibilities for ancient and future wisdom and current assistance with our life purposes.

a. Crystals

One of the areas of energy I am passionate about is using stones and crystals for healing and alchemical transformation. There are many books available which describe each stone's personal energy and many metaphysical properties. I have experienced their sentience in many ways, including being guided to use a specific stone in a circumstance when the usual properties do not apply and hearing about that rare application later.

Stones and crystals are used for physical, mental, emotional and spiritual healing, including balancing chakras, protection, attracting abundance, releasing specific low vibration feelings or attributes, enhancing high vibration energy, and connecting to All That Is.

"All solid matter is made up of atomic particles arranged in some definite crystalline structure. Certain crystals can act as resonators and transducers of electromagnetic energy. It is quite likely that we would be able to demonstrate that they can transform or amplify other forms of energy, if scientific equipment were sophisticated enough.[153]

The human body is made up of many crystal-like structures. It follows then, that we have an especially resonant connection with minerals and crystals. We can assimilate their energy and interact with it; therefore they can be very helpful allies to change our vibration.

Minerals in the earth vibrate with a specific frequency. Some minerals have a very specific energy and a narrow range of vibration. Others carry a much more extended range of energy. Crystals and stones carry the entire spectrum of light energy available to us. The lower frequency energies resonate with the physical realm and the high frequencies are associated with spirituality. They basically work by entrainment; your energy is brought into alignment or resonance with the stones. Robert Simmons, in his 'Book of Stones', explains two things that happen when we come in contact with stones and crystals. "First, the electromagnetic frequencies, carried by that stone will vibrate with related frequencies in our own energy field through the physical law of resonance, creating a third larger field of vibration."[154] This information is sent to the brain causing bio-chemical shifts in the physical, mental, emotional and spiritual systems. "Second, tiny particles of minerals in your body which also carry that frequency will move into resonance with the particles of minerals in the stone. This causes your body to believe that you actually have more of that material in your body, and it will react accordingly with additional biochemical shifts."[155]

Before you choose to work with crystals, it's important that you learn how to select the best crystal, how to cleanse and renew its energy. A list of helpful books is provided in the resources section at end of this book.

Anything physical, mental, emotional, and spiritual covered in this book has a crystal or stone which can enhance or diminish it. Here are some of the several stones that are helpful for shifting consciousness and awakening. [156, 157]

Energetic overload: Blizzard stone

Transform negativity: Euclase

Diminish fear: Blue Lace Agate, Andalusite, Aragonite, Danburite, Red Jade, Serpentine, Spirit Quartz, and many others.

There are a lot of stones that diminish or eliminate fear. Just as with Flower Essences, some are for specific fears and others are more general. Because stones are sentient, they will shift their energy to address the specific needs of the person using them. You have less need to consult with an expert if you use your intuition and communicate with the stone.

Here are some stones that are useful for the work that you're doing throughout this book. At some point you may wish to consult an expert resource to give you some tips and show you ways to select the most appropriate crystal for you. This is a complimentary service at many crystal shops. Be discerning about the person's abilities and use your own intuition if a stone attracts you that is not recognized for the characteristics you want. I am discouraged when a customer comes into the metaphysical store where I work and insists on getting the stones they identified by reading, on the net, or even from a well intentioned friend. It may be they need a certain frequency in that moment.

Energetic alignment; Barite.

Gratitude; Green Apatite, Hiddenite.

Personal evolution; Nirvana Quartz, or Moldavite.

Higher consciousness; Natrolite, Blue Tourmaline.

Raising vibration energies into resonance with higher worlds; combination of Natrolite, Danburite, Herderite, Phenacite, Azeztulite, Scolecite, Brookite, Satyaloka Quartz.

Building the optimal energy pattern for next stage of human evolution; the eight stones above plus Tanzanite, Moldavite and Tibetan Tektite.

Shifting perception; Smithsonite.

Spiritual activation; Selenite.

Raising vibrational level; Tektite

Awakening; Moldavite, Scolesite, Zoisite.[158] [159]

b. Power Animals

Another type of ally is used by many indigenous people and shamanic practitioners. They believe you can call on different animals to help you develop an attribute you wish to cultivate. Animals, birds, insects and water creatures have specific energies. So do trees, plants, feathers and other natural items. This is another specialized field of knowledge that is useful when you want to increase your vibration and move into higher consciousness.

If you are not familiar with power animals and nature symbols, but you feel the idea calling to you, I would recommend you consult the resource section at the end of the book. I really enjoy looking up the energetic attributes of animals and birds and insects that I see in dreams or in the wild. It's amazing the synchronicity that occurs between the creatures I see right when I have challenges they can help me with. If you live in an urban area, there are also different sets of Oracle cards which help you determine which power animal is best for you to work with to address a particular need.

c. Mother Nature as an Ally

Many indigenous people across the globe connect with the energy of natural objects. When they speak of "All My Relations", they may refer to the plant kingdom as "their cousins the standing people", stones as "the stone people", birds as "the winged ones", and animals as "the four leggeds". There is a website page which stirs my heart and soul and makes me tingle as I read it. I love this page about the standing people. If you are intrigued or resonate with connecting to nature, I strongly encourage you to read this online. http://www.manataka.org/page15.html.

Being in nature is an ideal way to enhance and sustain higher vibration energy. Spend as much time as you can connecting with nature, but if you need a quick lift, here is a technique you can do:

Stand outside, on the balcony, or even in front of an open window. Take three deep breaths of fresh air and connect with a tree, bush, flower, bird, rock, or any other natural item that draws your attention. Touch it if you can. Feel your oneness. Say good morning; listen for a reply. It could be as simple as a warm feeling that comes. Some people can actually communicate and get messages from a natural item. Open and allow your imagination free reign. As you receive its acknowledgment, tell it you love and respect or honour it. Thank it for being. This just takes a couple of minutes and relaxes and energizes you. Also connect with your houseplants. Ask a stone if you can take it with you. If it agrees, enjoy it for a day or two, then return it back outside. It might be quite an adventure for the rock - that's one way they can travel.

I want to wrap up this section of the book by offering a few more tools that will help you increase and sustain higher vibration emotions so you can live in peak consciousness. You could say I saved the best for last, certainly some are the most bizarre and fun.

Easy Tools to Increase and Sustain Your Vibration.

As I mentioned, When I teach stress reduction classes, my students have lots of fun with the following exercise. We brainstorm and identify activities you can do in 1 minute, 5 minutes, 15 minutes, 30 minutes, half a day, and more. I take their creative ideas and add them to ones from other classes and make flash cards. I suggest that they cut them out and pick one when they want to focus on enhancing their high vibrational energy.

- Borrow your nieces, nephews, grandchildren, or offer to babysit so that you can watch children play. This is usually a very quick way to help you sustain higher vibration energy.
- Dance or do some other movement.
- Connect with a pet by holding or playing with it.

- Choose to use all your senses for the next activity you're planning to do.
- Find humour in your challenges. My body has ears that sometimes don't hear what's being said accurately *(notice how I worded that without owning it as a problem. I chose that instead of "I have trouble hearing" which, by virtue of Universal Laws, is a self fulfilling prophesy)*. I actually perceive that it's kind of funny and like to think that the angels are helping me look at life as a comedy, which naturally shifts me into a higher vibratory state.
- Remember and re-live some happy memories using all your senses (even though it does mean being in the past).
- Be childlike. See through the eyes of a child as if you had never seen something before. Abandon decorum and throw yourself into the snow and make a snow angel. Run through a sprinkler on a hot day with your suit on. Jump in a puddle.
- Ask for help, and receive it. It feels so freeing and elevates your frequency when you actually do this without reservation.
- Make it your goal to find something to enjoy in every situation. For example, I prefer many activities to housework. But by committing to find something enjoyable in every situation in order to maintain higher vibration energy, I challenge myself to find something new every time I do a chore. I have really found pleasure in seeing a clean toilet, enjoyed using my sense of smell with the cleaning products I use. When the effect of the good smell no longer did it for me I imagined myself as Cinderella, cleaning just after I'd met Prince Charming (knowing of course that he would find me and hire someone to clean for me).

Here's another rather bizarre way I played with while cleaning the toilet. Now, as you know, I connect with plants and animals, so it wasn't that much of a stretch to play with the idea of connecting with the energy or the spirit of my toilet. I told it I was grateful it was an indoor toilet and that it flushed. I thanked it for working so well and staying leak free. Well, that was kind of unusual and funny, and my frequency rose even more when I thought about how my family and acquaintances would respond if I told them this was my new mindfulness practice. So, let go of your dignity. I have found being playful can lead to higher vibration, which leads to living more consistently in higher consciousness.

Summary

This chapter has provided more tips and tools for moving into and sustaining higher vibration. Section Three has lots of ideas you can select from. Remember to Focus on everything good in your life and be grateful. Focus on what you want; make healthy choices in your thoughts, emotions and beliefs. Practice healthy living, including healthy food and exercise. Remember moderation, but live passionately and fulfill your longing to make a difference.

Raise your vibration and live in higher consciousness by doing whatever pleases you; meditate, walk, read or hike; Watch movies, listen to music, attend workshops, connect with other like-minded people, nature and All That Is; Consciously choose to follow your Guided Path Sensors© (GPS); Allow yourself to be excited and enthusiastic; Be curious; Really *feel* higher frequency emotions like joy, peace, fulfillment, serenity; Laugh, Dance, Move, Hug, Sing, Yodel! These will all help change your neural pathways and sustain your higher vibration habits and beliefs.

It has been my desire in Section Three to provide you with a plethora of exceptional tips and tools to choose from. I know you now have the knowledge and skills to avoid being overwhelmed by the abundance of choices available to assist you. In this book you have a cornucopia of effective resources to dive into anytime you feel stuck, limited, and fearful, or are caught in other low vibration beliefs, thoughts and feelings. Moreover, you have a buffet of delightful possibilities, which you can nibble on whenever you want a bit of vibrational sustenance to sustain and intensify your higher consciousness.

Chapter 16

Hope for the Future.

> When you become peace inside,
> You will find only peace outside
> Gina-Dianne Harding

In this book I have offered you an opportunity to live a more fulfilled life. You now have a greater ability to manage your emotions and live in higher vibration. When you choose to incorporate these tips, tools and techniques and live in higher vibration, you will have a healthier life and better relationships; you will enjoy the work you do and realize the abundance all around you.

When you live in higher vibration, your energy is elevated and supports a higher collective human consciousness. You will recognize that you have a greater purpose in life. Just setting an intention and saying *yes* to higher-conscious living is contributing to the evolution of the whole. This book is not only meant to give you tools to live a happier, healthier, more fulfilled and abundant life in higher vibration consciousness, it is intended to be a call to action.

One of the key messages in this book is to connect and be aware of what's happening internally and externally. When I am playing in higher-conscious energies, I listen to music that stimulates gamma waves to open me to the highest creative connection centres in my brain. One morning, after I listened to an inspirational online energy shift program by Adela Rubio[160], I turned on the music and set my intention to let what wanted to be said to complete this book come through. I relaxed my body with three deep breaths and consciously connected with All That IS (universal divine energy) and All My Relations (every energy in physical or non-physical form). I expressed gratitude, focused internally and externally, and observed:

First, I hear the traffic helicopter sweep across the sky. Whup, whup, whup, it announces itself. Awareness comes to me, an explanation that the helicopter symbolizes a vigilant eye in the sky.

Next I expand to a cosmic view, looking through my collective super-conscious eye near the edge of the galaxy, relishing the evolutionary indicators radiating from that 3rd planet from the sun, almost 2,012,000 light years away.

Now I zoom to an observation deck at the core of the Milky Way galaxy, anti-gravity stabilizers set. Focusing on the earth, I observe the Truth: what is happening, stripped of the illusion of the 3rd dimension...

Hives of activity -- collaboration at its finest. Communication weaves throughout a matrix, a world wide web, attracting eager people passionate about designing, and co-creating their harmonious world. They're envisioning it into being and energizing its attributes...

Like-minded resonance with similar goals and flexible means of achieving it. No right and wrong in this new space. The how-tos' unfold easily and effortlessly, at the perfect time.

New words revealing themselves; they are non-dualistic, expressions of acceptance.

People conceiving the inconceivable, emerging, birthing unimaginable possibilities. Yet, the unimaginable is being imagined. Initiatives are underway. People are gathering in unlikely groupings, not groping blindly but being guided by visionary people, just ordinary citizens who want to make a difference. One change at a time. One person at a time.

I am aware of the message. "That is how it will happen."

I experience a bit of frustration. *"No rhetoric please,"* my mind screams. I'm aware that my throat is tight and my breath is shallow when I notice my mind-body-spirit connection. "Enough with the rhetoric" "How will it happen?" "Patience, keep going," I encourage myself.

Three crows sit in the tree across the road. I know from power-animal studies that they are messengers from the void, the nothingness where creation occurs. Three, the number of trinity. Father, mother, child. Positive, negative, neutral.

What have you been writing the book about? they ask. "How will it happen? It's simple really; check in, connect.*

What's the process? People just need to follow that. ...

Remind them: Intention. Know there is no lack. There is abundance. There is more than enough. Trust that. It's not a pipe dream. Believe. It is so"

Another crow flies from right to left, signifying movement from creative to logical, etheric to material. *First it happens in the etheric dimension then in the 3rd; the awareness comes.*

The crows in the tree are joined by a 4th, a 5th, and then there are 4, then 3, then 1, and none. They are now swooping and dancing in the early morning. What messages are they giving? I ask. *"Everything is always changing. They represent the new humans. They are engaging in order to collaborate, then departing to dance; there is activity, then rest; there is consultation and observation; checking in with the self and then with the group.*

Two birds are in the tree again. *Watchers, observers; apart and together.*

They demonstrate non-verbal communication, discernment, connection, relationship, longing, passion, heart-sharing, respect, and love. I continue to look at the tree. Are there two crows or one crow? I hear, *"twoness and oneness, united. There is no separation.*

Now, the words and the tune of a song enter my mind. I hear reminders that we are all the same despite our apparent different appearances Truth Bumps rise on my skin. More explanations come about the crows and how their actions represent the new humanity. *"They come together to create... They stay together, congregating to support like-minded beings. To experience a sense of belonging. Coming and going; going and coming."*

I see multidimensional bubbles rising as I look towards the trees. They represent the higher vibrations of peace, rest and being. I become aware of the sound of bubbles in the background music; percolating. I follow my thoughts to see where they take me. Bubbling up from the ground, reminding me of crude oil, black gold in abundance; reminding me of a bubbling caldron, of alchemy. Of being, of meditation for the morning, meditation for the mourning, mediation for the collective--- fanfare for the common man, soul stirring........

As I have been reflecting and asking for guidance for this last chapter, I noticed the music for 'Fanfare for the Common Man' by Aaron Copeland has been playing in my mind. Not only that, it appeared three times synchronistically for me lately. Once in the above meditation, then I heard it played two days ago at the beginning of the recent 25th annual World Congress on Illumination[161], and it appeared on You Tube when I went to research another project.[162] This music was one of my favourites when I played French horn in my high school band. And it has always stirred my soul when I hear it through the years. So, what is the significance of these happenings? Why now?

We, the common man and woman, are making a change. Individuals are awakening and projecting their high vibration memes into the collective, *truly* conscious mind. The change is occurring from the ground up. We are the leaders, the movers and the shakers in our own way: quiet and subtle, or noisy and overt. We are all activists.

There is an ancient Chinese saying: 'may you live in interesting times'. Some perceive it as a curse. Others say it is an opportunity. It reflects my knowing that we will thrive as we transition into the next age because of the opportunities around us. In this book, you have learned some tools that you can use to reframe how you look at your personal crises. You see them as situations that have come to pass to allow you to release lower vibration energy and evolve into a happier human being.

Some people believe our personal lives are a reflection of what is going on in the greater society. I look at this in a hopeful way. I believe we have enough people in the world who want a positive change, people who are choosing conscious awareness. There is a critical mass of people who are making The Shift into the upcoming age with grace and determination. When I look at the world from a higher-conscious perspective, I see many examples of people - and organizations - who want to make a difference and craft a better world. We have the creativity and knowledge to do this. When we undertake change from a higher frequency, ideas and actions flow easily and effortlessly. At this moment, I see systems and organizations operating independently to make positive changes. I envision smokestacks rising from each individual organization, with life-enhancing, evolutionary gifts wrapped in ribbons popping out of every smokestack. These organizations are not consciously cooperating in any way. People like you are standing below, catching the presents, opening them, comparing them creatively to see how they could be used together, combined to design something even more magnificent.

In this vision I also see the Internet and World Wide Web as a light matrix woven around the world, easily accessible by many people. I see that as it expands, many more keen minds can share ideas and inventions and can alchemically transform standard tried-and-true solutions to meet the needs of the now moment.

I envision common people, co-creating with our higher selves, and sharing ideas with other like-minded people through the Internet, where they have access to social sites with billions of members. This can be the key to our rapid evolution. By connecting successful, sustainable initiatives from every field, informally, it is possible to create a now solution. Connecting positive higher- conscious ideas, and energy will result in evolution into the next phase of humanity. The Shift is happening now and the process will continue well into next age. Conscious choices made by creative people working together cooperatively and non-judgmentally will establish a greater outcome than they would alone. When we integrate the separate gifts produced by individual organizations and apply our social, scientific and spiritual skills, we generate the limitless potential to move us through 2012, and into the next evolutionary cycle.

Remember, by just *'Being'* in higher vibration you are making a difference. But if you are inspired to participate in a more active way, there are opportunities for that as well. Many initiatives have been established with 2012 as their symbolic goal for change, including: Humanities Team[163] and 4 Years. Go.[164]

There are also some post-2012 initiatives. One that has captured my imagination is Birth 2012. Barbara Marx Hubbard, Stephen Dinan of The Shift Network and Devaa Haley Mitchell are drawing together a network of global citizens to assist with co-creating "a global celebration on December 22, 2012. Barbara has set this day as a 'due date' -- a vital evolutionary signal -- for all of us to wake up, synergize among ourselves, celebrate what is working and ignite a new way of being". [165]

They are connecting and communicating with other groups who are planning initiatives and hope to perhaps coordinate activities as well. "Many other respected thought leaders -- Jack Canfield, Neale Donald Walsch, Lynne Twist, Ken Wilbur and others -- have joined Barbara in this powerful vision, and more than 36,000 people so far have accessed our Birth 2012 Activation Calls."[166]

This initiative will no doubt feature many new ways of being in wisdom, intuition and other key skills, including how to live in high vibration consciousness.

I believe we are entering the "Age of Intuition™" where developing our capacity to receive energy thought-forms will be fully accepted, common place and more highly refined. ... Intuitive information enters our body-mind-heart unfiltered, unbiased, and undistorted. An entire answer-image drops in all at once, sometimes when we least expect it. ...Your presence – your charismatic illumination – grows along with your Intuitive Intelligence and informs the quality of energy you bring to and exchange with the world

International Academy of Intuitive Entrepreneurs http://iaie-connect.com/tricks-trade-e-newsletter/are -you-ready-age-of-ntuition/

In keeping with the advice from the crows that I end this book by reminding you of the process I have promoted in *From Fear to Eternity*, and in following the urging and desires of my heart, I express Gratitude: to the Maya wisdom teachers and other indigenous teachers, to ancient wisdom and current science, guidance that led me to information about the nature and practice of energetic co-creating, and for being introduced to 'woo woo'. I am grateful for everything that has occurred in my life; for my son, my parents, my marriage and relationships, my friends and colleagues.

I once said "I want to experience everything", and I was manifesting that -- until I realized that I need to be careful what I ask for! I changed my order to the universe to "I want to experience everything good, (w)holy and beautiful; easily and effortlessly". I make that choice whenever I need a vibrational energy shift. I am grateful for all my experiences because they have brought me to this point of deep-down joy, and the choice and ability to live in higher-conscious vibration, knowing that all is right in my world, no matter what is happening in the 3D illusion.

I Am connected to All That Is, and I see:

> *The Truth and perfection of our present moment.*

> > *That is All There Is.*

Along my path I learned an alternative to wishing someone good luck. And so I leave you with that blessing:

Go To Your Destiny

And, as you enjoy *your* journey from fear to eternity, may you relax and thrive in your higher-conscious vibration

So Be it. It is So. It is Done.

About the Author

Gina-Dianne Harding, B.Sc. Nursing, and Master Public Health was a successful public health nurse and administrator when she was hospitalized, during a period of extreme fear, anxiety and deep depression. During her recovery from overwhelming emotions and limiting beliefs, she developed several energy mastery techniques, which helped her reconnect with life and experience its limitless possibilities. She first experienced the bliss of connecting with the eternal energy of life during a tropical storm at an ancient Mayan ruin. She now regularly connects with this heart and soul expanding energy.

Gina-Dianne is an experienced adult educator, and combines her life-affirming techniques with a synergy of innate ancient wisdom and current science. She explains why everything in the universe has its signature energetic vibration and how to shift from lower vibrations and unconscious existence to vibrant, higher-conscious living. These are crucial skills, in our current fear based, unsustainable society.

She provides individual coaching and online classes designed to help you implement life-enhancing skills and increase your energetic frequency.

Learn more at

http://www.gina-dianneharding.com

Gina-Dianne loves living on the west coast in Vancouver Canada with her talkative Siamese cat, Sugar.

Depression Assessment Questionnaire

The Depression Assessment Questionnaire is used with the permission of The Well Being Project in Brisbane Australia.

Depression is defined clinically as a mood disorder. It's about feeling bad, most of the time, for over two weeks. It is a constellation of symptoms that affect different aspects of our lives. The following is a list of these. These criteria are based on those used by medical doctors and psychiatrists, from a diagnostic manual called the DSM IV (Criteria for Major Depressive Episode).

- Feeling sad or empty (or irritable), most of the day, nearly every day

- Loss of usual or former interest in, or pleasure and enjoyment in things, most of the day, nearly every day

If you find either or both of these first two apply to you, then continue to look at the next list of criteria. If neither of the above two criteria apply to you, then you are unlikely to be clinically depressed.

- Loss of appetite, or overeating
- Loss of weight, or weight gain
- Being agitated, or the opposite – being markedly slower in doing things
- Tiredness and lack of energy
- Having interrupted sleep patterns, insomnia, or over-sleeping
- Loss of concentration, poor memory, or inability to make decisions about things

- Loss of self-esteem and feelings of self-worth
- Inappropriate guilt
- Avoiding social contact
- Suicidal thinking

If you think you are depressed, having perused this symptom list, it is important to go to your Doctor for a formal diagnosis. **Your Doctor will determine whether there is some other medical condition to be investigated, and whether you need to consider anti-depressant medication**[or other treatment]**, and advise you accordingly.**

A more comprehensive self assessment is available at http://thewellbeingproject.com.au/amidepressed.htm

Appendix 2

More Limiting Belief Examples

I could never do that

I'm not thin enough, (pretty enough, tall enough)

If you want it done right you have to do it yourself

Nobody can do it but me

If you have time you have no money; if you have money you have no time to enjoy it

As soon as I put on white clothes they get a big spot

My parents wrecked my life

Nobody could stand being in a relationship with me I'm too sensitive,

If I go to the mall I'll be exhausted for days

Whenever I do (call, see) _____ I feel so exhausted

If I go out in the morning I'm such a psychic sponge I don't have the energy to _____

I can't watch movies I cry and then get a headache

Daydreaming is a waste of time

You have to hit rock bottom before you will change

Communication is muddled up when mercury goes retrograde

Never sign a contract in mercury retrograde

My was is the only way

This is the right way

Why would anyone want to read what I wrote when there are so many other books about it?

I'm alone

I'm separate from everyone else

The rich get richer, the poor get poorer

That only happens to ____

Everybody in my family is a smoker, (alcoholic, gets pregnant when they are 16 etc.)

Nobody in our family ever ____ ...graduated from school

What will the neighbours, friends, or parents say or think

People won't like me they'll think I'm a snob

Real friends keep secrets

I'll make them nervous if I sound too smart

I have to ____ to fit in

Men don't make passes at girls with glasses

I'm not good enough

It's up to me to make everyone happy, like their job

I'm a loser, I'm flawed I'm faulty

I am useless unless I'm doing something

I'll always be abandoned by men; my partner will always leave me

Life is a struggle

I'm a drain on society

I'd be better off dead (please get help if this is your thought)

Everyone in our family dies young

I'm a lousy cook

I can't stop ____

I'm so clumsy

I'm a Gemini – we all have lung problems

Men can't commit

Men can't talk about their feelings

I can only rest when I'm sick

End Notes

Preface

1. Dan Sewell Ward, "Age of Pisces." *The Library of Halexandriah.* 2003. Web. 22 July 2011. <http://www.halexandria.org/ dward207.htm>.

2. Mark Heley, *101 Things You Should Know about 2012:.* Avon, MA: Adams Media, 2011. Print. P.17

Introduction

3. Jim Self, "FAQs | Mastering Alchemy." *Mastering Alchemy | Energy Tools for Personal and Spiritual Growth | Mastering Alchemy.* Web. 22 July 2011. <http://www.masteringalchemy.com/faq>.

4. Ken Keyes Jr. "The 100th (Hundredth) Monkey - Story about Social Change (wowzone.com) WOW Poetry, Lyrics, Music, Stories, classics Wish Only Well." *Wish Only Well - Wowzone.com.* Web. 22 July 2011. <http://www.wowzone.com/monkey.htm>.

5. Value Based Management.net. "Innovation Adoption Curve of Rogers - Innovators, Early Adopters, Early Majority, Late Majority, Laggards - Innovations Diffusion Change Model." *Management Methods | Management Models | Management Theories.* Web. 22 July 2011. <http://www.valuebasedmanagement.net/methods_ rogers_innovation_adoption_curve.html>.

6. "Diffusion (business)." *Wikipedia, the Free Encyclopedia.* 6 Dec. 2010. Web. 22 July 2011. <http://en.wikipedia.org/wiki/ Diffusion_(business)>.

Chapter 1

7. Jerry Snider, and Richard Daab, "The Advocacy of Marcel Vogel." *Asunam - Reiki Master / Reiki Foundation*. Magical Blend Magazine. Web. 22 July 2011. <http://www.asunam.com/MarcelVogel03.html>.

8. Rich Young, "Can Plants Feel Pain?" *BIOSCI/Bionet Newsgroups*. 8 Dec. 1994. Web. 22 July 2011. <http://www.bio.net/bionet/mm/plantbio/1994-December/004565.html>.

9. Richard Gerber, *Vibrational Medicine: the #1 Handbook of Subtle-energy Therapies*. Rochester, VT: Bear &, 2001. Print. Pp 39,40

10. James Higgo, "A Lazy Layman's Guide to Quantum Theory." 1999. Web. 22 July 2011. <http://www.higgo.com/quantum/laymans.htm>. Although much of this article is tongue in cheek this quote is accurate

11. Lynne McTaggart, *The Intention Experiment: Using Your Thoughts to Change Your Life and the World*. New York: Free, 2007. Print. p.11

12. James Higgo

13. Unknown, "What Is Quantum Physics." *MSU Physics and Astronomy Department*. Web. 22 July 2011. <http://www.pa.msu.edu/courses/2000spring/phy232/lectures/quantum/quantum_def.html>.

14. "Woo Woo - Wiktionary." *Wiktionary, the Free Dictionary*. 13 July 2011. Web. 23 July 2011. <http://en.wiktionary.org/wiki/woo_woo>.

15. "Ascended Master." *Wikipedia, the Free Encyclopedia*. 13 July 2011. Web. 23 July 2011. <http://en.wikipedia.org/wiki/Ascended_master>.

16. Richard Gerber, *A Practical Guide to Vibrational Medicine*. New York: HarperCollins World, 2002. Print. P.32

17. "Inspiration from My Mentors, -Bruce Lipton the Biology of Belief." Interview by Lisa Garr The Aware Show. The Aware Show. Web. 27 Apr. 2011. <http://www.theawareshow.com/inspire/lipton/>.

18. "Moral Development-Stages of Moral Development." Developmental Studies Center. Oakland, CA. Web. <http://psychology.jrank.org/pages/431/Moral-Development.html#ixzz1Sx99t3Bw>.

19. The Aware Show 27 Apr.2011

20. David R. Hawkins, *Transcending the Levels Of Consciousness.* Sedona AZ: Veritas Publishing, 2006. Print pp. ix,x,

21. *Transcending the Levels Of Consciousness.* pp.28, 29

22. ibid.

23. ibid.

24. Andrew Zimmerman Jones, "Observations About Observers." *About.com Guide.* 12 Jan. 2011. Web. <http://physics.about.com/b/2011/01/12/observations-about-observers.htm>.

25. "What Is Quantum Physics." *Think Quest.* Oracle Education Foundation. Web. 23 July 2011. <http://library.thinkquest.org/3487/qp.html>.

26. *The Intention Experiment: Using Your Thoughts to Change Your Life and the World.* p.8.

27. "Meditation Experiment Arrests Crime." *A Transcendental Meditation (TM) Portal for Teachings of Maharishi Mahesh Yogi.* Web. 23 July 2011. <http://www.alltm.org/pages/crime-arrested.html>.

28. ibid.

29. John S. Hagelin Et Al. "Policy "Effects of Group Practice of the Transcendental Meditation Program on Preventing Violent Crime in Washington, DC: Results of the National Demonstration Project, June-July 1993"." *Institute of Science, Technology and Public Policy at Maharishi University of Management: John Hagelin, Director.* Web. 23 July 2011. <http://www.istpp.org/crime_prevention/>.

30. Lynn McTaggart. "THE INTENTION EXPERIMENT The Roy Water Experiment: April 26, 2008." *The Intention Experiment.*

Web. 23 July 2011. <www.theintentionexperiment.com/wp.../01/ the-roy-water-experiment.pdf>.

31. Darren R. Weissman, "Chapter 7." *The Power of Infinite Love & Gratitude: an Evolutionary Journey to Awakening Your Spirit.* Carlsbad, CA: Hay House, 2007. Print.

32. Jeanie Lerche Davis WebMD Feature Reviewed by Michael W. Smith, MD. "Can Prayer Heal?" *WebMD - Better Information. Better Health.* Web. 23 July 2011. <http://www.webmd.com/ balance/features/can-prayer-heal>.

33. Randy Peyser. "Peace in the New Millenium - An Interview of James Twyman by Randy Peyser." *Randy Peyser, Expert Book Editor, Writer, Home Page.* Web. 23 July 2011. <http://www. randypeyser.com/twyman.htm>.

34. Lynda Freeman. "Chapter 17." *MOSBYS COMPLIMENTARY AND ALTERNATIVE MEDICINE: A RESEARCH BASED APPROACH.* Mosby, 2004. pp.521, 531-547. Print.

35. Scott H. Young. "Energy Management « Scott H Young." *Scott H Young.* 14 July 2006. Web. 26 July 2011. <http://www. scotthyoung.com/blog/2006/07/14/energy-management>.

36. Darren R. Weissman, "Chapter 7." *The Power of Infinite Love & Gratitude: an Evolutionary Journey to Awakening Your Spirit.* Carlsbad, CA: Hay House, 2007. pp.42-43. Print.

Chapter 2

37. "The 100th (Hundredth) Monkey - Story about Social Change (wowzone.com) WOW Poetry, Lyrics, Music, Stories, classics Wish Only Well."

38. Dr. David Hawkins, "Power Vs. Force: Exploring Levels of Human Consciousness." I Can Do It Conference. Sands Expo, Los Vegas. 28 June 2008. Address.

39. "Are You Part of the 11%?" Marianne Williamson - YouTube." *YouTube - Broadcast Yourself.* Institute Of Noetic Science. Web. 11 Aug. 2011.http://www.youtube.com/watch?v=03N2irkKOho>.

40. Gina-Dianne Harding. *Signs and Symptoms of Waking Up*. 2008. Revised from class handout for Losing Limiting Beliefs and Manufacturing Miracles Classes. This List was compiled through a literature review and personal experience. Karen Bishop validated my experiences, as well as those of other Lightworkers in her 2 websites, 'Waking up On Planet Earth' and 'Emerging Earth Angels'. These websites are no longer active on line. If you search for Emerging Earth Angels, you will see the site belongs to someone else.

41. ibid.

42. Kryon, and Lee Carroll. *Alchemy of the Human Spirit: a Guide to Human Transition into the New Age*. Del Mar, CA: Kryon Writings, 1997. Print. P.32

43. Racie Allen, Intuitive Astrologer, Maple Ridge BC Canada. June 2010, personal conversation

Chapter 3

44. Dr. Richard Jelusich. "Endorsement and Comments." Message to the author. 17 Aug. 2011. E-mail.

45. "Rife Frequency List." *Royal Ramond Rife*. Web. 10 Aug. 2011. <http://altered-states.net/barry/newsletter135/frequecies.htm>.

46. William Shakespeare, 'As You Like It', personal Knowledge

47. Gregg Braden. "The Divine Matrix and the Science of Miracles: Shattering the Paradigm of False Limits." I Can Do It Conference. Sands Expo, Los Vegas. 29 June 2008. Address.

48. "Evolution - Conscious Evolution." *The Co-Intelligence Institute*. Web. 10 Aug. 2011. <http://www.co-intelligence.org/Evolution. html>.

Chapter 4

49. Catherine MacCoun, *On Becoming an Alchemist: a Guide for the Modern Magician*. Boston: Trumpeter, 2008. Print p. 149

50. Copyright 2007. Jim Self. This information is meant to circulate and may be freely disseminated, in whole or in part, provided

that this notice is included. This material may be used with the condition that all rights, including copyrights of translations of this material, remain with the original copyright holder. Further information about Jim Self and Mastering Alchemy may be found at: http://www.MasteringAlchemy.com ,**Thanks for helping to spread the Light!**

Chapter 5

51. Eric Pearl, *The Reconnection: Heal Others, Heal Yourself.* Carlsbad, CA: Hay House, 2001. Print.

52. Carl Calleman. "March 9 2011, The Dawn of Unity Consciousness Time." Web log post. The Dawn of Unity Consciousness Time Blog. Lovepeaceandharmony.ning.com, 22 Jan. 2011. Web. 5 Aug. 2011. <https://lovepeaceandharmony.ning.com/profiles/blog/show>. by David Dogan Beyo on January 22, 2011 at 12:35am

53. Major Jenkins, "The Origins of the 2012 Revelations." The Mystery Of 2012: Predictions, Prophecies & Possibilities. Boulder, CO: Sounds True, 2009. P.38. Print.

54. "Harmonic Convergence." Wikipedia, the Free Encyclopedia. Web. 06 Aug. 2011. <http://en.wikipedia.org/wiki/Harmonic_Convergence>.

55. José Argüelles. "Harmonic Convergence Update." 2012 Unlimited. Web. 06 Aug. 2011. <http://www.2012.com.au/harmonic_convergence.html>.

56. ibid.

57. ibid.

58. Yahweh, The Story Teller, through Chuck Little. Brought to Canada by Carole Webber, Reflections Books, Coquitlam, BC. 2008. Lecture.

59. Caroline Preston, and Nicole Wallace. "Donations to Aid Haiti Exceed $528-Million - News - The Chronicle of Philanthropy-Connecting the Nonprofit World with News, Jobs, and Ideas." Home - The Chronicle of Philanthropy- Connecting the

Nonprofit World with News, Jobs, and Ideas. 27 Jan. 2010. Web. 07 Aug. 2011. <http://philanthropy.com/article/Donations-to-Aid-Haiti-Exce/63756/>.

60. ibid.

61. New Reality Transmission â 11.11.2010 One Million Person Meditation - YouTube. YouTube - Broadcast Yourself. New Reality Transmission, Oct. 2010. Web. 05 Aug. 2011. <http://www.youtube.com/watch?v=hMvxtV9pcqg>.

62. "Women On The Edge of Evolution Update." Message to the author. Nov. 2009. E-mail

Chapter 6

63. Sacred Earth Journeys Tour Company. Vancouver, Canada http://www.sacredearthjourneys.ca/current-tours

64. Ervin Laszlo. *WorldShift 2012: Making Green Business, New Politics, and Higher Consciousness Work Together*. Rochester, VT: Inner Traditions, 2009. p. xix Print

65. World Shift p 24.

66. "The Origins of the 2012 Revelations." *The Mystery Of 2012: Predictions, Prophecies & Possibilities. p.38*

67. Gregg Braden. *Fractal Time: the Secret of 2012 and a New World Age*. Carlsbad, CA: Hay House, 2009. p.40 Print.

68. Dr. Richard Jelusich. "Mayan Cosmology and 2012." Sacred Journey to 2012. Campeche, Mexico. 3 Dec. 2009. Lecture.

69. *The Mystery Of 2012: Predictions, Prophecies & Possibilities. P.38*

70. ibid. p.38

71. Miguel Angel Vergara. "Understanding Mayan Calendars." Mayan Wisdom Series. Merida Mexico. Nov. 2009. Lecture.

72. Carl Calleman. "The Question of the Mayan Calendar End Date." *The Mayan Calendar*. Web. 08 Aug. 2011. <http://www.calleman.com/content/articles/question_end_date.htm>.

73. Carl Calleman. "March 9 2011,The Dawn of Unity Consciousness Time." Web log post. *The Dawn of Unity Consciousness Time Blog.* Lovepeaceandharmony.ning.com, 22 Jan. 2011. Web. 5 Aug. 2011. <https://lovepeaceandharmony.ning.com/profiles/blog/show>. by David Dogan Beyo on January 22, 2011

74. ibid..

75. ibid..

76. "Understanding Mayan Calendars." Mayan Wisdom Series.

77. Mark Heley. *101 Things You Should Know about 2012: Countdown to Armageddon or a Better World?* Avon, MA: Adams Media, 2011. p.106 Print.

78. Fractal Time p.67

79. Mark Heley, *101 Things You Should Know about 2012:* Avon, MA: Adams Media, 2011. Print. P.17

80. Amazon.com: Serpent of Light: Beyond 2012 - The Movement of the Earth's Kundalini and the Rise of the Female Light, 1949 to 2013 (9781578634019): Drunvalo Melchizedek." *Amazon. com:* Web. 06 Aug. 2011. <http://www.amazon.com/gp/product/images/1578634016/ref=dp_readdesc_b?ie=UTF8>.

81. *101 Things You Should Know about 2012. p.17*

82. Dan Sewell Ward, "Age of Pisces." *The Library of Halexandriah.* 2003. Web. 22 July 2011. <http://www.halexandria.org/dward207.htm>.

83. *101 Things You Should Know about 2012. p.17*

84. "The Aware Show with Guest Bruce Lipton." Interview by Lisa Garr. *Www.brucelipton.com.* Apr. 2010. Web. 6 Aug. 2011. <http://www.brucelipton.com/calendar/042711-the-aware-show-with-lisa-garr>.

85. *Fractal Time.*

86. *Fractal Time. p.* 156

87. *Fractal Time. p.202*

88. "Geomagnetic Reversal." *Wikipedia, the Free Encyclopedia*. Web. 07 Aug. 2011. <http://en.wikipedia.org/wiki/Geomagnetic_ reversal>.

89. Gregg Braden. *Walking Between the Worlds: the Science of Compassion*. Bellevue, WA: Radio Store, 1997. Print.

90. Alex Morales. "Chilean Quake Likely Shifted Earth's Axis NASA Scientist Says" *Http://www.freerepublic.com/*. Business Week, 21 May 2010. Web. 6 Aug. 2011. <http://www.freerepublic.com/ focus/f-news/2461896/posts>.

91. Geomagnetic Reversal." *Wikipedia, the Free Encyclopedia*

92. ibid.

93. *101 Things You Should Know about 2012. p.141*

94. Carl Calleman, March 9 2011,The Dawn of Unity Consciousness Time

95. *101 Things You Should Know about 2012. p.141*

96. ibid.

Chapter 7

97. Jim Self. "*The Shift E-Book*." www.masteringalchemy.com. Mastering Alchemy, 2009. Web.

98. JOHN MAJOR JENKINS. "The 2012 Story: Reconstructing Ancient Maya Science and Wisdom Teachings." The Tipping Point Conference. Simon Fraser University, Vancouver Canada. 23 July 2012. Address. Personal notes

99. Reckoning, Danielou's. "*Hindu Theory of World Cycles.*" Baharna. Web. 09 Aug. 2011. <http://baharna.com/karma/yuga.htm>.

100. "*Belief & Anticipation—The Basics - Belief & Anticipation.*" Judaism, Torah and Jewish Info - Chabad Lubavitch. Web. 09 Aug. 2011. <http://www.chabad.org/library/moshiach/article_ cdo/aid/1121885/jewish/The-Basics.htm>.

101. "*What the Kabbalah Says About 2012.*" December 21 2012, The Official Website for 122112 Information. Web. 09 Aug.

2011. <http://www.december212012.com/articles/news/What_Kabbalah_Says_About_2012.htm>.

102. Meg Blackburn Losey. *"Message from the Masters March 7 2011 Online Message."* Spirit Light Resources & Dr. Meg Blackburn Losey - Radio Show, Sessions & More. 7 Mar. 2011. Web. 02 Aug. 2011. <http://www.spiritlite.com/messages.php>.

103. Quote by BuckMinster Fuller in Email from Stephan Dinan, The Shift Network. *"The Sacred Way of Conscious Evolution Course Outline."* Message to the author. 22 Apr. 2010. E-mail.

104. Barbara Marx Hubbard. *"The Sacred Way of Conscious Evolution Course Outline."* Message to the author. 22 Apr. 2010. E-mail.

105. Barbara Marx Hubbard. *"Birthing the Universal Human Within Ourselves."* Sacred Way of Conscious Evolution Course Week 2. The Shift Network. 05 May 2010. Lecture.

106. *"Noosphere."* Wikipedia, the Free Encyclopedia. Web. 09 Aug. 2011. <http://en.wikipedia.org/wiki/Noosphere>. Quoting from Teilhard de Chardin, "Hominization" (1923)

107. *"The Sacred Way of Conscious Evolution Course Outline."*

108. *"Noosphere."* Wikipedia, the Free Encyclopedia

109. Barbara Marx Hubbard. *"Gaining Evolutionary Eyes."* The Sacred Way of Conscious Evolution Class 1. The Shift Network, 28 Apr. 2010. Lecture

110. ibid.

111. Barbara Marx Hubbard. *"Birthing Co-Creative Society."* The Sacred Way of Conscious Evolution Class 5. The Shift Network. 26 May 2010. Lecture

112. *"Wisdom University - Personal Transformation, Wisdom Studies, Wisdom Spirituality, Emerging Wisdom Culture, Cultural Creatives, Sacred Activism, Deep Ecumenism, Chartres, Mystery School, Wisdom School."* Wisdom University - Graduate Studies with World Renowned Leaders. Web. 09 Aug. 2011. <https://www.wisdomuniversity.org/syllabus60136.htm>.

113. *"Birthing Co-Creative Society."*

114. *"Birthing the Universal Human Within Ourselves."*

115. *The Shift E Book*

116. *The Shift E Book* p.3, 4.

117. *101 Things You Should Know about 2012.* p. 202

118. *101 Things You Should Know about 2012.* p.201

119. *101 Things You Should Know about 2012.* p.200

120. *Serpent of Light.*

121. *101 Things You Should Know about 2012* .p.197-199

122. Personal Opinion

123. *101 Things You Should Know about 2012*

124. ibid.

125. Karen Bishop *'Emerging Earth Angels'. This websites is no longer active on line.* If you search for Emerging Earth Angels, you will see the site belongs to someone else.

126. Tom Kenyon, The Hathors. *"Partaking From the Solar Winds."* Tomkenyon.com. 27 Jan. 2011. Web. 10 Aug. 2011. <http:// tomkenyon.com/partaking-from-the-solar-winds>.

127. *"The Aware Show with Guest Bruce Lipton."* Interview by Lisa Garr. www.brucelipton.com. Apr. 2010. Web. 6 Aug. 2011.

128. Dyer, Dr. Wayne. *"The Difference Between Beliefs and Knowings."* Nightingale Conant: World Leader in Success, Personal Development and Motivation. 2010. Web. 10 Aug. 2011. <http://www.nightingale.com/Newsletters/402. aspx?promo=INLACx402v2>.

Chapter 8

129. Jerome Kagan, PhD *PEDIATRICS Vol. 104 No. 1 Supplement July 1999 The Role of Parents in Children's Psychological Development*, Harvard University, Cambridge, Massachusetts. , pp. 164-167

130. Joe Vitale. *The Key: the Missing Secret for Attracting Anything You Want!* Hoboken, NJ: John Wiley & Sons, 2008. Print.

131. Deepak Chopra. "Meditation Q and A." *Deepak Chopra Newsletter -May 2007 | Chopra Center.* May 2007. Web. 14 Aug. 2011. <http://www.chopra.com/namaste/may07>.

132. "60,000 Thoughts - What Are You Thinking?" *Zen Minute.* Web. 14 Aug. 2011. <http://zenminute.com>.

Chapter 9

133. I was unable to find a citation attributing this to Wayne Dyer. I did find a similar story at "Frames: Attitude." *Quotes About Attitude.* Web. 14 Aug. 2011. <http://pw1.netcom.com/~spritex/att_fr.html>.

Your attitude and behavior are a function of your paradigm. For example: It's Sunday morning, you are enjoying a quiet ride in the subway - no crowds. A man with several children gets on. The children act rowdy, shouting, disturbing others. You become irritated and finally say "Sir, your children are really disturbing a lot of people, I wonder if you couldn't control them a little more." The reply comes slowly: "I guess I should... We just came from the hospital... Their mother just died about an hour ago and I guess... I don't know what to think.... I guess they don't know how to handle it either..." You have just experienced a paradigm shift that puts the situation in new light. We all see things differently.

134. theuniverse@tut.com

Chapter 10

135. *"VISUALIZATION AND SPORTS PERFORMANCE." Free Articles Directory | Submit Articles - ArticlesBase.com.* 3 Jan. 2010. Web. 17 Aug. 2011. <http://www.articlesbase.com/sports-and-fitness-articles/visualization-and-sports-performance-1660889.html#ixzz0ytu6P5tF>.

136. ibid.

137. *"Ultra Height Vibrational Hypnotherapy Experience."* Personal interview with Joy Borthwick CH, HC, CHt Certified Clinical Hypnotherapist, Quantum Focusing Practitioner and Pain Relief Educator, Author October 2010 <http://www.joyhypnotherapy.com/Virtual-Gastric-Band.page>.

138. ibid.

139. http://en.wikipedia.org/wiki/Emotional_Freedom_Technique

140. *Introduction to EFT Video.* Gary Craig, 24 July 2010. Web. <www.youtube.com/watch?v=dYhYp3IziX8>.

141. *"A to Z Index of Mind Body Spirit Therapies."* About Holistic Healing - Body Mind Spirit - Chakras - Energy Medicine. Web. 17 Aug. 2011.

142. "Matrix Energetics: What Is Matrix Energetics?" *Matrix Energetics Healing Seminars Taught by Richard Bartlett.* Web. 17 Aug. 2011. <http://www.matrixenergetics.com/WhatIs.aspx>.

143. "Theta Healing with Grace Talson." Telephone interview. Oct. 2010. <http://www.movingforwardwithgrace.com/reiki.html >

144. Viana Stibal, founder Theta Healing http://www.youtube.com/watch?v=Eze_j-HwWFE

145. Eric Pearl, The Reconnection: Heal Others, Heal Yourself. Carlsbad, CA: Hay House, 2001. Print.

146. Pat Donworth. "What Is The Reconnection?" *Welcome to The Reconnection & Reconnective Healing in Miami, Florida.* Web. 17 Aug. 2011. http://www.reconnectyourself.com/reconnection.html>.

Chapter 14

147. Daniel G.Amen . *Healing the Hardware of the Soul: Enhance Your Brain to Improve Your Work, Love, and Spiritual Life.* New York: Free, 2008. Print. p.7

Chapter 15

148. Abraham, and Esther Hicks. "A Simple Choice: Which Thought Feels Best? Abraham Hicks." *Spirit Library - Articles, Channelings, Books and Other Spiritual Information.* 27 Nov. 2007. Web. 16 Aug. 2011. <http://spiritlibrary.com/abraham-hicks/a-simple-choice-which-thought-feels-best>.

149. Diane M Cooper. "Unwinding Your Emotions with Sound with Tom Kenyon by Diane M. Cooper." *The Spirit of Ma'at.* Vol 3.No3. Web. 16 Aug. 2011. <http://www.spiritofmaat.com/archive/oct3/kenyon.htm>.

150. "Dr Bach's System of 38 Flower Remedies." *The Bach Centre.* Web. 26 Aug. 2011. <http://www.bachcentre.com/centre/firstpag.htm>.

151. Patricia Kaminski, and Richard Katz. *Flower Essence Repertory: a Comprehensive Guide to North American and English Flower Essences for Emotional and Spiritual Well-being.* Nevada City, CA: Flower Essence Society, 2004. Print.

152. Simmons, Robert, and Naisha Ahsian. *Book of Stones.* United Kingdom: New Agency, 2006. Print. p.xix

153. ibid. p. xxviii

154. ibid. p.xxix

155. ibid.

156. Melody. *Love is In the Earth A Kaleidoscope of Crystals :update : the Reference Book Describing the Metaphysical Properties of the Mineral Kingdom.* Wheat Ridge, CO.: Earth-Love Pub. House, 1995. Print

157. ibid.

158. Book of Stones

Chapter 16

159. Adela Rubio, "Events." *Adela Rubio — Creating Conscious Business through Partnership and Community.* Web. 22 Aug. 2011. <http://adelarubio.com/events/#>.

160. Patricia Cota Robles. "25th Annual World Congress on Illumination - Webcast." *Healing With The Masters – Volume 8.* Jennifer McLean, 18 Aug. 2011. Web. 21 Aug. 2011. <http://www.healingwiththemasters.com/WorldCongress/webcast.htm>.

161. StarRider8008. "Aaron Copland - Fanfare For The Common Man - YouTube." *YouTube - Broadcast Yourself.* 28 Nov. 2009. Web. 21 Aug. 2011. <http://youtu.be/4NjssV8UuVA>.

162. "Humanities Team." *Humanities Team Facebook Page.* Web. 22 Aug. 2011. <https://www.facebook.com/#!/HumanitysTeamWorldwide>.

163. *Four Years. Go.* Web. 22 Aug. 2011. <https://www.facebook.com/#!/fouryearsgo>.

Resources

Dr Richard Jelusich: http://lightnews.org/ healers training, books, newsletter

Miguel Angel Vergara, Maya Wisdom Teacher, Maya Cosmic Institute http://www.casakin.org/ Shamanism Workshops and sacred tours.

Iluminado Tours http://www.iluminado-tours.com/sacred-maya-tours.html

Sacred Earth Journeys http://www.sacredearthjourneys.ca/
Maya Sacred Journey to 2012 , and travel worldwide.

Websites for connection with other higher conscious persons or inspiration

adelarubio.com Free Your Essence, Activate Your Business (conscious business tribe, energy shifts)

iliveineasyworld.com –Julia Rogers Hamrick

joyhypnotherapy.com/Books-CDs.page

Heartmath.org

www.glcoherence.org and clicking the Global Care Room link

http://www.manataka.org/page15.html.

Power animals and symbols in nature

Ted Andrews
Animal speak
Animal Wisdom
Nature Speak

Stephen Farmer- Animal Spirit Guides

Medicine Oracle Cards and Book

Recommended Reading

Buried Treasure: Finding Enchantment Within *Joy Borthwick*

Healing Power of Water *Matsura Emoto*

Ask and it is Given *Ester and Gerry Hicks and Abraham (Universal Laws)*

Happy for No Reason *Marci Shimoff*

Eye of the Lotus: Psychology of the Chakras Dr.Richard Jelusich

Vibrational Medicine *Richard Gerber*

Power vs Force *Dr.David Hawkins*

Healing the Hardware of the Soul *Dr.Daniel Amen*

Emissary of Light: a Vision of Peace. James F Twyman,

Crystal Allies

Love is in the Earth, *Melody*

Book of Stones, *Robert Simmons, and Naisha Ahsian*

Crystal Bible, *Judy Hall*

Oracle Cards and Positive Thought Cards

Louise Hay
Wayne Dyer
Esther and Gerry Hicks
Path of the Soul Fractal Cards
The Mayan Oracle Return Path to the Stars

CD's to stimulate focus and creativity

Tom Kenyon, The Ultimate Brain Ambient Support
Kelly Howell Pure Focus Gamma Waves
Steven Halpern Accelerated Learning